"This new book from Anne Hunt is one that we have long needed, not only in theology, but also in the wider Christian community. An obvious gap in the current renewal of the theology of the Trinity has been that we have yet to retrieve the rich insights of the Christian mystics. Anne Hunt brings eight great mystical writers to life, and leads us into a deep appreciation of their experience and understanding of the triune God. This is a beautiful book, well-structured, well-written, abounding in insights, and accessible, a book that draws the reader to wonder and to prayer."

> —Denis Edwards
> Professor of Theology
> Flinders University, Australia
> Author of *Breath of Life: A Theology of the Creator Spirit*

"With unusual insight and clarity, Anne Hunt has shown how central to Christian life the experience and worship of the Trinity should be by appropriating for contemporary spirituality and theology the extraordinary Trinitarian consciousness of eight mystical titans."

> —Harvey D. Egan, SJ
> Professor of Systematic and Mystical Theology
> Boston College

"A feature of post-conciliar theology has been the recovery of the centrality of the Blessed Trinity both for the daily life of believers and for theology. A major contributor to this development is the eminent Australian theologian, Anne Hunt. In books such as *Trinity* (2005) Professor Hunt communicates the riches of contemporary Trinitarian theology, while in a volume such as *The Trinity and the Paschal Mystery* (1997) she connects the Trinity and the Cross, communicating the thought of the principal authors in the field and then proposing further possible developments. Now in this new volume she presents the experience of the Blessed Trinity on the part of eight mystics of the second millennium— William of St. Thierry, Hildegard of Bingen, St. Bonaventure, Meister Eckhart, St. John of the Cross, St. Teresa of Avila, Julian of Norwich and Blessed Elizabeth of Dijon. Her goal is 'to probe through their witness to the mystery of the Trinity,' convinced that they offer 'rich seams of data for systematic theology.' She notes that they would all want us to reflect on the Trinity as the eternal event of love by which believers are welcomed into the very midst of the Eternal Three, attaining an entry into the Trinitarian relations. This work—each chapter a fascinating portrait of both the life and the Trinitarian experience of a particular mystic—presents 'new ways of knowing the Trinity.' Professor Hunt has enriched again the theology of the Trinity."

> —Thomas J. Norris
> Professor in Systematic Theology
> Maynooth, Ireland

THE TRINITY

INSIGHTS FROM THE MYSTICS

ANNE HUNT

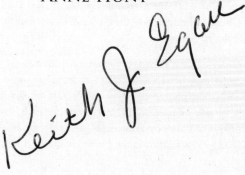

A Michael Glazier Book

LITURGICAL PRESS
Collegeville, Minnesota

www.litpress.org

A Michael Glazier Book published by Liturgical Press

Cover design by Ann Blattner. Illustration: *True Trinity in True Trinity* by Hildegard of Bingen, c. 1180.

Library of Congress Cataloging-in-Publication Data

Hunt, Anne, date
    The Trinity : insights from the mystics / Anne Hunt.
      p. cm.
    "A Michael Glazier book."
    Includes index.
    ISBN 978-0-8146-5692-1 – ISBN 978-0-8146-5731-7 (e-book)
    1. Trinity–History of doctrines–Middle Ages, 600–1500. 2. Mysticism. I. Title.
BT109.H85 2010
231'.044–dc22
                                    2009048453

CONTENTS

Introduction   vii

Chapter 1: William of St. Thierry (ca. 1080–1148)   1

Chapter 2: Hildegard of Bingen (1098–1179)   23

Chapter 3: Bonaventure (ca. 1217–1274)   48

Chapter 4: Meister Eckhart (ca. 1260–1328)   73

Chapter 5: Julian of Norwich (1342/3–ca. 1416)   98

Chapter 6: Teresa of Avila (1515–1582)   122

Chapter 7: John of the Cross (1542–1591)   144

Chapter 8: Elizabeth of the Trinity (1880–1906)   168

Conclusion   182

Index of Names   188

INTRODUCTION

The mystery of God as Trinity stands at the center of the Christian faith. The radically trinitarian shape of the church's faith has its origins in the post-Easter consciousness of Jesus' disciples. Through their experience of the paschal mystery of Jesus' death and resurrection, their perception of the mystery of God was profoundly reshaped. They came to understand, however strange it seemed to their Jewish monotheistic faith, that the unity of God implies a divine *communion* of life and love. Thus it was that the Christian conviction that God is somehow both Three and One emerged. It took root in the prayer and liturgy of the early Christian community. In the following centuries, it led to the articulation of the doctrine of the Trinity.[1]

Throughout the two millennia since those heady days of Jesus' post-resurrection appearances, the best and brightest of Christian minds have struggled to express the mystery in a coherent and plausible way. In their efforts, they have most often looked for analogies for this Three-in-Oneness with things known in the natural world, the world of our everyday experience. St. Patrick took the example of the shamrock. St. Augustine of Hippo took the human mind and its activities or faculties of memory, understanding, and love. Richard of St. Victor took the example of interpersonal love to demonstrate that God is necessarily threefold in divine

1. See Sebastian Moore's very imaginative and very plausible reconstruction of the disciples' experience, what he calls "the grass-roots derivation of the mystery," in *The Fire and the Rose Are One* (London: Darton, Longman and Todd, 1980). For a study of the biblical evidence concerning the emergence of trinitarian belief, see Larry Hurtado, *Lord Jesus Christ: Devotion to Jesus in Earliest Christianity* (Grand Rapids, MI/Cambridge, UK: Eerdmans, 2003); also *How on Earth Did Jesus Become a God? Historical Questions about Earliest Devotion to Jesus* (Grand Rapids, MI: Eerdmans, 2005). See also Anne Hunt, "The Emergence of Devotion to Jesus in the Early Church: The Grass-Roots Derivation of the Trinity," *Australian E-Journal of Theology*, issue 4 (February 2005), http://dlibrary.acu.edu.au/research/theology/ejournal (accessed October 25, 2009).

personhood, for, Richard argued, the perfection of interpersonal love requires not just two coequals who love each other, but their shared love for
a third coequal. An understanding of the mystery was also advanced, albeit
less frequently, by an exploration of the interconnection of the mystery of
the Trinity with other mysteries of Christian faith, for example, with grace
or with the Eucharist. Philosophical resources were also brought to bear
in explicating the mystery, a strategy that reached its brilliant apogee in
the highly refined and metaphysically elegant theology of St. Thomas
Aquinas and his masterful appropriation of Aristotelian philosophy.
Throughout the centuries, theology sought in these ways to further faith's
understanding of this most sublime and ineffable mystery.

Meanwhile, at various times in the history of Christianity, in the Eastern as well as the Western tradition, there are mystics who, in their profound encounters with God, have gleaned distinctly trinitarian insights.
Of course, in all Christian mysticism, by virtue of the Christian faith from
which it issues, God is necessarily trinitarian. But for some mystics, such
as Julian of Norwich and John of the Cross, their consciousness of God
as Trinity is heightened to a more intense and explicit degree in and
through their mystical encounters.

As is right and fitting, theology recognizes the beauty and the drama
of the mysteries of faith unfolding in the very lives as well as the testimonies
of the mystics. What is rather remarkable, however, is that in fact theology,
in its task of faith seeking understanding, has paid little systematic attention to the insights offered by the mystics. Theology, by and large, has not
probed Christian mysticism as a rich seam of data for the understanding
of Christian faith. Yet surely, if theology is to be true to itself, it must attend
to the actual witness of the mystics and the intense consciousness of the
mysteries that they manifest.[2]

Not a few theologians, including the great Karl Rahner, SJ, have be-
moaned the divide between mystical consciousness and doctrinal theology.
Rahner, for example, speaks of bridging "the rift" between "lived piety
and abstract theology," and of "how religious experiences of a spiritual or
mystical kind can overflow and be transposed into the idiom of theological
reflection."[3] More recently, then-president of the Catholic Theological

2. Joan M. Nuth suggests that the rift between theology and mysticism perhaps has its
origins in the distinction between scholastic theology and monastic theology in the Middle
Ages. See Nuth, "Two Medieval Soteriologies: Anselm of Canterbury and Julian of Norwich,"
Theological Studies 53 (1992): 611–45, at 613.

3. Karl Rahner, *Experience of the Spirit, Source of Theology,* vol. 16 of *Theological Investigations,*
trans. David Morland (New York: Crossroad/Seabury Press, 1979), 72, n.12.

⊙ *Locus theologicus*

Society of America, theologian Michael J. Buckley, SJ, also posed the question: "Is it not extraordinary that so much Catholic formal theology for centuries . . . has bracketed this actual witness [the spiritual experiences of the saints/mystics] as of no cogency. . . ? Is it not a lacuna in the standard theology, even of our day, that theology neither has nor has striven to forge the intellectual devices to probe in these concrete experiences the warrant they present for the reality of God and make them available for so universal a discipline?"[4] Buckley, like Rahner, challenges theologians to find in the consciousness and insights of the mystics a *locus theologicus*, a source and a resource for theological reflection on the mysteries of Christian faith.

The aim of this book is to take up that challenge and at least to examine a number of mystics who have had what could be described as distinctly trinitarian insights. Our goal is to probe, through their witness, the mystery of the Trinity, and so to deepen faith's understanding of the mystery. Such an approach has the advantage of avoiding the philosophical issues that have proved so problematic in trinitarian theology in recent times, such as the relationship between the immanent and the economic Trinity, or the relative virtues of the psychological analogy compared to, say, the social model in explicating the mystery. Instead, the mystics offer not an explication of the mystery per se but rather, as near as possible in this world, a rendering of an unmediated experience of the Trinity. What is also interesting is that, whereas women are by and large eclipsed in the classical theological tradition of Christianity, their voices deemed to have very limited authority, they figure just as strongly as the men in the tradition of Christian mysticism.[5] Indeed women mystics are apparently more numerous than their male counterparts, certainly in the Middle Ages. In

---

4. Michael J. Buckley, Presidential Address, *The Catholic Theological Society of America Proceedings* 47 (1992): 77.

5. Bernard McGinn recounts that the scholastic theologian Henry of Ghent, around 1290, in his *Summae Quaestionum Ordinarium*, Art XI, quaest. 11, ff 77v–78r, addressed the question: "Whether a woman can be a doctor of theology?" Henry argued that women cannot be doctors of theology because (ex officio) they cannot have the four public marks required for doctoral status: constancy, efficacy, authority, and effect. Henry added a further note, however: "Speaking about teaching from divine favour (ex beneficio) and the fervour of charity, it is well allowed for a woman to teach just like anyone else, if she possesses sound doctrine. But this should be done privately and in silence, not in public and before the church" (and, moreover only to other women and girls, not to men as it might incite lust). See McGinn, *Meister Eckhart and the Beguine Mystics: Hadewijch of Brabant, Mechthild of Magdeburg, and Marguerite Porete* (New York: Continuum, 1994), 1.

the tradition of Christian mysticism, their voices are by no means silenced. Moreover, women's mystical insights are particularly noteworthy, given that most of them did not have access to the education and scholarly training that was granted to their male contemporaries.

Methodological and Hermeneutical Issues

Given the necessarily limited scope of the project, we have chosen William of St. Thierry (ca. 1080–1148), Hildegard of Bingen (1098–1179), Bonaventure (ca. 1217–1274), Meister Eckhart (ca. 1260–1328), Julian of Norwich (1342/3–ca. 1416), Teresa of Avila (1515–1582), John of the Cross (1542–1591), and Elizabeth of the Trinity (1880–1906) for this study. We hope that a further study will include mystics from the early Christian centuries and also mystics from the Christian tradition of the East.

Of our chosen mystics, all are continental or English. All belong to the Western tradition of Christianity. Four are women, four men. Most are monastic in their formation, some scholastic; one is an anchorite. They range from the eleventh century (William of St. Thierry) to the twentieth century (Elizabeth of the Trinity). Some lived in that richly creative period, the Middle Ages (1100–1450), but by no means all. Some are visionaries, some not; some indeed have little interest in visions or ecstasies. Some are teachers and preachers, some prophets, some poets, some artists indeed. All of them are relatively well known, with the exception of William of St. Thierry who is included because of the significant role he played in the development of trinitarian devotion in the Cistercian tradition, albeit his writings were mistakenly ascribed to his friend Bernard of Clairvaux for some centuries. What unites our chosen mystics is that each offers penetrating insights into the mystery of the Trinity and the soul's mystical union with it. Each communicates a distinctly trinitarian encounter with God and invites others to enter into the mystery of God who is Trinity.

The men—William of St. Thierry, Bonaventure, Meister Eckhart, John of the Cross—are all well educated, trained in Latin, the Sacred Scriptures, and theology. William and John belong to the monastic tradition. Bonaventure belongs to the newly founded Order of Friars Minor (Franciscans). Meister Eckhart of the Order of Preachers (Dominicans) is the brilliant Master of Paris, master of scholastic theology and meister of the spiritual life. None of the women—Julian of Norwich, Hildegard of Bingen, Teresa of Avila, and Elizabeth of the Trinity—had the privilege of the high level of education in theology and Scripture that was given to their male contemporaries. Admittedly, Julian is clearly well educated in Latin and well read in the spiritual classics, and Hildegard has at least working knowledge of Latin but, nevertheless, neither has training in theology as such. Julian, Teresa, and Elizabeth write in the vernacular, while Hildegard, with the assistance of her secretary-scribe, writes in Latin. Three of the women have remarkable visionary experiences, particularly Julian and Hildegard. Their visions, together with the claim that their writings are divinely inspired, give their teachings an authority otherwise not granted—indeed not permitted—to them as women.

They write for a variety of reasons—some for teaching on prayer and contemplative practice, others for exhortation, others for more classically theological purposes, but rarely for precise elucidation of the mystery of the Trinity. Consequently, their writings show a variety of forms of mystical discourse, ranging from scholastic treatises and biblical commentaries, through accounts and interpretations of their visions, to sermons and letters and poems. All call for a rather different kind of reading and comprehending, for more of a kind of *lectio divina*, a rumination, a meditation, rather than a linear analytic examination of a text, not that such a method is totally excluded. Hildegard's writings also include a remarkable series of intricately detailed illuminations, which are by no means mere illustrations of or a supplement to the written text, but integral to her theology. Indeed, for Hildegard, the two forms of communication are inextricably connected; her theology is as much visual as it is verbal.

Together, our chosen mystics exemplify different styles of theology, which can be broadly classified as monastic, scholastic, and vernacular. On the one hand, monastic theology strives for an understanding of the mysteries of faith that is the fruit of prayer, liturgy, and contemplation. Focused on interpretation of the Sacred Scriptures, it is basically exegetical in method. Its goal is experience, contemplation: believe in order to experience. Its most common genres are the biblical commentary, the letter-treatise, and the written rhetorical sermon. Scholastic theology, on the other hand, is the fruit of the more explicitly scholarly endeavor of faith seeking understanding. It took root in the universities, which emerged in the eleventh and twelfth centuries, and flourished with the advent of Aristotelian philosophy into Europe in the thirteenth century. Its goal is knowledge, understanding, rationality, the demonstration of the reasonableness of Christian faith: believe in order to understand. Its typical genres are *lectio, disputatio, quaestio,* and *summa.* Vernacular theology also surfaced with considerable vigor in the twelfth century, not from the academic schools of the professional theologians, but more often from those who were barred from entry to university. It flourished not among the scholarly trained—though there were some exceptions, such as the erudite Master of Paris, Meister Eckhart, who championed it—but among devout souls, formed by prayer and contemplation and informed by a wide reading of the spiritual classics available to them in the vernacular. Women, such as Julian of Norwich, played a particularly significant role in the development of this style of theology. More fluid in style and content, and technically less precise, vernacular theology is not as easily characterized as the monastic and scholastic. It includes visionary experiences and their explanation, hagiography, and poetry.

Clearly, the experiences and the insights of the mystics into the mystery of the Trinity do not come out of nowhere. Each of the mystics—along with the rest of us—is influenced and limited by the creedal statements as well as the images and concepts of God that prevail in his or her milieu and time. Our chosen mystics come to their profound consciousness of the mystery with a strong faith in and conception of it, as intimated in the New Testament and as defined by the church in its creeds and doctrines. They also come with knowledge, in varying depth, of Augustine's exploration of the mystery of the Trinity in terms of what is now called the psychological analogy, wherein the mystery is understood in terms of the human mind's operations or faculties. There is, then, no doubting that their revelations and insights are grounded in a prior familiarity with doctrinal formulations as well as iconographic and theological expressions of the mystery. The influence of trinitarian iconography is evident to varying degrees. Teresa and Elizabeth, for example, make reference to particular visual images of the Trinity.

It is hardly surprising that a flourishing of trinitarian mysticism would coincide with a period of sustained attention to matters trinitarian, such as occurred in the centuries following the split between East and West in the eleventh century over the procession of the Holy Spirit. Both the Fourth Lateran General Council in 1215 and the Second General Council of Lyons in 1274 attempted reunion and affirmed the *filioque*.[6] The Council of Ferrara-Florence in 1438 and 1439 made another attempt at reunion and reiterated the double procession of the Spirit as well as affirming the legitimacy of its insertion into the Creed for the sake of clarity.[7] The feast

---

6. H. Denzinger and A. Schönmetzer, eds., *Enchiridion Symbolorum: Definitionum et Declarationum de Rebus Fidei et Morum*, 36th ed. (Freiburg: Herder, 1976), 850 and 853 (hereafter DS); J. Neusner and J. Dupuis, eds., *The Christian Faith in the Doctrinal Documents of the Catholic Church*, 6th rev. and exp. ed. (New York: Alba House, 1996), 321 and 24 (hereafter ND).

7. DS 1300–1302.

of the Trinity, which is celebrated on the first Sunday after Pentecost, was eventually proclaimed for inclusion in the Roman Church calendar in 1334. At the same time, the eleventh and twelfth centuries saw a remarkable flourishing of trinitarian devotion and trinitarian iconography. The *Gnadenstuhl* iconographic form (Throne of Mercy or Seat of Grace as it is often known), which combines representation of the mystery of the Three with the crucifixion of Christ, proved especially popular at this time. The explosion of images for private devotion that occurred in the fourteenth and fifteenth centuries prompted another flourishing of trinitarian iconography, also witnessing to the interconnection between mysticism and the visual arts.[8]

Some Practicalities and Limitations

We have arranged our studies of the chosen mystics in chronological order, though they can be approached in any order. We have also tried not to rely too greatly on a prior knowledge of the tradition of trinitarian theology. We have sought to give sufficient background about the mystics' lives and times to assist the reader in better appreciating the particular insights of each. Each mystic, after all, is grounded in a particular time and place and their context shapes the theological and doctrinal insights that they offer to us. Admittedly, there is the question as to whether a biography is even possible in many cases, with sources tainted and the biographical records, such as they are, often written in the style of hagiography.

In each chapter, then, we have first provided a brief overview of the mystic's life and times, his or her writings, and, to the degree that is possible, the mystical experience or, better, the mystical consciousness on which those writings are based before moving to an exploration of the insights into the mystery of the Trinity that the mystic offers. Our task is to plumb the writings of mystics, not just for their spiritual richness, but for their distinctly theological and doctrinal insights. We have kept footnotes to a minimum and, at each chapter's end, we have provided further sources, both primary and secondary, as well as recommended readings for those readers who wish to pursue the subject more deeply. We have included numerous quotations in the studies, in order to allow the mystics'

---

8. See, for example, Henk van Os, et al., *The Art of Devotion in the Late Middle Ages in Europe, 1300–1500*, trans. Michael Hoyle (Princeton, NJ: Princeton University Press, 1994); also Michael Camille, *Gothic Art: Glorious Visions* (Upper Saddle River, NJ: Perspectives, Prentice Hall Art History, 1996).

own voices to be heard as much as practicable. Throughout, our primary focus is the distinctly doctrinal nature and caliber of their insights into the mystery of the Trinity.

We shall not, in this study, enter into the discussion of the complex issues concerning the phenomenon of mysticism itself. We shall instead adopt Bernard McGinn's notion of mysticism as a special consciousness of God and the ensuing transformation of person that results from immediate or direct encounter with God. We recognize that this immediately and intensely personal encounter with the transcendent reality of God, by its very nature, defies conventional modes of expression, and hence the mystics' strong use of metaphors and figures of speech and the metaphoric complexity and lyrical quality of their mystical writings. We recognize too that a probing of the mystics' writings is consequently more akin to a contemplative *lectio divina* than scholarly exegesis, a rumination rather than a linear analysis. As McGinn explains, comparing their use of language to poetry: "Mystical masterpieces . . . are often close to poetry in the ways in which they concentrate and alter language to achieve their ends . . . [and use] verbal strategies in which language is used not so much informationally as transformationally, that is, not to convey a content but to assist the hearer or reader to hope for or to achieve the same consciousness."[9]

In his discussions of mysticism, McGinn highlights the problems associated with the use of the word *experience* and opts instead for the word *consciousness*, for *consciousness*, he argues, expresses the reality that "mysticism (as the mystics insisted) is more than a matter of unusual sensations, but essentially comprises new ways of knowing and loving based on states of awareness in which God becomes present in our inner acts, not as an object to be grasped, but as the direct and transforming centre of life."[10] The particular focus of our probing of the mystics is the new ways of knowing the Trinity that emerge from their heightened consciousnesses of the mystery. It is those new ways of knowing the Trinity that we offer to our readers, that they too will come to a new and deeper understanding of this great mystery. Our hope is that the study will be of assistance to students of trinitarian theology as well as to the interested lay reader in deepening an understanding and appreciation of the mystery of the Trinity.

9. Bernard McGinn, *Foundations of Mysticism*, vol. 1 of *The Presence of God: A History of Western Christian Mysticism* (New York: Crossroad, 1992), xiv, xvii.

10. Bernard McGinn, *The Essential Writings of Christian Mysticism* (New York: The Modern Library, Random House, 2006), xiv. See also McGinn, "Mystical Consciousness: A Modest Proposal," *Spiritus* 8, no. 1 (2008): 44–63.

In conclusion, I wish to express an enormous debt of gratitude to the many writers and commentators on the mystics whose studies have made this study possible. This contribution, by way of synthesis and perspective, would be impossible were it not for the many superb specialist studies already undertaken by many fine scholars in the field. Theirs is the groundwork on which this contribution humbly stands. In particular, I salute Professor Bernard McGinn for the magisterial and monumental contribution that he has made to the study of the Christian mystical tradition.

Anne Hunt
Australian Catholic University
Trinity Sunday 2009

1

WILLIAM OF ST. THIERRY
(CA. 1080–1148)

Although relatively unknown to contemporary Christians, William of St. Thierry is one of the great masters of twelfth-century monasticism, a period that came to be known as the golden age of Western monasticism. With strong currents of reform astir, monasticism was at a crossroads. William himself straddles the two great currents of the Western monastic tradition of the period: Benedictine, in the tradition of the renowned abbey of Cluny, and the Cistercian renewal movement, which had taken root at the abbey of Cîteaux in 1098. After spending many years of his life as a Benedictine monk, William, inspired by the reforming zeal of Bernard, abbot of the abbey at Clairvaux, set aside the black habit of the Benedictines to take on the white habit of the Cistercians.

Monk, mystic, and theologian, William was a man of deep faith, piety, and prayer, great learning, and considerable speculative skill. He is famed as a contemporary and friend—and biographer—of the charismatic Mellifluous Doctor, Bernard of Clairvaux, and as a spiritual writer and teacher. His so-called *Golden Epistle,* a letter written to the Carthusian monks at Mont Dieu, was highly esteemed by generations of monks and nuns, of various monastic observances, as an authority on the contemplative life. It continues to be regarded as one of the classics of medieval spirituality.

William himself, however, fell into obscurity soon after his death. Within just a few years of his passing, William's writings were confused with those of Bernard and came to be ascribed to Bernard. William was almost completely forgotten for a few hundred years, known only as Bernard's friend and biographer. Following a revival of interest in William in the twentieth century, William is now out of Bernard's shadow, once again recognized in his own right as a master of the spiritual life, in no way of lesser importance than or a mere reiteration of the thought of the Mellifluous Doctor, but rather of genuine individuality and originality,

1

creativity, and richness of thought. Indeed, it may well be the case that Bernard made at least some of William's thought his own.

Étienne Gilson writes in glowing terms of William: "William of Saint-Thierry has everything: power of thought, the orator's eloquence, the poet's lyricism, and all the attractiveness of the most ardent and tender piety."[1] Bernard McGinn writes: "William may have been less influential in the later tradition than Bernard and the Victorines, but he yields to no twelfth-century mystic in the depth and sophistication of his theology."[2] In a succinct summary of his penetrating studies of William's writings, Odo Brooke writes: "The great contribution of William of St. Thierry is to have evolved a theology of the Trinity which is *essentially* mystical and a mystical theology which is *essentially* trinitarian."[3] Here indeed lies our particular interest in William: the deeply and distinctly trinitarian character of his mysticism and, at its center, the soul's union with God in and through the person of the Holy Spirit.

William's Life and Times

Although William is now recognized as one of the great lights in the medieval monastic movement, we know very little about the details of his life.[4] He was born in Liège, a thriving intellectual center, known in the eleventh century as the "Athens of the North," in the last quarter of the twelfth century, a few years before Bernard (b. 1090). The Norman invasion and conquest of England had occurred just a few years earlier in 1066. The first crusade had been waged in 1095, the second in 1145. The monasteries were the repositories and the intellectual hubs of Christian thought, but the era of the schools and universities was about to blossom. New intellectual centers were emerging, and a new humanism was taking root. A new movement in theology was also stirring, and one that would find rich resources for reflection, not only in the liturgy, the Scriptures, and the fathers, as had been the classical monastically fashioned way of approach

1. Étienne Gilson, *The Mystical Theology of Saint Bernard*, trans. A. H. C. Downes (New York: Sheed & Ward, 1955), 198.

2. Bernard McGinn, *The Growth of Mysticism*, vol. 2 of *The Presence of God: A History of Western Christian Mysticism* (New York: Crossroad, 1994), 225.

3. Odo Brooke, *Studies in Monastic Theology*, Cistercian Studies Series 37 (Oxford: Mowbray, 1980), 8. Italics are Brooke's.

4. For a more detailed introduction to William of St. Thierry's life and works, see John Anderson's introduction to *The Enigma of Faith*, Cistercian Fathers Series 9 (Kalamazoo, MI: Cistercian Publications, 1973).

until then, but in philosophy and in new methods that were more obviously scientific and speculative, more scholastic than monastic.

We know next to nothing of William's family, childhood, and education. In his ninth *Meditation*, he thanks God for a happy childhood. He also speaks of a measure of waywardness in his youth: "For by pursuing my desires and my heart's vanities, I lost my youth, and almost embarked on the way of the flesh" (*Meditation* 9).[5] It is possible, however, that this waywardness is due more to the influence of Augustine's *Confessions* on William's construction of his autobiography than to historical veracity.

Tradition has it that William studied at Reims, a flourishing and respected center of learning since the tenth century. He entered and received the habit at the Benedictine monastery of St. Nicaise in Reims, where the Rule of St. Benedict was observed according to the Cluniac usage, and in a way that was reputedly stricter than most Cluniac houses of the time. By all accounts William was greatly respected for his piety and ability, and, in 1119 or 1120, he was elevated to the abbacy of the monastery of St. Thierry, a few kilometers from Reims. He exercised the responsibilities of abbot for about fifteen years, reputedly with exemplary discipline and spiritual leadership. In spite of the demanding responsibilities of his office, William wrote a number of his treatises at this same time.

At some stage, perhaps as early as in 1118, before becoming abbot of St. Thierry, William visited the newly founded religious house at Clairvaux and met Bernard, the first abbot of the abbey of Clairvaux. Clairvaux was a daughter house of Cîteaux, the center from which the then-flourishing Benedictine reform movement, the Order of Cîteaux, had emerged about twenty years previously. Bernard was a leading light in this Cistercian reform and his reputation was already considerable. William was enthralled by Bernard and by the ideals of Cistercian reform that he epitomized. Indeed William later sought Bernard's approval to come and live at Clairvaux, but Bernard disapproved of William's plan and urged him to stay at St. Thierry and to continue with his duties as abbot and his work in the Benedictine Cluniac reform. In 1134 and 1135, however, after about fifteen years as abbot of St. Thierry,[6] William resigned his abbatial office

---

5. See also *Meditation* 4 which gives a more explicit confession. Translations are taken from the editions cited at the end of the chapter.

6. That period has been described as the "golden age of the Abbey of St Thierry." See M. Basil Pennington, "Abbot William, Spiritual Father of Saint Thierry," in *William, Abbot of St. Thierry: An International Colloquium*, trans. Jerry Carfantan, Cistercian Studies Series 94 (Kalamazoo, MI: Cistercian Publications, 1987), 225–39.

and retreated to a life of solitude and simplicity, taking the Cistercian habit—not at Clairvaux where he feared that Bernard, having counseled him against the transfer, might have refused to accept him—at the newly established Cistercian abbey at Signy in the Ardennes in the diocese of Reims. In the event, Bernard expressed no disapproval or displeasure. The two men enjoyed an enduring friendship. William was devoted to Bernard and, perhaps more than anyone else, understood and appreciated Bernard's thought.

Never having enjoyed a robust state of health, in fact of a rather delicate constitution, and now older and infirm, William was exonerated from the Cistercian requirement for manual work, and devoted himself to writing. This was to prove the most fruitful and prolific period of writing of his life. Eleven of his treatises were written at this stage, including his refuta- tion of Peter Abelard, his commentary on the Song of Songs, and his famous *Golden Epistle*.

William died after a brief illness on September 8 in 1147 or 1148.[7] A few decades later, by way of tribute to him, William's remains were exhumed from the cloister where his body had first been interred and reburied in a wall in the church at Signy. Although never canonized, he is honored as one of the great stars in the sky of the medieval Cistercian movement, a *beatus* in the Cistercian Order.

William lived in a time of profound development and reform in Western monasticism. Benedict of Nursia had written his Rule for Monks around AD 500, and this Rule had exercised a profound influence on monastic life and observance, particularly with the rise of the abbey of Cluny in the tenth century and of the Cluniac family of monasteries under Cluny's authority. Over the course of the years, however, the abbey of Cluny had adopted a moderate or mitigated interpretation of St. Benedict's Rule. Manual labor, an important element in Benedict's vision of monastic life, along with a careful balance of liturgy, sacred reading, and personal prayer, had yielded to a greater emphasis on psalmody and liturgical prayer, and a much expanded liturgy. By the twelfth century, many monasteries were drawing substantial incomes, and their prosperity had brought them considerable power, prestige, and influence. This had contributed to relaxation in observance of the Rule, as well as involvement in temporal affairs of society and the world. Observance in some monasteries had

7. For a translation and brief discussion of the events recounted in the *Vita Antiqua of St. William of St. Thierry* (MS Lat. 11782 of the Bibliothèque Nationale), see David N. Bell, "The Vita Antiqua of William of Saint Thierry," *Cistercian Studies* 11 (1976): 246–55.

slackened considerably. Some had succumbed to lukewarmness; some had slipped even further into carelessness.

The monastery of Cîteaux, near Dijon, was founded in the early twelfth century as a corrective to the mitigation and laxity of Cluny. With enormous zeal and vigor, it heralded a restoration of the spirit of St. Benedict and observance of the authentic letter of the Rule. It championed a return to the manual work that St. Benedict had espoused and a faithful observance of the Rule. It sought to strip away the many customs, embellishments, and additional observances that had become entrenched over the years and that were actually superfluous to and a distraction from the authentic observance of the Rule. The reform movement strove to revitalize the monastic tradition of old by following the Rule, simply and strictly, without compromise or mitigation. At root, it was motivated by a fervor for the original purity of monastic life, a zeal for the pristine ideals of monasticism, and a yearning for the simplicity, silence, and solitude, the austerity and asceticism of monastic life.

Tension inevitably emerged between Cîteaux and Cluny, between the Cistercian Order and the traditional Benedictine monasticism of the Cluniac form. There was thus deep conflict in the Benedictine world of Cluny to which William belonged. While not a member of the Cluniac Order per se, the abbey of St. Nicaise, where William had taken the black habit of the Benedictines, and the abbey of St. Thierry, where he was abbot, had both adopted the mitigated usages of Cluny.

Meanwhile, as monasticism was facing a radical challenge and impetus to reform, new currents were also emerging in theology, currents that would eventually flower in the scholastic theological synthesis that would be the achievement of the thirteenth century. Peter Abelard and his followers were bringing the method of dialectic and a heavy reliance on metaphysics and logic to the task of theology. Concerned to conserve and defend the tradition, William was relentless in his opposition to such novelties that, according to William's assessment, were imperiling the tradition. With a keen eye for error, William was a severe critic of Abelard's theology in particular, denouncing Abelard's errors to the by then powerful Bernard of Clairvaux, and urging Bernard to censure Abelard. At root was the perennial question of the relationship of faith and reason, and the proper application of Anselm's notion of theology as faith seeking understanding (*fides quaerens intellectum*) in the exploration of the mysteries of faith, a question that continues to challenge us today.

This issue of faith in relation to reason is especially pertinent in trinitarian theology. Against Peter Abelard, William insisted that the mystery of the Trinity does not yield to the faculty of human reason, but is rather to be approached by way of loving contemplation. William emphasized the utter transcendence of God, and the sheer incomprehensibility and ineffableness of the mystery of the Trinity. Faith, William insisted, is the key to an understanding of the mystery.

William's Writings

As Bernard McGinn explains, William writes with "a distinctive style—complex, often knotty, capable of passion and precision, though at times bordering on opacity."[8] William writes in fluent Latin and, as is the norm for the period, uses the Vulgate Bible.[9] He was clearly well educated in Scriptures and in the writings of the patristic fathers, including some of the Greek fathers. Contemporary scholarship is unresolved in regard to William's knowledge of Greek and on the level of influence of the Greek fathers in his thought, particularly regarding the notion of the trinitarian image and likeness in the human person. While some argue that William has quite a wide knowledge of Eastern sources, it is much more probable that William knew those sources only through translations and the writings of Latin masters.

William clearly knows Augustine's work well and his writings show the clear influence of Augustine's thought. But William's work is by no means a mere repetition of Augustine's approach and method and is distinctly his own. Indeed, as Odo Brooke has noted in his incisive study of William's work: "the Augustinian images undergo a profound transformation, through William's greater emphasis on the dynamic conception of the 'image' as an imprint impelling the soul towards the final 'resemblance' of participation in the trinitarian life."[10] William is also clearly alert to contemporary theological questions of his day and to newly emerging

8. McGinn, *The Growth of Mysticism*, 227.

9. The Vulgate Bible is the Latin translation of the Bible attributed to St. Jerome in the late fourth century and later accorded official status by the church.

10. Odo Brooke, "The Trinitarian Aspect of the Ascent of the Soul to God in the Theology of William of St. Thierry," in *Studies in Monastic Theology*, Cistercian Studies Series 37 (Kalamazoo, MI: Cistercian Publications, 1980), 14. For a discussion of the relationship of Augustine's approach to the mystery of the Trinity and that of William of St. Thierry, see Brooke, "The Trinitarian Aspect," esp. 19–20, 34; J. M. Déchanet, *Exposition on the Song of Songs*, trans. Columba Hart (Kalamazoo, MI: Cistercian Publications, 2006), xl–xlvi; and David N. Bell, *The Image and Likeness: The Augustinian Spirituality of William of St. Thierry* (Kalamazoo, MI: Cistercian Publications, 1984).

theological methods, as is well attested, for example, by his vehement refutation of the work of Peter Abelard and of William of Conches.

Currently, eighteen theological and mystical treatises are considered to be the work of William.[11] *On Contemplating God* (*De contemplando Deo*) is fashioned along lines of St. Augustine's *Confessions* and *Soliloquies*, and has a sequel, *The Nature and Dignity of Love* (*De natura et dignitate amoris*), in which William presents a comprehensive account of human love enlightened and transformed by God's grace, under the impetus of the Holy Spirit. In *The Mirror of Faith* (*Speculum fidei*) and its companion volume, *The Enigma of Faith*, William expounds a distinctly trinitarian mysticism and theology. The latter is effectively a tract on the Trinity, a rigorous theological exposition of the mystery of the Trinity. *On the Sacrament of the Altar* (*De sacramento altaris*) treats the manner of the presence of Jesus Christ in the Eucharist. *Meditativae orationes* is a collection of meditations. The *Exposition on the Song of Songs* (*Expositio super Cantica canticorum*) provides William, as for so many other mystics, with the opportunity to express the role of Jesus Christ and of the Holy Spirit in the soul's search for the joy of union with its Lover, God. A biography of Bernard of Clairvaux remained unfinished on William's death.

Without doubt, William's best-known work is *Epistle to the Brothers of Mont Dieu* (*Epistola ad Fratres de Monte Dei*), or the *Golden Epistle*, as it came to be known. This was written about 1144 when William was at Signy. It is the last of William's spiritual writings. Though never intended for the public eye, this is the work that has captured the most attention and secured William's place for posterity as a master of the spiritual life. It was written for the Carthusian community of monks at the charterhouse at Mont Dieu, following a series of talks that William had given to them while staying with them around 1144. William clearly had particular affection and admiration for the Carthusian monks, who were renowned for their holiness and for their life of personal solitude. Despite explicit references to William's other works in the introduction to the letter, not long after William's death, the letter came to be attributed to Bernard, and was so for about four hundred years hence.

The *Golden Epistle* is a remarkable letter in a number of ways, not least because it witnesses, par excellence, to the golden age of Western monasticism. It is not a theological treatise as such, but rather a kind of apologia for the monastic ideal and a summa of mystical theology. In it, William stresses humility, fidelity, and the constant exercise of prayer in monastic life–the

11. Translations of most of his works are found in the Cistercian Fathers Series, published by Cistercian Publications.

Divine Office and prayers according to the Rule, but also private prayer. Other masters and teachers of the spiritual life, including Bonaventure, Anthony of Padua, Jan van Ruusbroec, Francis de Sales, and Hadewijch refer to it with admiration, albeit thinking it to be the work of Bernard.

In regard to himself, William offers only the scantiest autobiographical comment and does not provide a personal account of his mystical experience. What we can however sense in his writings, perhaps most especially in his commentary on the *Song of Songs*, the *Meditations*, *On Contemplating God*, and the *Golden Epistle*, is an indication of the mystical heights that he himself must have experienced in order to be able to write with such warmth, lucidity, and profundity about the contemplative life. His writings evince a profound intuition of union with God and the knowledge that union in love affords. William's writings also evince a richness and sophistication of thought. He is clearly an insightful thinker with a strong capacity for speculative thought. By virtue of his own experience and context, he is more aptly described as a mystical theologian than a speculative theologian.

William's Insights into the Mystery of the Trinity

It is in William's *The Mirror of Faith* and its companion volume, *The Enigma of Faith*, that William most fully expounds his trinitarian theology. Other writings, such as the *Exposition on the Song of Songs* and the *Golden Epistle*, attest more clearly to the mystical experience in which William's thought has its deeply experiential roots. On the other hand, his treatise against Abelard (*Disputatio adversus Petrum Abelardum*) is a counter to the rationalist approach of his contemporary.

In his Prefactory Letter to the Brethren at Mont Dieu, William explains that he wrote *The Mirror of Faith* and *The Enigma of Faith* for the Carthusian monks as an encouragement to their faith and a consolation in their solitude. *The Mirror of Faith* deals mainly with faith as the means of seeing and knowing God in this life, while *The Enigma of Faith* treats the object of faith, God, Trinity of Father, Son, and Holy Spirit, in a more speculative fashion. William explains: "That work is divided into two books, the first of which, because it is straightforward and easy, I entitled *The Mirror of Faith*: the second, because it will be found to contain a summary of the grounds and the formulations of faith according to the words and the thought of the Catholic Fathers and is a little more obscure, *The Enigma of Faith*" (Prefactory Letter §7, *Golden Epistle*). The titles of the works are inspired by Paul's words in the First Letter to the Corinthians: "For now we see in a mirror, dimly [lit. an enigma], but then we will see face to face. Now I know only in part; then I will know fully, even as I have been fully known" (1 Cor 13:12). This Pauline text is highly significant for William, encapsulating the interrelatedness of seeing and knowing, of vision and understanding that permeates his thinking.

As for many of his medieval contemporaries, William shows a certain predilection for triads. He engages a number of them, including that of the three theological virtues (faith, hope, and charity) and Augustine's psychological triad of memory, intellect, and love, and its variants, to describe the human person's progress to union with God. But unlike Augustine, with whose work William is clearly well acquainted, William shows no great interest in detailed exploration of trinitarian analogies. William's concern is not an explication or even an exploration of the mystery of the Trinity per se, and of questions such as how the procession of the Holy Spirit differs from that of the Son, which so vexed Augustine. William writes to refute and correct certain errors of method and approach that he detects in some spheres of theological speculation of his time, most notably in the work of Peter Abelard, and to describe the ascent of the soul to union with God. William understands that the soul's capacity for ascent to God and entry into trinitarian communion is grounded in the imprint of the Trinity in the human person, an imprint there indelibly from the very beginning. It is this imprint of the Trinity on the soul that constitutes the human person as *imago Dei, imago Trinitatis*, and therein lies the possibility of the human person's attainment of similitude or likeness to the Trinity, *similitudo Trinitatis*, and participation in the innertrinitarian communion.

An understanding of the human person as *imago Dei* lies at the heart of William's theology. For William, the divine image is really imprinted, like an indelible seal of the divine persons, from the very first moment of creation of the human person, in the faculties of memory, reason, and will. William explains:

> When [God] infused the breath of life into the face of, and by infusing created, the new man . . . He established in his, as it were, fortress the power of memory so that he might always remember the power-fulness and goodness of the Creator. Immediately and without any delay, memory of itself begets reason, then both memory and reason from themselves bring forth the will. . . . These three (memory, reason, and will) are one yet effectively three, just as in the supreme Trinity there is one substance and three persons. As in that Trinity the Father is the one who begets, the Son the one begotten, and the Holy Spirit the one who proceeds from both, so reason is begotten

from memory and from both memory and reason proceeds the will. (*Nature and Dignity of Love* §3)

William then draws a direct correspondence between the three faculties and the three divine persons, and, moreover, describes each of the divine persons as laying claim to the respective faculties:

> So that the rational soul created in man may adhere to God, therefore, the Father claims the memory for himself, the Son the reason, and the Holy Spirit, who proceeds from both, claims the will proceeding from both. (*Nature and Dignity of Love* §3)

It is because of this indestructible imprint of the Trinity that the soul, by its very nature and structure, is naturally inclined to and positively drawn to union with the Trinity. By no means a static *imago*, the soul is impelled, in a distinctly trinitarian dynamic, to ever closer resemblance or similitude to its trinitarian Creator. The ground for the experience of union with God is grounded precisely here in this primordial image, indelibly imprinted from the very first moment of creation.

Sin, on the other hand, causes a disturbance of this likeness, a disruption to the soul's movement toward God. Because of sin, the image of the Trinity in the human person, and thus the human person's capacity to know God, is blighted. William recognizes that faith is the first vital step in restoration of the divine image, as is exemplified in Mary, the Mother of God, and her *fiat* in response to God. Here William understands the restorative, creative, and transformative dynamism of grace. By illuminating the soul's faculties of memory, reason, and will, grace restores the image to its original representation of the trinitarian image and likeness. The restoration of the image into a likeness or resemblance is the human person's perfection, the end for which the human person was created. William explains: "Resemblance to God is the whole of man's perfection. . . . For to this end alone were we created and do we live, to be like God; for we were created in his image" (*Golden Epistle* §259).

A text from the First Letter of John is particularly influential in William's understanding of the soul's ascent to union with God: "Beloved, we are God's children now; what we will be has not yet been revealed. What we do know is this: when he is revealed, we will be like him, for we will see him as he is" (1 John 3:2-3). The text provides the basis for William's understanding of the interconnection and reciprocity of vision (i.e., knowledge) and likeness. To see God is to be like God. Correlatively, to be like God (similitude) is to see (and to know) God. Without ever collapsing one into the other, William recognizes a reciprocity, indeed an equivalence, between knowledge and likeness.

A text from Matthew's gospel is also highly instructive for William: "No one knows the Son except the Father, and no one the Father except the Son and anyone to whom the Son chooses to reveal him" (Matt 11:27). William explains: "as for the Father to know the Son is nothing else but to be what the Son is, and for the Son to know the Father is simply to be what the Father is, . . . and as for the Holy Spirit to know and understand the Father and the Son is simply to be what the Father and Son are, so is it with us . . . to love and to fear God is nothing other than to be of one spirit with him" (*On Contemplating God* §11). Again, William stresses the reciprocity of knowledge and likeness. The greater the likeness, the greater the knowledge. The greater the likeness, the greater also is the union. Here William is particularly mindful of a text from the farewell discourse in John's gospel, which connects knowledge with mutual abiding: "On that day you will know that I am in my Father, and you in me, and I in you" (John 14:20).

In *The Mirror of Faith*, William treats the trinity of virtues—faith, hope, and charity—by which one attains union with the Trinity of Father, Son, and Holy Spirit. William understands that it is precisely through this trinity of virtues that one is restored to the image and likeness of the Trinity and thus initiated into the life of the Trinity. In the opening paragraph of *The Mirror of Faith*, William explains:

> Among all the saving acts of God, our Salvation, which our God, the God who saves us, has proposed to men to be observed for his salva-tion, these three, as the Apostle says, remain: Faith, Hope, and Charity. And they are to be observed in a special way by all who are to be saved. For the mind of the faithful soul the Holy Trinity has constituted this trinity to His image and likeness. By it we are renewed in the inner person to the image of him who created us. (*Mirror of Faith* §1)

Indeed, William brings *The Mirror of Faith* to conclusion with a prayer for this trinity of virtues and for union with God, union with the Trinity:

> O You whom no one truly seeks and does not find, . . . find us that we may find you! Come within us that we may go to you and live in you, for surely this comes not from the person willing, nor from the person running but from you who have mercy! Inspire us first that we may believe! Strengthen us that we may hope! Call us forth and set us on fire that we may love. May everything of ours be yours "that we may truly be in you," in whom we live and move and have our being. (*Mirror of Faith* §32)

William frequently stresses the necessity of grace in the exercise of the virtues and the transforming power of grace in the restitution of the divine image:

> Anyone who truly seeks the Triune God therefore must strive to have the trinity of these powers in himself and must eagerly study to conform himself to their teaching. Consciousness of them is a paradise of delights that enjoys an abundance of graces along with chaste delights of the holy powers. Here man, native to this paradise, converses with God. He often sees Him, he often hears Him speaking, he often speaks with Him. (*Mirror of Faith* §3)

Not only does the human person, restored to the divine image and likeness, enjoy the grace of conversing with God, seeing him, hearing him, speaking with him, but the human person finds him- or herself in the very midst of the divine persons, united to God by that *same love* whereby the Father and Son are united in love *in the very person of the Holy Spirit*:

> Such is the astounding generosity of the Creator to the creature; the great grace, the unknowable goodness, the devout confidence of the creature for the Creator, the tender approach, the tenderness of a good conscience, that man somehow finds himself in their midst, in the embrace and kiss of the Father and Son, that is, in the Holy Spirit. And he is united to God by that charity whereby the Father and Son are one. He is made holy in Him who is the holiness of both. (*Mirror of Faith* §32)

For William, the soul's ascent to union with the Trinity occurs, not simply *through the agency of the Holy Spirit*, but actually *in the very person of the Holy Spirit* as bond of union of Father and Son, their kiss, their embrace, their love, the unity and oneness of Father and Son. Alluding to the psalmist's vision of abyss calling to abyss (Ps 42:7), and contrasting the Spirit's role in our human earthly existence and in the Trinity, William insists that it is "absolutely the same Spirit":

> This embrace is the Holy Spirit. He is the Communion, the Charity, the Friendship, the Embrace of the Father and of the Son; and he himself is all these things in the love of the Bridegroom and Bride. But on the one hand stands the majesty of consubstantial Nature; on the other, the gift of grace. On the one hand, dignity; on the other, condescension. Nevertheless, it is the same, absolutely the same Spirit. True, this embrace is begun here, to be perfected elsewhere. This deep calls on another deep. (*Song of Songs* §132)

It is the Holy Spirit who effects the restored likeness to God. It is in and through the person of the Holy Spirit, who is, in person, the bond of union of Father and Son, that the human person enters into the very midst of the trinitarian relations and into the communion of the Trinity, "to become not God but what God is." As William again explains, clearly recognizing the distinction between God and the soul in this state of union:

> The soul in its happiness finds itself standing midway in the Embrace and the Kiss of Father and Son. In a manner which exceeds description and thought, the man of God is found worthy to become not God but what God is, that is to say man becomes from grace what God is by nature. (*Golden Epistle* §263)

Throughout his writings, William stresses the particular role of the Holy Spirit as bond of union between Father and Son and bond of union between the human person and God. The Holy Spirit is not simply one *with* the Father and Son, but their very oneness. William recognizes the same mutuality in our love and knowledge of God as between the divine persons in the Trinity.

In contradistinction to any notion that the mystery of God can be approached by way of reason, such as William detected in Abelard's thought, William insists that the reality and the mystery of God can *only* be grasped by love. He recognizes that love is "the sense of the soul" in regard to the things of God, divine things. Thus William speaks in terms of the "*sensus amoris.*" It is the sense of the soul, akin to a blind person's sense of touch, by which the human person not only loves God but feels God, senses God, and comes to an understanding of God. William explains:

> When it senses things rational, reason goes out to them and once it has returned, the mind is transformed to these realities and understanding occurs. But in those things which pertain to God, the sense of the mind is love. By this it senses whatever it senses of God, according to the spirit of life [*Spiritus vitae*]. And, the spirit of life is the Holy Spirit; by him anyone loves who loves what truly ought to be loved. (*Mirror of Faith* §27)

Here William appeals to an understanding of the knowledge of the senses— that we know what we sense when and because we are transformed in some way into what it is that we sense. In other words, a knower's knowledge of some object comes about by the formation of—and the mind's conformation to—a likeness, a "similitude" (*similitudo*), of the object in the mind of the knower. William thus understands and indeed insists that we know God in and through being transformed into a likeness of God. We note again the interconnection and interpenetration of knowledge and likeness that is so important in William's theology, inspired by 1 John 3:2-3 in which vision and likeness go hand in hand.

William understands that this transformation into the likeness of God occurs by way of the love that is the Holy Spirit. It is by participation in the person of the Holy Spirit, who is the mutual love and union of Father and Son, that we become like God and, in becoming like God, know God. It is through the Holy Spirit that the human person participates in the love and the knowledge that is the trinitarian communion. Our union with God is thus effected in and through the person of the Holy Spirit.

In this way, William, without ever resiling from the sheer transcendence of God, articulates in very explicit trinitarian terms, and indeed distinctly *innertrinitarian* terms, the soul's ascent to union with God and the knowledge of God *in se* that is thus attained, not by way of theological speculation, but by way of love and the *sensus amoris* by which the human person loves, senses, and knows God. It is love, he insists, that grasps the ungraspable and comprehends the incomprehensible:

> This process [of transformation into what one senses] happens in a more forceful and more worthy manner when he, the Holy Spirit, who is the substantial will of the Father and the Son, so attaches the will of a person to Himself that the soul, loving God and, by loving, sensing Him, will be unexpectedly and entirely transformed, not into the nature of divinity certainly, but into a kind of blessedness beyond the human form yet short of the divine, in the joy of illuminating grace and the sense of an enlightened conscience. (*Mirror of Faith* §30)

For William, it is therefore the Holy Spirit who is the great master of the spiritual life. It is the Holy Spirit who attracts the memory, enlightens the intellect, and enkindles the heart. It is the Holy Spirit who waits, prompts, teaches, and draws the human person ever more deeply into the mystery of God and lets him or her "see" God. It is in and through the Holy Spirit that our likeness to God is restored and we come to participate in the innertrinitarian communion and thus come to share in the very love and knowledge with which God loves God's self.

Much more than mere appropriation is implied here in William's understanding of the role of the Holy Spirit, though in his treatment of appropriation per se (in *The Enigma of Faith*) William follows the classical approach. He offers no account of how to reconcile these two approaches. Odo Brooke makes a helpful and thought-provoking observation in this regard:

It should be noticed that the texts treating of appropriation are con-cerned with another problem from that of the texts on the restoration of resemblance. The texts treating of appropriation are concerned with the attributes of the divine essence in opposition to Abelard's supposed attempt to make the attributes of power, wisdom and love constitutive of the person, whereas the texts treating of resemblance are concerned with our participation in the life of the Holy Ghost, conceived as the mutual unity of the Father and the Son. . . . But the essential point of these texts does not lie in the conception of an action *ad extra*, but in the participation in the life of the Holy Ghost in what William conceived as proper to the Holy Ghost, the mutual unity of the Father and the Son.[12]

Despite the conundrum it raises, in William's theology the role of our sanctification and participation in the mystery of the Trinity is proper to the person of the Holy Spirit. It is important to note that, for William, the Holy Spirit is the bond of *both mutual knowledge and mutual love* that unites Father and Son, not just, as for Augustine, the bond of mutual love. This is well demonstrated in the following passage, in which the inspiration of Matt 11:27 is also clear:

But the recognition which is mutual to the Father and Son is the very unity of both, which is the Holy Spirit. The recognition by which they recognize one another is nothing other than the substance by which they are what they are. Yet in this recognition no one learns to know the Father except the Son and no one learns to know the Son except the Father and him to whom He chooses to reveal Him. These are the Lord's words. The Father and the Son reveal this to certain persons then, to those to whom They will, to those to whom They make it known, that is, to whom They impart the Holy Spirit, who is the common knowing or the common will of both. Those therefore to whom the Father and the Son reveal [Themselves] recognise them as the Father and the Son recognise Themselves, because they have within themselves Their mutual knowing, because they have within themselves the unity of both, and their will or love: all that the Holy Spirit is. (*Mirror of Faith* §31)

For William, the Holy Spirit is not just mutual love but mutual knowl-edge. The Holy Spirit is, in a sense, *amor-intellectus*, the love that is knowl-edge and the knowledge that is love. Here is another vital notion in William's theology and another counter to the notions that he detected

12. Brooke, *Studies in Monastic Theology*, 31.

we become the Holy Spirit.

and rejected in Abelard's thought. In the Holy Spirit, and thus in our union with the Holy Spirit, love is understanding. It is not that William collapses the distinction between love and knowledge; it is rather a matter of the interpenetration of love and the knowledge that is born of love and that goes beyond all human understanding. Hence, only reason humbled by love, as William insists,[13] can fruitfully probe the mysteries of faith.

William would have us understand that, in the soul's loving union with God, reason passes over into love and into an understanding that surpasses the capacity of reason alone. In other words, in the soul's ascent to union with God, love gradually subsumes and transcends reason, and leads the human person to union of spirit (*unitas spiritus*). In this, the highest stage in the ascent of love, we *become* the Holy Spirit, who is, in person, the very unity and oneness, the mutual love and knowledge of Father and Son. In his *Exposition on the Song of Songs*, William describes the intimacy of this blissful union in terms of the kiss and embrace of bride and bridegroom, reiterating that "all this is the Holy Spirit":

> They are named Bride and Bridegroom, while words are sought that may somehow express in human language the charm and sweetness of this union, which is nothing else than the unity of the Father and the Son of God, their Kiss, their Embrace, their Love, their Goodness and whatever in that supremely simple Unity is common to both. All this is the Holy Spirit—God, Charity, at once Giver and Gift. Upon this bed are exchanged that kiss and that embrace by which the Bride begins to know as she herself is known. And as happens in the kisses of lovers, who by a certain sweet, mutual exchange, impart their spirit each to the other, so the created spirit pours itself out wholly into the Spirit who creates it for this very effusion; and the Creator Spirit infuses himself into it as he wills, and man becomes one spirit with God. (*Song of Songs* §95)

In that state of union, William explains, echoing the Pauline text, 1 Corinthians 13:12, the soul "begins to know as she herself is known." Self-knowledge comes with God-knowledge. Only with God-knowledge does the human person attain authentic knowledge of self.

William's notion of *unitas spiritus* (unity of spirit) is inspired by Paul's words: "But anyone united to the Lord becomes one spirit with him"

---

13. Reason is humbled in the sense that love has priority over reason. William is clearly arguing against the scholastic notion—a dangerous pretension, in William's view—that reason is the greater faculty. Both are necessary in the ascent, William argues, but love has the priority.

(1 Cor 6:17).[14] William explains: "There is yet another likeness . . . It is so close in its resemblance that it is styled not merely a likeness but unity of spirit. It makes man one with God, one spirit, . . . It is called unity of spirit not only because the Holy Spirit brings it about or inclines a man's spirit to it, but because it is the Holy Spirit himself, the God who is Charity" (*Golden Epistle* §262-63). *Unitas spiritus* means that the love and the knowledge with which God loves and knows God's self innertrinitarianly is the love and the knowledge with which God loves us and we, God. It is a grace, it is gift, indeed it is the Holy Spirit himself. It is a unity that *is* the Holy Spirit. In other words, the Holy Spirit, the love of God, may so transform our human love into divine love and our faith into understanding (*intellectus*), that we become one spirit with God. The human soul can then sense God, because its senses, its ways of knowing, have been transformed into the very being they sense.

There is no hint of pantheism in William's thinking, however. He has no doubts about the distinction between this *unitas spiritus* and the trinitarian mystery of the unity of the divine persons. William stresses that the Holy Spirit's indwelling in the human person is not to be equated with the Holy Spirit's indwelling in the Trinity, where Holy Spirit is consubstantially one with Father and Son. The Holy Spirit's indwelling in the human person is by grace, not by nature as in the Trinity wherein the Holy Spirit is of the same nature and substance as Father and Son. As William explains:

> Yet this [presence of the Holy Spirit] is so in one way in the divine substance wherein he himself is consubstantially one with the Father and Son, but in another way in inferior matter. . . . There [in God] the mutual recognition of the Father and Son is unity. Here [in us] it is a likeness of man to God; of it the Apostle John says in his epistle: We will be like to him because we will see him as he is [1 John 3:2]. (*Mirror of Faith* §31)

William continues, describing that blessed state of union with God wherein the human person will see God and be like God:

> There, to be like God will be either to see or to recognise him. One will see or recognise him, will see or recognise to the extent that he will be like Him. He will be like Him to the extent that he will see and recognise Him. For to see or to recognise God there is to be like to God and to be like to God is to see or to recognise Him. (*Mirror of Faith* §32)

14. See Jacques Delesalle, "On Being 'One Single Spirit' with God in the Works of William of Saint-Thierry," *Cistercian Studies Quarterly* 33, no. 1 (1998): 19–28.

Here too we see the profound influence in William's thought of those Johannine words that connect knowledge (seeing) with likeness: "we will be like him, for we will see him as he is" (1 John 3:2). But notice that William also reverses the order of seeing and being like God. Where John writes that "we shall be like him, for we shall see him as he is," William explains that we shall see him, for—and to the extent that—we shall be like him.

Here is the heart of the matter, as William understands it: vision comes through participation. It is participation in the divine life that allows the vision, the sense, the understanding, an understanding that reason unaided can never attain. Hence William's adage, *Amor ipse intellectus est*.[15] Love itself is understanding. There is an understanding that is only accessible by love. As William explains in his *Exposition on the Song of Songs*: "For love of God itself is knowledge of him; unless he is loved, he is not known, and unless he is known, he is not loved. He is known only insofar as he is loved, and he is loved only insofar as he is known" (*Song of Songs* §76). In this state of grace, love and understanding mutually interpenetrate each other, as they do in the very person of the Holy Spirit in the innertrinitarian mystery. The human person then loves and knows, not in a human way, but *in divino modo*, a divine mode of knowledge, that is otherwise utterly beyond our understanding. As William reiterates: "But from the Bride to the Bridegroom, knowledge and love are all the same, for here love itself is understanding" (*Song of Songs* §57). *Amor ipse intellectus est*. William intends neither a tautology nor a reduction nor an identification of understanding and love. Rather, he comprehends that there is an understanding attained by love that is utterly beyond the capacities and boundaries of human reason. It is not just a knowing *about* God but knowing God *in se*.[16]

For William, it is only by entry into and participation in the mystery of the Trinity that we come to understand it. That the mystery is beyond rational penetration does not mean that it is beyond experience. Indeed, an understanding is only possible through experience. Hence William's insistence: *Credo ut experiar*! (Believe in order to experience.) Augustine's *Credo ut intelligam* (Believe in order to understand) thus yields, in William's mystical theology, to *Credo ut experiar*. For William, that experience is ultimately the

15. As has been noted by several scholars, the immediate background to William's *Amor ipse intellectus est* is Gregory the Great's *Amore ipse notitia est*.

16. In a similar way, William often speaks of *intellectus amoris*, that higher level of knowledge and understanding than is accessible by reason alone, an interpenetration of knowledge and love, without loss of distinction between the two. See Patrick Ryan, "*Sensus Amoris*: The Sense of Love in Two Texts of William of Saint Thierry," *Cistercian Studies Quarterly* 40, no. 2 (2005): 163–72.

experience of the Trinity, the communion of the Father and the Son and their mutual union in reciprocal love and knowledge, the Holy Spirit.

In *The Enigma of Faith*, William, in more speculative style, treats five key themes—(1) vision and knowledge of God; (2) faith in the Trinity; (3) degrees of knowledge; (4) divine names; and (5) contemplation of the mystery of the Trinity—and in the course of the tract treats such matters as the divine subsistent relations, persons, the divine names, and the strategy of appropriation. Fashioned in reaction—and as a corrective—to the rationalist approach that William perceived in Peter Abelard's *Theologia scholarium*, William is there concerned to develop a methodology by which to speak of the mystery of the Trinity, without exceeding the capacities and limitations of human reason. Reason alone, he again insists, is incapable of coming to a knowledge of God. Two eyes, love and reason, are involved in seeing God, as William explains in the *Nature and Dignity of Love*:

> The sight for seeing God, the natural light of the soul therefore, created by the Author of nature, is charity. There are, however, two eyes in this sight, always throbbing by a sort of natural intention to look toward the light that is God: love and reason. When one attempts to look without the other, it does not get far. When together they help one other, they can do much, that is, when they become the single eye. (*Nature and Dignity of Love* §21)[17]

William demonstrates considerable reliance on Augustine's terms and concepts in *The Enigma of Faith*. While he remains ever close to the thought and conceptuality of Augustine, this is by no means mere repetition, however. Distinct differences and developments are evident, most obviously in William's understanding of the person of the Holy Spirit as the mutual bond of union of Father and Son. He writes:

> There, as in the Trinity, which is God, the Father and the Son mutually see one another and their mutual vision consists in their being one and in the fact that the one is what the other is, so those who have been predestined for this and have been taken up into it will see God as he is, and in seeing him as he is they will become like him. And there, as in the Father and the Son, that which is vision is also unity; so in God and man that which is vision will be the likeness that is to come. The Holy Spirit, the unity of the Father and the Son, is himself the love and likeness of God and man. (*Enigma of Faith* §5)

17. Hence William's notion of "humbled reason." See also *Song of Songs* §92, and *Golden Epistle* §196.

To see, to know, to participate in the mutual knowledge and love of the Father and Son, this is the soul's ultimate transformation, the perfection of the *similitudo Dei*. And this transformation, which is heaven for us, is achieved in the very person of the Holy Spirit, as William reflects in one of his meditations:

> As I see it then our dwelling in you and yours in us is heaven for us. But for you the heaven of heavens is your eternity, where you are what you are in your own self. The Father is in the Son and the Son in the Father; and the bond that unites you, Father and Son, is the Holy Spirit, who comes not as it were from somewhere else to be the link between you, but who exists as such by virtue of his unity of being with you both. It is in the Holy Spirit too, who creates and sets in order the unity that makes us one among ourselves and in you. (*Meditations* 6, §7)

As William never fails to stress, returning always to his notion of the indelible imprint of the Trinity in the very constitution of the human person: "For to this end alone were we created and do we live, to be like God; for we were created in his image" (*Golden Epistle* §259).

Conclusion

Thomas Merton said of William, "There is not a line of his writing that is not filled with the light and unction of the Holy Spirit."[18] Indeed, it is the Holy Spirit who dominates William's insights into the mystery of the Trinity.[19] While he understands the soul's union with God as the action of the whole Trinity, the Holy Spirit stands at center stage in his theology. William understands that our experience of the Trinity, our entry into the trinitarian communion, is grounded in the very person of the Holy Spirit as bond of union, mutual love *and knowledge* of Father and Son, their kiss and embrace, their very oneness; and that too for the human person in union with God. William would have us understand that the very desire to enter into union with God is itself the embrace of the Holy Spirit that carries us into the mystery of the Father and the Son. There is no sense

18. Thomas Merton, "Blessed William of Saint-Thierry: Monk of Signy," *Cistercian Studies Quarterly* 35, no. 1 (2000): 5.

19. This emphasis on the role of the Holy Spirit is all the more interesting, given that William writes at a time when a theology of person of the Holy Spirit and of the Spirit's role and gifts is not particularly well developed and precise, in the way that it would later become in the hands of Thomas Aquinas.

of the dark night, such as emerges so prominently in John of the Cross's understanding, but rather a much more positive process of attracting the memory, illuminating the intellect, and enkindling the will. In the person of the Holy Spirit, directly and immediately at work in us, the human person is inserted into the very midst of the Trinity, so to speak, and there enters into the Trinity's knowledge and love of itself. There too the human person also begins to know as he or she is known.

William engages Augustine's conceptual schema to describe the mystery of the Trinity, albeit with some significant modifications, which attest to the originality, independence, depth, and sophistication of his thought.[20] For William, the Holy Spirit is not love as such (as in Augustine's thinking), but the reciprocity of love. Moreover, the Holy Spirit is love *and knowledge*.

Utterly critical to William's theology is the mystery of the human person as created in the image of the Trinity, with the trinitarian image indelibly imprinted on the soul from the moment of creation, impelling it to union with God. In William's theology, the triad of memory, intellect, and will is not just a psychological parallel or image, an illustrative strategy, but a real ontological participation in God, embedded in the very being of the human person. The perfection of the human person lies in the restoration of the image and likeness of the Trinity, effected in and through the person of the Holy Spirit, and thereby participation in the very love and knowledge of the divine persons and entry into the trinitarian communion.

William insists that an understanding of the mystery of the Trinity is only possible through experience, not through the powers of human reason. Hence his dictum, *Credo ut experiar*: Believe in order to experience. Experience in order to love and understand. In love is understanding: *amor ipse intellectus est*. The more we love God, the more we know and understand God. Love is the way of entry into participation in the divine being. It is not so much a matter of an unveiling of the mystery, but a deeper entry into the incomprehensibility of the mystery of unity in Trinity. In that entry into the mystery, love and understanding, similitude (or likeness) and participation (or union) are profoundly and dynamically interconnected. Indeed they interpenetrate each other circumincessively. To love is to know, and with knowledge comes likeness, and with likeness comes

---

20. It is interesting to note that William rejects the definition of Boethius of the person as individual substance of rational nature (whereas Thomas Aquinas will appropriate it into his trinitarian theology); see *Enigma of Faith* §34. McGinn observes that "William understands the nature of the Spirit as essentially intersubjective . . . and circumincessive" (McGinn, *The Growth of Mysticism*, 270–71).

unity of spirit. The greater the participation, the greater the vision, the greater the understanding, the greater the union.

William is rightly described as one of the great masters of trinitarian mysticism, so intrinsically trinitarian is his understanding of the soul's constitution and its journey to union with God. His theology is correspondingly deeply trinitarian, and essentially mystical. Indeed, his is arguably the most profound theology of the Trinity of the twelfth century.

References and Further Reading

Primary Sources

William of Saint Thierry. *The Mirror of Faith*. Translated by Thomas X. David. Cistercian Fathers Series 15. Kalamazoo, MI: Cistercian Publications, 1979.

———. *The Enigma of Faith*. Translated by John D. Anderson. Cistercian Fathers Series 9. Kalamazoo, MI: Cistercian Publications, 1973.

———. *On Contemplating God, Prayer, Meditations*. Translated by Penelope Lawson. Cistercian Fathers Series 3. Kalamazoo MI: Cistercian Publications, 1977.

———. *The Golden Epistle: A Letter to the Brethren at Mont Dieu*. Translated by Theodore Berkeley. Cistercian Fathers Series 12. Kalamazoo, MI: Cistercian Publications, 1971.

———. *The Nature and Dignity of Love*. Translated by Thomas X. Davis. Cistercian Fathers Series 30. Kalamazoo, MI: Cistercian Publications, 1981.

———. *Exposition on the Song of Songs*. Translated by Mother Columba Hart. Cistercian Fathers Series 6. Kalamazoo, MI: Cistercian Publications, 2006.

———. *Exposition on the Epistle to the Romans*. Translated by John Baptist Hasbrouck. Cistercian Fathers Series 27. Kalamazoo, MI: Cistercian Publications, 1980.

Secondary Sources

Bell, David N. *The Image and Likeness: The Augustinian Spirituality of William of St. Thierry*. Kalamazoo, MI: Cistercian Publications, 1984.

Brooke, Odo. *Studies in Monastic Theology*. Kalamazoo, MI: Cistercian Publications, 1980.

McGinn, Bernard. "William of St. Thierry: Spirit-Centered Mysticism." In *The Growth of Mysticism*. Vol. 2, *The Presence of God: A History of Western Christian Mysticism*. 225–74. New York: Crossroad, 1994.

William, Abbot of St. Thierry: An International Colloquium. Translated by Jerry Carfantan. Cistercian Studies Series 94. Kalamazoo, MI: Cistercian Publications, 1987.

2

HILDEGARD OF BINGEN
(1098–1179)

Paris was a flourishing center of learning in the twelfth century, but it was not the only one. The Rhineland was another, and it was there that Hildegard of Bingen emerged. One of the most celebrated women of the Middle Ages, she came to be revered as the Sybil of the Rhine. She described herself more humbly as a feather (*penna*), having no weight of its own, flying or winging on the breath of God: "But I stretch out my hands to God so that he might raise me up like a feather, which, having no weight of its own, flies on the wind" (L103r).[1]

A letter written to her in 1148 by Odo of Soissons, a Master of the University of Paris, seeking Hildegard's advice on a theological issue, illustrates the high regard in which she was held.[2] Odo writes: "It is reported

---

1. Translations from her letters will be taken from *The Letters of Hildegard of Bingen*, trans. Joseph L. Baird and Radd K. Ehrman, 3 vols. (New York: Oxford University Press, 1994–1998). By permission of Oxford University Press. Letters L1–L90 are found in vol. 1; letters L91–L217 in vol. 2; and letters L218–L390 in vol. 3.

In reference to herself as feather, see also Scivias 1.4.2, 112; also *The Life of Hildegard* 2.17, 180, in *Jutta and Hildegard: The Biographical Sources*, trans. Anna Silvas, Brepols Medieval Women Series (University Park: The Pennsylvania State University Press, 1999).

All translations from *Scivias* are taken from *Hildegard of Bingen: Scivias*, trans. Columba Hart and Jane Bishop, Classics of Western Spirituality (New York: Paulist Press, 1990). *Scivias* consists of three parts with twenty-six visions. In references to *Scivias*, e.g., 1.4.2 means book 1, vision 3, part 2.

2. In response to Odo, she writes: "Whoever says that God is not paternity and divinity names a point without a circle, and if he wants to have a point without a circle, he denies Him who is eternal. And whoever denies that God is paternity and divinity denies God, because he wants there to be some void in God. And this is not the case. But God is plenitude, and that which is in God is God. For God cannot be shaken out nor strained through a sieve by human argument, because there is nothing in God which is not God. And since creation has a beginning, it follows that man's reason discovers God through names, for reason itself, by its very nature, is full of names" (L40r).

that, exalted, you see many things in the heavens and record them in your writing, and that you bring forth the melody of a new song" (L40). Pope Eugenius in one of his letters to her writes: "your honourable reputation has spread so far and wide that many people regard you as 'the odour of life unto life' [2 Cor 2:16]" (L4). The monk, Guibert of Gembloux, who in 1177 became her secretary and remained so until her death, writes of her in even more lofty terms:

> Truly, save for her through whose Son we attain our salvation, your grace is unique among women. For although we find in the Scripture some songs and prophecies of Miriam, the sister of Aaron and Moses, or of Deborah or Judith, you seem to us coequal, if I may say so, to those contemplators of the highest mysteries through visions or revelations from the Lord, bedewed much more by the floods of the Spirit. O the wondrous and unceasing mercy toward humankind of our gracious Redeemer! For through the same sex by which death entered the world, life has been restored—through His mother. And the same hand that served us the deadly cup of perdition has now poured out for us the antidote of recovery through your salvific teaching. (L102)

Centuries later, Pope John Paul II in a letter in 1979, commemorating the eight hundredth anniversary of Hildegard's death, refers to her as *Saint Hildegard* and describes her as "a light to her people and her time."[3]

Extraordinarily gifted in many ways, Hildegard of Bingen was a mystic, a visionary, a prophet in the Old Testament tradition, a Benedictine nun, leader of her community, spiritual advisor and counselor, writer, composer, poet, playwright, and physician, as well as theologian. Among her many accomplishments, she invented a secret language, with an alphabet of twenty-three letters, and a vocabulary of about nine hundred words. She founded two monasteries and established a hospice. A constant stream of visitors and correspondents, from Germany and beyond, sought her advice. With ecclesiastical authority, she undertook extensive preaching tours toward the end of her life, urging monastic and clerical reform. She was the author of six major works, and some of her manuscripts include illustrations of the visions on which the writings were based. Indeed, Hildegard was one of the earliest writers to include illustrations alongside the written text. By no means mere decoration to the written text, these illuminations are integral to her theology.

3. See http://www.vatican.va/holy_father/john_paul_ii/letters/1979/documents/hf_jp-ii_let_19790908_800-ildegarda_lt.html (accessed October 25, 2009).

She was a charismatic and capable woman, strong and independent, influential and powerful. A few hundred of her letters survive and they show that she corresponded with the rich and powerful, with leaders of church and society, as well as with simple laypeople. She was not afraid to engage in polemic when she judged it fit, and at one point reproved her patron, the Emperor Frederick I (Barbarossa), for his role in the papal schism.[4] In fact, it was Barbarossa who, in a charter that she obtained from him in 1163, referred to her as abbess; canonically, she was actually not abbess but *magistra*, teacher, under the jurisdiction of the abbot of the monastery of Disibodenberg, through his appointed representative, the *prepositus* or provost of her community of nuns.

As a woman, albeit the *magistra* of a Benedictine community of nuns, she did not have the formal authority of the masters of the schools of Paris. Nevertheless she was renowned for her spiritual insight and enjoyed a reputation comparable with that of the great masters. In an era of renewed interest in trinitarian theology she had a distinctive contribution to make, inspired by her visions. She often used feminine images to articulate the Godhead and its work in the world, again inspired by her visions. She did indeed bring forth "the melody of a new song."

Hildegard's Life and Times

Hildegard was born in the summer of 1098 in the village of Bermersheim, in the German province of Rheinhessen, not far from the cathedral city of Mainz.[5] Her family belonged to the local nobility. She was the tenth child of her parents and, when she was eight years old, her parents offered her, reputedly by way of a tithe, to God, entrusting her to the care of a recluse, ascetic and teacher Jutta von Sponheim (1092–1136), who was just a few years older than Hildegard and a daughter of Count Stephen of Sponheim.

Jutta and Hildegard lived in an anchorhold attached to the Benedictine monastery of Disibodenberg, their lives ordered around the Divine Office.[6] Under Jutta's tutelage, and through immersion in the Psalter that lies at

---

4. Letters 312, 313, 315, 316.

5. For a more detailed introduction to Hildegard's life and works, see Barbara Newman, ed., *The Voice of the Living Light: Hildegard of Bingen and Her World* (Berkeley and Los Angeles: University of California Press, 1998); also the introduction in Baird and Ehrman, *The Letters of Hildegard of Bingen*, vol. 1.

6. See *The Life of Jutta*, in Silvas, *Jutta and Hildegard*, 65–84.

the center of monastic prayer and worship, Hildegard developed at least a rudimentary knowledge of Latin. The precise details of Hildegard's early years and her education are unclear. Sometime around 1112 or 1113, when she was about fifteen, Hildegard chose to make her monastic profession and to follow the Benedictine Rule. It seems that, together with Jutta, Hildegard underwent solemn enclosure.[7]

Jutta gradually built up her own school as other young women joined Jutta and Hildegard. The group eventually became a small community of Benedictine nuns, with monks from the adjoining monastery providing administrative and liturgical services. When Jutta died in 1136, Hildegard, then approaching forty, was elected to take up Jutta's role as *magistra* of the growing community. Hildegard continued in this role until her own death.

Hildegard had visions and mystical experiences from early childhood.[8] In 1175, toward the end of her life, in one of her letters to Guibert, a learned monk from the monastery of Gembloux, in response to whose bidding she spoke of her experiences, Hildegard stressed that her visions, while not perceived by means of her physical senses, were not the outcome of ecstasy. She insists that she saw them with eyes wide open, fully awake, fully conscious.[9] She writes:

> I am now more than seventy years old. But even in my infancy, before my bones, muscles, and veins had reached their full strength, I was possessed of this visionary gift in my soul, and it abides with me still up to the present day. In these visions my spirit rises, as God wills,

7. See *The Life of Jutta* 3, in ibid., 69.

8. From her third year of age, even before she could convey it, according to her, in *The Life of Hildegard* 2.2, in ibid., 158; the age of five years according to *Scivias* Declaration, 59.

9. Some have speculated that these visions, which she received for forty years before experiencing a dramatic prophetic call, were physiologically related to the chronic ill-health, which possibly included migraines, that Hildegard suffered throughout her life. See Oliver Sacks, *Migraine: Understanding a Common Disorder* (Berkeley: University of California Press, 1985), 57, 106–8; Sabina Flanagan, *Hildegard of Bingen, 1098–1179: A Visionary Life*, 2nd ed. (London and New York: Routledge, 1998), 191–201. In autobiographical insertions in *The Life of Hildegard*, for example, Hildegard often refers to her ills: "Indeed, so great was the pressure of pains in my flesh that if they were not from God, I could not have survived for long. However racked I was by these things, still, I continued dictating, singing, and writing through the heavenly vision whatever the Holy Spirit wished to announce through me" (*The Life of Hildegard* 2.10, in *Jutta and Hildegard*, 171); "I have never taken my rest—rather I have been worn out by many trials, till at length God rained down the dew of His grace upon me" (*The Life of Hildegard* 2.14, in *Jutta and Hildegard*, 177).

to the heights of heaven and into the shifting winds, and it ranges among various peoples, even those very far away. And I see in such a fashion, my perception of things depends on the shifting of the clouds and other elements of creation. Still, I do not hear these things with bodily ears, nor do I perceive them with the cogitations of my heart or the evidence of my five senses. I see them only in my spirit, with my eyes wide open, and thus I never suffer the defect of ecstasy in these visions. And, fully awake, I continue to see them day and night. (L103r)

Hildegard kept her visionary experiences to herself, confiding only in Jutta and Volmar, a monk of St. Disibodenberg, who was her teacher, confidant, and confessor, as well as secretary and provost to her convent.[10] Later in her life, however, Hildegard experienced a distinctly different kind of vision, as she recounted to Guibert. She writes:

It happened that, in the eleven hundred and forty-first year of the Incarnation of the Son of God, Jesus Christ, when I was forty-two years and seven months old, Heaven was opened and a fiery light of exceeding brilliance came and permeated my whole brain, and inflamed my whole heart and my whole breast, not like a burning but like a warming flame, as the sun warms anything its rays touch. And immediately I knew the meaning of the exposition of the Scriptures, namely the Psalter, the Gospel and the other catholic volumes of both the Old and the New Testaments, though I did not have the interpretation of the words or their texts or the division of the syllables or the knowledge of cases or tenses. But I had sensed in myself wonderfully the power and mystery of secret and admirable visions from my childhood—that is, from the age of five—up to that time, as I do now. (*Scivias*, Declaration)

In this different kind of vision, there was "a fiery light of exceeding brilliance," a flood of light or fire, rather than images as such, and with it she experienced an infused knowledge—an intuitive grasp—of the meaning of the Scriptures and the mysteries of faith.

Hildegard explained to Guibert that, in this second kind of vision, with its fiery light of exceeding brilliance, she sometimes sees "another light," which she calls "the Living Light." The sight of this Living Light is a source of refreshment and rejuvenation. She explains:

10. In another autobiographical insertion in *The Life of Hildegard*, Hildegard describes her spiritual experiences in childhood, including her first vision. See *The Life of Hildegard* 2.2, in *Jutta and Hildegard*, 157–59.

And sometimes, though not often, I see another light in that light, and this I have called "the Living Light." But I am even less able to explain how I see this light than I am the other one. Suffice it to say that when I do see it, all my sorrow and pain vanish from my memory and I become more like a young girl than an old woman. (L103r)

With this markedly different kind of vision, Hildegard experienced a distinctly prophetic call, a call to write down and speak out about her visions. Nevertheless, she did not make the transition in role from visionary to prophetess with ease. Hildegard confided in Volmar and he urged her to set aside her reluctance and her fear and to follow this call. With his editorial help, Hildegard eventually took up the task of writing, though a certain unease and diffidence persisted. Seeking further confirmation, between 1146 and 1147 she wrote to Bernard of Clairvaux, abbot of the newly founded Cistercian foundation at Clairvaux, asking for his counsel as to whether or not she should speak out about her visions. Bernard replied approvingly, if very briefly, and urged her to exercise the gift that she had been given. He replied: "We rejoice in the grace of God which is in you. And, further, we most earnestly urge and beseech you to recognise this gift as grace and to respond eagerly to it with all humility and devotion" (L1r).

Despite Bernard's assurances, Hildegard was still not entirely sure and sought the validation of her visionary experiences and an authorization of her gifts from the official church. Volmar and the abbot of the monastery of Disibodenberg informed the archbishop of the Diocese of Mainz who authorized an investigation. Hildegard's prophetic gifts were eventually approved at the Synod in Trier by Pope Eugenius III, a Cistercian monk and disciple of Bernard. The pope read from Hildegard's then-incomplete text of the *Scivias* to the assembled prelates at the synod. Bernard of Clairvaux was present at the time and urged reception of Hildegard's gifts, as did Heinrich, archbishop of Mainz. Her writings were received and endorsed with enthusiasm. The pope subsequently instructed her to continue with her writing and to make known all that had been revealed to her. With papal blessing and approval, Hildegard then had the highest ecclesial endorsement possible. She remained in correspondence with Eugenius III.[11]

---

11. Bernard McGinn comments: "Her road to fame was probably a good deal more difficult than her surviving *Epistolarium*, the collection of letters that is our main source, lets on. The text was carefully edited to construct a myth of papal approval and to highlight the rapid recognition of her powers" ("Withdrawal and Return: Reflections on Monastic Retreat from the World," *Spiritus* 6 [2006]: 149–72, at 160).

Hildegard's reputation as a holy and inspired woman spread quickly. Her visions ultimately resulted in the writing of three visionary works: *Scivias* (an abbreviation of *Scito vias Domini*, *Know the Ways of God* or *Know the Ways*), *Liber vitae meritorum* (*The Book of Life's Merits*), and *Liber divinorum operum* (*The Book of Divine Works*).

New aspirants joined Hildegard's convent, eventually necessitating a relocation of the growing community to more adequate accommodation.[12] Despite the abbot's disapproval, Hildegard determined to move to Rupertsberg near Bingen on the Rhine, about twenty miles from Disibodenberg, to a site revealed to her in a vision. The abbot eventually conceded, though the relationship between Disibodenberg and Rupertsberg would be strained for some years. With the support of Heinrich, the archbishop of Mainz, she secured the property. She oversaw the building of her new abbey church and monastery. Hildegard and eighteen nuns with her took up residence in the new foundation. Hildegard retained the services of the monks of the monastery of Disibodenberg for liturgical and administrative services. The convent at Rupertsberg prospered and, in due course, a daughterhouse was established in Eibingen in 1150. Music played a vital part of the liturgical life of her convent.

At age sixty, despite chronic ill-health, Hildegard, with ecclesiastical endorsement, set out on a preaching tour, calling for conversion, especially among monastic communities, but also preaching to clergy and laity on occasion. In fact, Hildegard conducted four extended preaching tours in these latter years, including one in Cologne against the Cathar heresy that was gathering support.[13]

---

12. A letter to Hildegard from Mistress Tengswich of Andernach, who was superior of a foundation of canonesses, indicates some of the unusual features of the convent under Hildegard's leadership. Tengswich speaks, with a certain unmistakable measure of disapproval, of hearing of "certain strange and irregular practices that you countenance. They say that on feast days your virgins stand in the church with unbound hair when singing the psalms and that as part of their dress they wear white, silk veils, so long that they touch the floor. Moreover, it is said that they wear crowns of gold filigree, into which are inserted crosses on both sides and the back, with a figure of the Lamb on the front, and that they adorn their fingers with golden rings. . . . Moreover, that which seems no less strange to us is the fact that you admit into your community only those women from noble, well-established families and absolutely reject others who are of lower birth and of less wealth" (L52).

13. Sabina Flanagan argues the following: "The cases where Hildegard appeared 'before the clergy and people' suggest that she sometimes preached in the cathedral, while the other occasions would have been internal addresses, delivered most probably in the chapter house of the monastery, or possibly in the monastic church" (See Flanagan, *Hildegard of Bingen*, 165).

Toward the end of her life, Hildegard suffered a bitter controversy over the burial of a nobleman in the consecrated ground of the graveyard of Hildegard's convent. Because the nobleman had been excommunicated, his burial in sacred ground was forbidden by the church. Church authorities in Mainz thus demanded that the body be disinterred on pain of Hildegard's own excommunication together with that of her convent. In the course of the controversy, an interdict was imposed on Hildegard's convent, prohibiting the celebration of the Mass and the reception of the sacraments, and also specifically proscribing the singing of the Divine Office.[14] All turned on whether or not the nobleman in question had been reconciled to the church before his death. Hildegard believed that he had and she had witnesses to support her in this conviction (see L24). She refused to accede to the demand for exhumation. The interdict was eventually revoked, just a few months before her death, as it happened. During this period of enforced suppression of the music that was so strong and vibrant a feature of the liturgical life of her convent, Hildegard wrote what amounted to a theology of music, describing music as reflecting the celestial harmony and the delights of paradise (L23).

Hildegard died on September 17, 1179, aged eighty-one. Guibert of Gembloux had commenced the writing of a *vita* during his time as her secretary, but he was unable to complete the project. Another monk, Theodoric of Echternach, was later commissioned to recommence and complete the project, which when finished included extensive autobiographical passages plus a description of many miracles worked by Hildegard.[15]

Veneration of Hildegard flourished almost immediately after her death, including reverence for her shrine. Hildegard continues to enjoy popular devotion in Germany. The Rupertsberg convent was destroyed in 1632 in the Thirty Years' War, but a convent at Eibingen, in close proximity to the site of the original one there, continues today as a place of pilgrimage and veneration.

Proceedings for her canonization commenced in 1233. In 1237, Pope Gregory IX, having received certain documents, wrote in response that the depositions of the witnesses had not been recorded in sufficient detail. Due to technical problems, however, the canonization process was never concluded. Following the unsuccessful canonization attempts, the produc-

14. See Hildegard's letter (L23) to Christian, archbishop of Mainz, who was away at the time of the dispute, where Hildegard informs Christian of the cause of the dispute.

15. See *Jutta and Hildegard: The Biographical Sources.*

tion of copies of her works declined and eventually stopped. Her works enjoyed renewed interest in a modest revival of interest in medieval spiritual and manuscript copying in the fourteenth century, on the eve of the Renaissance. Jacques Paul Migne, in his epic series, *Fathers, Doctors and Writers of the Church*, devoted a volume to Hildegard (PL 197), and she is counted in the Roman Martyrology, with her feast day celebrated on September 17.

The influence and respect that Hildegard enjoyed during her lifetime are all the more remarkable given that she lived in an age when the church authorities were particularly suspicious of the gifts of women. Following the New Testament prohibition on women teaching (most especially 1 Tim 2:9ff), when and if women had authority to teach, it was only in the private, never the public sphere.[16] The Second Lateran Council in 1139 proscribed women not living in common according to the Rule of St. Benedict, Basil, or Augustine (canon 26) as well as nuns singing psalms in the same choir as men (canon 27).[17] The Synod of Reims in 1148, over which Pope Eugenius III presided, declared that nuns and canonesses must at all times live in a convent, divest themselves of their private possessions, and follow strictly the Rule of St. Benedict or that of St. Augustine (canon 4) on pain of the prohibition of the Divine Office in their chapels and Christian burial.

Hildegard herself scorned her era as "an effeminate age" (*mulierbre tempus*), and contrasted it with what she described as the "masculine strength" of the apostolic era.[18] She was very critical of the decadence that she saw in the church and, in particular, the clergy whom she chastised for being lukewarm and sluggish, weak and fickle. In her eyes, the Cathar heresy epitomized the failure of the hierarchy in its leadership of the people.[19] She was a vigorous supporter of the Gregorian reforms instituted under Pope Gregory VII (1073–1085), addressing issues of integrity, independence, and discipline of the clergy.

16. See Elisabeth Schüssler Fiorenza, *In Memory of Her: A Feminist Theological Reconstruction of Christian Origins* (New York: Crossroad, 1983). See also Bernard McGinn, ed., *Meister Eckhart and the Beguine Mystics: Hadewijch of Brabant, Mechthild of Magdeburg, and Marguerite Porete* (New York: Continuum, 1994), 1.

17. See http://www.papalencyclicals.net/Councils/ecum10.htm (accessed October 25, 2009).

18. For her criticisms, see *Scivias* 1.1; L15r; L23; L26r.

19. See L15r for Hildegard's strident criticism of the clergy; see also L16r where she is critical of the failure of those in episcopal office.

Hildegard's Writings

Hildegard, as a woman monastic theologian, is very unusual for her era. First, all of Hildegard's works are written entirely in Latin. Most women of her time received only a limited education and were confined to use of the vernacular. Under the tutelage of her *magistra* Jutta, Hildegard developed at least a rudimentary knowledge of Latin. Admittedly, her writing style is peculiarly and idiosyncratically her own and is frequently dense and opaque. Barbara Newman observes: "Much of the strangeness is due to her diction [i.e., style or phraseology], which has acquired a reputation for difficulty. But her language is not at all precious or studied. The problem is that her basic vocabulary—like that of the Provençal troubadours—was quite small, and she relied heavily on certain polyvalent key words [including *viriditas, virtus*]."[20] But, thanks to Jutta and particularly to her secretary-scribe Volmar, she was deeply formed in and informed by the monastic tradition and way of life. Her writings indicate that she was well read. It is difficult to ascertain her sources, however, because they are not explicitly acknowledged.

Her visions are her source of inspiration for her distinctly theological works. They conferred on her an authority otherwise totally precluded for her, given that, as a woman, formal training in scholastic Latin and in the methods of theology was not available to her. She frequently stresses the divine authorship of her visionary writings. In her declaration at the start of *Scivias*, for example, she reiterates several times that the message to her was to speak and write the things that she saw and heard and that what she writes is not of her own invention or of any other person, but from God. In a letter, she insists: "These words do not come from a human being, but from the Living Light; let the one who hears see and believe where these words come from" (L52r). Throughout her visionary texts, she reiterates that these are not her words, but God's words. She is but the messenger, the prophet, the lowly woman, "a poor little creature" (*paupercula*; L103r), "a poor woman" (L103r; L31r), chosen by God who "chose what is low and despised in the world, things that are not, to reduce to nothing things that are, so that no one might boast in the presence of God" (1 Cor 1:28-29).

While her descriptions of her visions and the accompanying illuminations are justly famous, her primary concern is not to describe her own

20. Hildegard of Bingen, *Symphonia: A Critical Edition of the* Symphonia Armonie Celestium Revelationum, ed. and trans. Barbara Newman (Ithaca, NY: Cornell University Press, 1988), 38.

visionary experiences (which she did only when pressed by her hagiographers), nor to offer instruction on the spiritual life or a cartography of the soul and its union with God or instruction on the ways of contemplative prayer. As is indicated by the very title of her most famous work, *Scivias* (*Know the Ways*), salvation is her foremost concern. She recognizes that salvation requires the effort of both God and the human person and, indeed, that spiritual combat was required of the Christian. In this sense, she is more a prophet than a mystic. Indeed, her correspondents frequently compare her to the biblical prophets, such as Deborah, Miriam, and Judith.[21] Her style is distinctly prophetic, with strong measures of prophetic indignation and proclamation, passion, and urgency. She seldom refers to God in the second person (you), for example.

In dealing with salvation, she treats creation, the fall, and the return to God that the Son's incarnation enables, and the continuation of the Son's work by the church and its mediation of the sacraments. She sees that the redemption that is our salvation is grounded in God's trinitarian life and love, and so her treatment of salvation is thoroughly and profoundly trinitarian. What is particularly unusual is that she includes pictorial representations of her visions together with meticulously detailed commentaries on them.

She worked for about a decade (1141–1151) on her first and most celebrated book of her visions, *Liber Scivias*, or *Scivias*. Pope Eugenius III's unqualified endorsement of it, even when the manuscript was incomplete, assured its success and it remained the best known of her works during Hildegard's lifetime. She reputedly wrote it herself, in Latin, with a stylus on wax tablets, not by dictation. Volmar then transferred the writing from the wax tablets to parchment.

An illuminated *Scivias* manuscript was prepared in Hildegard's scriptorium at Rupertsberg at some stage, date uncertain, perhaps around 1175 to 1180, but possibly earlier. This so-called *Rupertsberg Scivias* includes thirty-five superb illuminations or manuscript paintings that accompany the written text. Their iconography is extraordinary. The production of the illuminations, using gold and silver leaf as well as color, clearly involved considerable expense. Most scholars agree that these superb illustrations were executed either under Hildegard's direction or supervision, or, at least, in her immediate tradition. More than merely illustrations for the purpose of decoration of the manuscript, they are illuminations, properly speaking, into the mystical world of her visions. As Bernard McGinn explains: here,

---

21. See Guibert of Gembloux's letter quoted above, L102.

in Hildegard, "theology is as much visual as verbal—neither side can be neglected in trying to gain an understanding of her teaching."[22]

Scivias is effectively a kind of medieval summa, a guide to Christian doctrine. It describes the creative, redemptive, and sanctifying work of the Trinity. The manuscript is divided into three sections, each section into visions, each vision into a varying number of chapters of varying lengths. Accompanying each vision is a detailed commentary, which is frequently introduced with the formula, "And I heard a voice from heaven, saying . . ." In total, the illuminated manuscript depicts and describes twenty-six visions, illustrated with thirty-five illuminations. In each case, Hildegard first recounts the vision then describes its meaning. The text begins with a declaration (in Latin, *Protestificato veracium visionum a Deo fluentium*), in which Hildegard stresses that what she writes is not of her own invention or of any other person, but from God.[23]

Part 1 of *Scivias* deals with the order of creation, treating God, creation, the fall, humanity, and life. This first part pertains to God the Father. It comprises six chapters and eight illuminations. Part 2 of *Scivias* deals with the order of redemption. It treats Christ's work of salvation and the continuation of that work of salvation by the church, which figures as Mother Church, the great maternal figure of Ecclesia. This second part of *Scivias* pertains to the second person of the Trinity, the Son. It comprises seven chapters, and features seven visions. Eight illuminations feature here. It is in part 2 that Hildegard's famous image of the Trinity, featuring the man in sapphire blue, is found (illumination 11). Part 3 of *Scivias* treats the order of sanctification and treats Christ, the church, the virtues, and the end times. This third part of *Scivias* pertains to the person and power of the Holy Spirit, the third divine person. It comprises thirteen chapters and features thirteen visions. A second image of the Trinity, Column (or Pillar) of the Trinity (illumination 28), figures in this third part of the *Scivias*. Part 3 culminates in the vision of the symphony of heaven, with hymns to Mary, the angels, the patriarchs and prophets, apostles and martyrs, confessors and virgins. Unfortunately, the original illuminated manuscript of *Scivias*, the *Rupertsberg Scivias* (formerly Weisbaden,

22. See Bernard McGinn, "Theologians as Trinitarian Iconographers," in *The Mind's Eye: Art and Theological Argument in the Middle Ages*, ed. Jeffrey F. Hamburger and Anne-Marie Bouché (Princeton, NJ: Princeton University Press, 2006), 186–207.

23. For an overview of the manuscript tradition see Albert Derolez, "The Manuscript Transmission of Hildegard of Bingen's Writings: The State of the Problem," in *Hildegard of Bingen: The Context of Her Thought and Art*, ed. Charles Burnett and Peter Dronke (London: The Warburg Institute, School of Advanced Study, University of London, 1998), 17–28.

Hessische Landesbibliothek, MS 1) was lost in 1945, during World War II, having been evacuated to Dresden. It is known now only through early black-and-white photographs and a handwritten, hand-painted copy that was made by the nuns of Eibingen in the late 1920s.

While *Scivias* is Hildegard's most celebrated work, she produced several other works. Around 1158 to 1163, she wrote a second visionary book, this time treating ethics, *Liber Vitae Meritorum (Book of Life's Merits)*. This manuscript treats sin and virtue, the virtues and vices, and is more practical and moral than the other two mystical works (*Scivias* and *Liber divinorum*). Hildegard's third visionary book, *Liber divinorum operum simplicis hominis* (or *De operatione Dei, The Book of Divine Works*), was written around 1163 to 1174. This work treats cosmology, explaining how humankind and creation are related to God and to each other. Like *Scivias*, it is accompanied by illustrations of the visions on which the written text is based.

Hildegard's vast corpus is also remarkable for the extraordinary diversity of her writings and the encyclopedic knowledge and breadth of talent that they evince. Standing in the well-established tradition of the Rhineland abbeys in the eleventh century of interest in the natural world, Hildegard had an exceptional knowledge of natural science, medicine, and herbal remedies. Hildegard's *Physica* is a book of natural history, a kind of scientific encyclopedia or compendium, while her *Causae et Curae* is a medical treatise. In addition to several nonvisionary books, she wrote biographies of St. Disibod and St. Rupert and commentaries on the Rule of St. Benedict and on the Athanasian Creed.[24] She was talented musically and composed liturgical music as well as poetry. The *Symphonia armoniae celestium revelationum (Symphony of the Harmony of Celestial Revelations)* is a corpus of songs set to music.[25] In *Symphonia 26, Laus Trinitati, Antiphon for the Trinity*, she famously describes God as music:

> To the Trinity be praise!
> God is music, God is life
> that nurtures every creature in its kind.
> Our God is the song of the angel throng
> and the splendor of secret ways
> hid from all humankind.
> But God our life is the life of all.[26]

24. The Athanasian Creed (*Quicumque Vult*). See *An Explanation of the Athanasian Creed*, trans. Thomas M. Izbicki (Toronto: Peregrina Publishing Co., 2001). Also at http://monasticmatrix .usc.edu/cartularium/article.php?textId=2462#biblioID (accessed October 25, 2009.)

25. See Newman, *Symphonia*.

26. Ibid., 143.

As well as her manuscripts, several hundred extant letters written by or to her have survived.

In terms of her sources, Hildegard's writing is replete with biblical allusions, albeit sparing with regard to direct quotations. Echoes of the Latin Vulgate, especially the Song of Songs and the Psalms reverberate through her writings.

As a woman, Hildegard did not have access to the scholastic training in Latin or in biblical exegesis. Hildegard is thus not schooled in the categories of being and form and the refined distinctions of scholastic theology. Instead, she engages a rich realm of symbolic imagery and language drawn from life itself. She engages a vast array of metaphors, as Barbara Newman describes:

> Even in the context of twelfth-century symbolics, Hildegard had no peer in her kaleidoscopic array of metaphors, her figures within figures, her synesthetic language. In the midst of a routine bit of exegesis, she would suddenly convey some new insight with an arresting turn of phrase, or use a familiar typological image in a wholly new sense. Expressive flashes of alliteration punctuate otherwise plodding texts. At times a passage will rise to a pitch of lyric intensity, almost to incantation, then as quickly return to bare expository prose.[27]

Hildegard's Insights into the Mystery of the Trinity

Hildegard's letter to Bernard, abbot of Clairvaux, written in 1146 to 1147, seeking his advice as to whether she should speak openly about her visions, provides an instructive introduction to her trinitarian thought, and the richness of her imagery with which she expresses her theological vision:

> And so I beseech your aid, through the serenity of the Father and through His wondrous Word and through the sweet moisture of compunction, the Spirit of truth [cf. John 14:17; 16:13], and through that holy sound, which all creation echoes, and through that same Word which gave birth to the world, and through the sublimity of the Father, who sent the Word with sweet fruitfulness [*viriditate*] into the womb of the Virgin, from which He soaked up flesh, just as honey is surrounded by the honeycomb. And may that Sound, the power of the Father, fall upon your heart and lift up your spirit so that you may respond expeditiously to these words of mine, taking care, of course, to seek all

---

27. Barbara Newman, *Sister of Wisdom: St. Hildegard's Theology of the Feminine* (Berkeley: University of California Press, 1987), 24.

these things from God—with regard to the person or the mystery itself—
while you are passing through the gateway of your soul, so that you
may come to know all these things in God. (L1)

Hildegard articulates her understanding of God not in technically
refined scholastic categories, but in a rich array of highly evocative metaphors. Her language and imagery is very sensual and luscious: the serenity
and sublimity of the Father, the sweet moisture of compunction of the
Spirit, the holy sound that all creation echoes, the sending of the Word
with sweet fruitfulness (*viriditate*, an allusion to the Holy Spirit), the taking
flesh of the Son in the Virgin's womb as like honey in the honeycomb.
With images of sweetness, moisture, sound, honey in the honeycomb, she
conjures up each of the senses of hearing and sight, taste and touch, and
even smell—and all this, she avers, that Bernard "may come to know all
these things in God." Guided by her, the reader is led to a sumptuous feast
of sensual delights, a divinely inspired supersaturation of the senses. It is
as if in her experience of God every sense is quickened and enthralled,
stimulated to overflowing.

She hopes and prays that Bernard will be awakened and enlightened
in making his response to her, not by his knowledge or insight or even
wisdom per se, but rather by the three divine persons and their particular
attributes, "which all creation echoes." It is through them, she avers, that
"you may come to know all these things in God." Here too we find one
of Hildegard's most highly privileged metaphors, associated most particularly with the Holy Spirit, that of *viriditas*. Virtually untranslatable into
English, *viriditas* literally means greenness, verdure (*viridis*, green, fresh)
and in her hands it is richly evocative. For Hildegard, it connotes life, vitality, freshness, life force, fecundity. By it, she means all life, physical as well
as spiritual, as quickened, nurtured, and sustained by the Holy Spirit, giver
of life. In its freshness, moistness, and fecundity, *viriditas* is also redolent
of the feminine in God and the life-giving nature of God.

Hildegard's insights into the mystery of the Trinity are nowhere more
clearly and vividly expressed than in her much celebrated illumination of
her vision of the Trinity, which occurs in *Scivias* 2.2, and in the accompanying description of the mystery.[28] In this rectangular illumination, a human

---

28. For colored reproductions of the illumination, see *Hildegardis Scivias*, eds. Adelgundis
Führkötter and Angela Carlevaris, vol. 43 of *Corpus Christianorum Continuatio Mediaevalis*
(Türnhout: Brepols, 1978), T.11.2.2, opp. 124; Heinrich Schipperges, *The World of Hildegard
of Bingen: Her Life, Times, and Visions*, trans. John Cumming (Tunbridge Wells: Burns & Oates
and Collegeville, MN: Liturgical Press, 1998), 72; Adelgundis Führkötter, *The Miniatures*

figure (*species hominis, homo*), the color of sapphire blue, stands at the center, looking directly out at the viewer. The figure is very simply dressed and has long hair. With neither beard nor veil, the figure is not obviously male or female. Its hands are raised in what would seem to be a gesture of prayer or blessing. There are no signs of the crucifixion on hands or feet. The left knee is a little forward, compared to the right. The figure is surrounded by two concentric halos of light, the inner one a bright fiery flame-like color, the outer one a brilliant shimmering silvery white. The same watery sapphire blue surrounds the outer circle and fills the exquisite border of the illumination.[29] The composure of this central figure exudes a sense of humility, gentleness, compassion, and serenity. The illumination as a whole radiates an energy and vitality. The quivering lines in the circles of light heighten this effect. The color of sapphire blue dominates the illumination. Hildegard describes the vision as follows:

> Then I saw a bright light, and in this light the figure of a man the color of sapphire, which was all blazing with a gentle glowing fire. And that bright light bathed the whole of the glowing fire, and the glowing fire bathed the bright light; and the bright light and the glowing fire poured over the whole human figure, so that the three were one light in one power of potential. (*Scivias* 2.2)

Here Hildegard employs the bathing motif, perceiving a reciprocal bathing of the bright light and the glowing fire, with both pouring over the central human figure. The bathing motif is redolent of the notion of circumincession, the mutual indwelling or interpenetration of the three divine persons. The interpretation of the vision then follows, describing how each of the three divine persons is portrayed:

> You see a bright light, which without any flaw of illusion, deficiency or deception designates the Father; and in this light the figure of a man the color of a sapphire, which without any flaw of obstinacy, envy or iniquity designates the Son, Who was begotten of the Father

---

from the Book *Scivias—Know the Ways—of St. Hildegard of Bingen from the Illuminated Rupertsberg Codex, Armaria Patristica et Mediaevalia* (Türnhout: Brepols, 1977). See also Art Resource at http://www.artres.com/c/htm/Home.aspx, Image Reference ART129323 (accessed January 8, 2009).

29. The sapphire is one of Hildegard's favorite gems. In the Middle Ages, sapphire was used to describe what would now be called lapis lazuli, the extremely expensive precious stone that was crushed to form the blue pigment, ultramarine, so prized by artists, especially in the Middle Ages.

in Divinity before time began, and then within time was incarnate in the world in Humanity; which is all blazing with a gentle glowing fire, which fire without any flaw of aridity, mortality or darkness designates the Holy Spirit, by Whom the Only-Begotten of God was conceived in the flesh and born of the Virgin within time and poured the true light into the world. (*Scivias* 2.2.2)

It is Christ the incarnate Son who stands at the center of the image, his hands raised and open, in blessing or in prayer. The inner fiery circle of flame-like red light represents the Holy Spirit, who appeared at Pentecost in tongues of flame over the disciples' heads, while the outer shimmering rim of radiant silvery white light represents the Father. Hildegard proceeds to explain how the three divine persons are inseparable, constituting one God, one unchanging indivisible divinity:

And that bright light bathes the whole of the glowing fire, and the glowing fire bathes the bright light; and the bright light and the glowing fire pour over the whole human figure, so that the three are one light in one power of potential. And this means that the Father, Who is Justice, is not without the Son or the Holy Spirit; and the Holy Spirit, Who kindles the hearts of the faithful, is not without the Father or the Son; and the Son, Who is the plenitude of fruition, is not without the Father or the Holy Spirit. They are inseparable in Divine Majesty, for the Father is not without the Son, nor the Son without the Father, nor the Father and the Son without the Holy Spirit, nor the Holy Spirit without Them. Thus these three Persons are one God in the one and perfect divinity of majesty, and the unity of Their divinity is unbreakable; the Divinity cannot be rent asunder, for it remains inviolable without change. (*Scivias* 2.2.2)

The resonances with the Athanasian Creed are strong[30] and continue when Hildegard stresses both the distinction of the Three in relation to each other (the Father is the Father and not the Son, etc.) and their inviolable unity:[31]

You must understand that no misfortune or change can touch God. For the Father is the Father, the Son is the Son, and the Holy Spirit

30. Athanasian Creed §25–26: "And in this Trinity none is afore or after another; none is greater or less than another. But the whole three persons are coeternal, and coequal" (http://www.ccel.org/creeds/athanasian.creed.html; accessed October 25, 2008).

31. Athanasian Creed §4: "Neither confounding the persons nor dividing the substance." And §5: "For there is one person of the Father, another of the Son, and another of the Holy Spirit."

is the Holy Spirit, and these Three Persons are indivisible in the Unity
of the Divinity. (*Scivias* 2.2.4)

Hildegard, drawing on images from nature, proceeds to give three
analogies for this unity of the three persons. She first considers the triad
of properties of a stone, an analogy reminiscent of the biblical image of
the Son as cornerstone (Mark 12:10):

> In the stone is cool dampness and solidity to the touch and sparkling
> fire. It has cool dampness that it may not be dissolved or broken;
> solidity to the touch that it may make up habitations and defenses;
> and sparkling fire that it may be heated and consolidated into hard-
> ness. Now this cool dampness signifies the Father, Who never withers
> and Whose power never ends; and the solidity of touch designates
> the Son, Who was born of the Virgin and could be touched and
> known; and the sparkling fire signifies the Holy Spirit, Who enkindles
> and enlightens the hearts of the faithful. (*Scivias* 2.2.5)

Again, Hildegard uses sensual imagery: cool dampness and solidity to
the touch and sparkling fire. She then proceeds to identify a triad of properties of a flame:

> A flame is made up of brilliant light and red power and fiery heat. It
> has brilliant light that it may shine, and red power that it may endure,
> and fiery heat that it may burn. Therefore, by the brilliant light un-
> derstand the Father, Who with paternal love opens His brightness to
> His faithful; and by the red power, which is in the flame that it may
> be strong, understand the Son, Who took on a body born from a
> Virgin, in which His divine wonders were shown; and by the fiery
> heat understand the Holy Spirit Who burns ardently in the minds of
> the faithful. (*Scivias* 2.2.6)

Hildegard then finds another triad to serve as an analogy for the unity
of the Trinity of three divine persons in an analysis of the production of
words in human speech. She writes:

> In a word there is sound, force and breath. It has sound that it may
> be heard, meaning that it may be understood, and breath that it may
> be pronounced. In the sound, then, observe the Father, Who manifests
> all things with ineffable power; in the meaning, the Son, Who was
> miraculously begotten of the Father; and in the breath, the Holy Spirit,
> Who sweetly burns in Them. But where no sound is heard, no mean-
> ing is used and no breath is lifted, there no word will be understood;

so also the Father, Son and Holy Spirit are not divided from one another, but do Their works together. (*Scivias* 2.2.7)

The imagery here is similar to that which Hildegard used in a letter between 1163 and 1164 to Eberhard, bishop of Bamberg, who had written to seek her advice on a precise theological point, for, as he says to her "you are imbued by the Holy Spirit." There Hildegard describes the Trinity and unity of the Godhead. She explains:

> Rational expression, also, has three forces: sound, word, and breath. The Son is in the Father the same way that a word is in a sound, and the Holy Spirit is in each, just as breath is found both in sound and in word. And these three persons are one God, as I said earlier. The essential quality of the Father is eternity, for there was no one before Him, since eternity (unlike the works of God) had no beginning. The essential quality of the Son is equality because the Son has never been separated from the Father, nor the Father from the Son. But the essential quality of the Holy Spirit is the connection [*connexio*] between the two, for the Son has always remained in the Father and the Father with the Son, since the Holy Spirit is the fiery life in them, and they are one. (L31r)

While describing the distinctions between the Three, Hildegard never fails to stress their inseparable unity of substance and in their work as, for example, in the following text in another place in the *Scivias*:

> The Father, the Son and the Holy Spirit testify that they are in no way disunited in power, even though they are distinguished in Persons, because they work together in the unity of the simple and immutable substance. . . . And so these three Persons are in the unity of insepa-rable substance; but they are not indistinct among themselves. How? He Who begets is the Father; He Who is born is the Son; and He Who in eager freshness [*ardentissima viriditate*] proceeds from the Father and the Son, and sanctified the waters by moving over their face in the likeness of an innocent bird, and streamed with ardent heat [*igneo ardore*] over the apostles, is the Holy Spirit. (*Scivias* 3.7.9)

Hildegard brings *Scivias* 2.2 to conclusion with a triple exhortation to her hearers: to understand the one God in Three divine persons; to rec-ognize in these three divine persons the one God, who is our Creator and Redeemer; and to embrace God:

> Thus, O human, understand the One God in Three Persons. In the foolishness of your mind you think that God is so powerless that He cannot truly live in three Persons, but only exist weakly in one. What

does this mean? God is, in three Persons, the true God, the First and the Last. . . . Therefore, O human, in these Three Persons recognise your God, Who created you in the power of His Divinity and redeemed you from damnation. . . . Therefore, O human, embrace your God in the daylight of your strength, before the hour comes for the purgation of your works, when all things will be manifest and nothing will be overlooked, when the times come that will be complete and will never end. (*Scivias* 2.2.7-9)

This triple exhortation—to understand the one God in three persons, to recognize your God, and to embrace your God—effectively brings to a crescendo an earlier exhortation in this same chapter: let no person ever forget to invoke the sole God in these three persons. Indeed, it is for this very reason that the mystery was revealed: that we may burn more ardently in God's love:

Let no person ever forget to invoke Me, the sole God, in these Three Persons, because for this reason I have made Them known to Man, that he may burn more ardently in My Love; since it was for love of him [humankind] that I sent my Son into the world, as My beloved John testifies, saying: "By this the charity of God has appeared toward us: that God has sent His Only-Begotten Son into the world, that we may live by Him. In this is charity, not that we have loved God, but that he has loved us, and sent His Son to be a propitiation for our sins" [1 John 4:9-10]. (*Scivias* 2.2.3-4)

Here is the vital key to an understanding of Hildegard's vision of the Trinity: the Father's sending of the Son and the revelation of the mystery of the Trinity in and through the Son (for it is the Son who declares both Father and Holy Spirit) is a mystery of love, a mystery of charity. It was for charity, as Hildegard explains in an earlier passage:

Before any creatures were made the Infinite Word was indivisibly in the Father; Which in course of time was to become incarnate in the ardor of charity, miraculously and without the stain or weight of sin, by the Holy Spirit's sweet freshness [*per viriditatem suavitatis*] in the dawn of blessed virginity. But after He assumed flesh, the Word also remained inseparably in the Father; for as a person does not exist without the vital movements within his viscera, so the only Word of the Father could in no way be separated from Him. (*Scivias* 2.1.3)

That charity is the meaning of the mysteries of incarnation and redemption is recapitulated in response to the question:

What does this mean? That through this fountain of life came the embrace of God's maternal love, which has nourished us unto life and is our help in perils, and is the deepest and sweetest charity and prepares us for penitence. (*Scivias* 2.2.4)

The revelation of the mystery of the Trinity is thus of singular *soteriological* importance. The fullness of the mystery of God is revealed in order that the Trinity be worshiped and invoked. Herein lies our salvation. It is, as the creeds of Nicaea and Constantinople declare, "for us and for our salvation" that the revelation of the mystery of the Trinity is revealed to us.

The revelation issues from the Trinity as fountain of life, from which creation and all life issues and which envelops us in the embrace of God's maternal love. The metaphor of embrace functions as a kind of inclusion here. The last imperative in the concluding triple exhortation—to embrace your God—both harkens back to God's embrace in maternal love for fallen humankind, and looks forward to a mutual embracing of God and humanity, indeed all creation, in the eschaton, "when the times come that will be complete and will never end" (*Scivias* 2.2.9). Here too is the key to the color blue that dominates this illumination. Hildegard herself, inspired by John's gospel, provides the clue to its meaning: it is charity, "the dearest and sweetest charity."

In *Scivias* 3, Hildegard, in a description of the seven principal virtues (among which humility is described as the queen and charity the most important), associates charity with the sky-blue color of a hyacinth. Again connecting the mystery of the incarnation with charity, she explains:

> And the second figure designates Charity; for, after the Humility with which the Son of God deigned to become incarnate, the true and ardent lamp of Charity was lighted when God so loved humanity that for its love He sent his Only-Begotten to take a human body. She *is a deep sky-blue like a hyacinth both in person and in tunic*; for through His humanity, the incarnate Son of God enlightened faithful and heavenly people, as a hyacinth illumines any object on which it is put down. (*Scivias* 3.8.19)

Just as a hyacinth illumines any object on which it is placed, she explains, so the incarnate Son of God illumines the world and everything in it. Here is the reason for the color blue, which in her illumination fills the entire area surrounding the Trinity. With the incarnation, all creation is illuminated by and suffused with the radiant blue hue that is his love.[32]

---

32. It is not clear why Hildegard speaks of these different blues: the Son as sapphire blue, charity as hyacinth blue. Certainly Hildegard and her sisters were no strangers to

Describing the Trinity as depicted in the image of the man in sapphire blue, Hildegard engages evocative language and sensual images: the sapphire blue of the Son, he "Who washed and dried our wounds. And He exuded the sweetest balm" (*Scivias* 2.2.4); the eager freshness, ardent heat, and viridity of the Holy Spirit, all blazing with a gentle glowing fire, enkindling power; Who burns ardently and sweetly in the hearts and minds of the faithful; and the cool dampness of the Father.

Interestingly, Hildegard makes no reference to a particularly intriguing feature of this illumination, which is the aperture above Christ's head and the thin rim of white that surrounds his entire body. The visual effect would seem to suggest the relationship of generation or begetting of the Son from the Father, as is expressed in the Creed of the Council of Nicaea, "he is begotten of the Father, one in being with the Father, God from God, Light from Light, true God from true God." There is indeed a certain womb-like quality to the illumination, which accords with an understanding of the Son as begotten from the Father, in the Spirit. It also connotes the *eternal* begetting of the Son from the Father, a notion that clearly figures in Hildegard's writing, again echoing the Athanasian Creed. Notice too that the perspective of the image remains ambiguous. It is unclear as to whether the central figure is coming forward toward the viewer, or receding and drawing the viewer inward. This also serves to augment the sense of energy and dynamism that exudes from the illumination.

A second illumination of the Trinity figures in *Scivias* 3.7. This trinitarian illumination, Pillar of the Trinity, is completely nonfigural, with no anthropomorphic figure.[33] The illumination shows a huge compound pier or column, at the corner of a building, its ends disappearing out of sight, a visual metaphor for the indivisibility of the components. Three sharp sword-like metallic edges represent the Trinity. The scattered straw (on the viewer's right-hand side, representing heretics), feathers (on the left side, representing Jews), and the dead branches in the center (representing pagans) together represent the errors of those who do not profess the mystery of the Trinity, and are hence "cut off by those sharp edges for their temerity." Hildegard writes:

---

precious jewels and she often makes reference to them and their beautiful colors. It is plausible that the Son, by virtue of his divinity, is depicted by the precious stone.

33. For colored reproductions of this illumination, see Führkötter and Carlevaris, *Hildegardis Scivias*, vol. 43A, T.28.3.7, opp. 464; Führkötter, *The Miniatures from the Book Scivias*, pl. 28. See also Art Resource at http://www.artres.com/c/htm/Home.aspx, Image Reference ART170111 (accessed October 25, 2009).

> Then I saw in the west corner of the building a wondrous, secret and supremely strong pillar, purple-black in color. . . . The outside part had three steel-colored edges, which stood out like sharp sword-edges from the bottom to the top. One of these faced Southwest, where a great deal of dry straw lay cut and scattered by it; another faced Northwest, where a lot of little wings had been cut off by it and had fallen; and the middle edge faced West, where lay many decaying branches that it had cut away. All of these had been cut off by those edges for their temerity. (*Scivias* 3.7)

Here Hildegard stresses that the mystery of the Trinity must be accepted in faith and not rashly scrutinized (*Scivias* 3.7.1-2). The mystery and the power of the Trinity is simply ineffable, she insists. She explains: "No one can comprehend the extent of Its glory and the limits of Its power as It shines with the immense sweetness and the brightness of Divinity" (*Scivias* 3.5.14).

Conclusion

In her articulation of the mystery of the Trinity, Hildegard's concern is to foster knowledge of the one true God, and thereby invocation and worship of the Trinity, for therein lies salvation. She finds rich resources and evocative imagery to express the mystery of the Trinity in the natural world and in human experience, rather than in the abstract categories and distinctions of her scholastically trained male contemporaries. She also engages feminine imagery, but without displacing or rejecting masculine imagery. No one particular trinitarian image or analogy dominates.

Her perception of the Holy Spirit is particularly vivid, and she employs images of fire, heat, moisture or water, warmth, freshness, and unction or salve to elucidate the mystery of this divine person who is physician and healer, ardently working to vivify the soul. The Holy Spirit is fiery but not arid. To the contrary, the Holy Spirit is life-giving, inundating and hydrating the soul, bringing greenness and fruitfulness, *viriditas*.

While she engages sometimes startling imagery, she is thoroughly orthodox in her teaching on the Trinity. Resonances with the Athanasian Creed are strong. The one indivisible God exists in three coequal and coeternal persons, who are one in substance and in action. She shows little concern for the innertrinitarian relations or the inner life of the Trinity, simply asserting the unity and inseparability of the three divine persons, while insisting on their personal distinction. She is primarily interested in the relationship between the triune God and creation, not in the doctrine of the Trinity per se. Her articulation of the mystery of the Trinity is always in the context of creation, redemption, and salvation. What is remarkable is the cosmic scope of her vision. All creatures, all creation, not just humankind, fall within her purview. As she sees it, creation is ordained to the incarnation from the very beginning, and the incarnation, and within it and integral to it the paschal mystery, is the preeminent manifestation of the charity of God.

What is also especially striking are her illuminations and moreover that she does not depict the Trinity in the usual iconographic style of the twelfth century, with the two figures with a dove representing the Father, Son, and Holy Spirit, in the Throne of Mercy (Gnadenstuhl) iconographic form. Instead, she presents a highly innovative and extraordinarily sophisticated image of the Trinity, with the figure of sapphire blue representing the incarnate Son, surrounded by two radiant concentric haloes of light representing Father and Holy Spirit. There is no other visualization of the mystery of the Trinity that compares with it in terms of theological sophistication as well as sheer beauty.

References and Further Reading

Primary Sources

Hildegard of Bingen: Scivias. Translated by Columba Hart and Jane Bishop. Classics of Western Spirituality. New York: Paulist Press, 1990.

Hildegardis Scivias. Edited by Adelgundis Führkötter and Angela Carlevaris. Vols. 43 and 43A, *Corpus Christianorum Continuatio Mediaevalis.* Turnhout: Brepols, 1978.

The Letters of Hildegard of Bingen. Translated by Joseph L. Baird and Radd K. Ehrman. 3 vols. New York: Oxford University Press, 1994–1998.

The Life of Hildegard in *Jutta and Hildegard: The Biographical Sources.* Translated by Anna Silvas. Brepols Medieval Women Series. University Part: The Pennsylvania State University Press, 1999.

Hildegard of Bingen. *An Explanation of the Athanasian Creed.* Translated by Thomas M. Izbicki. Toronto: Peregrina Publishing Co., 2001.

Hildegard of Bingen. *Symphonia: A Critical Edition of the Symphonia Armonie Celestium Revelationum* (Symphony of the Harmony of Celestial Revelations). Edited by Barbara Newman. Ithaca, NY, and London: Cornell University Press, 1988.

Secondary Sources

Flanagan, Sabina. *Hildegard of Bingen, 1098–1179: A Visionary Life*. 2nd ed. London and New York: Routledge, 1989.

Führkötter, Adelgundis. *The Miniatures from the Book Scivias–Know the Ways–of St. Hildegard of Bingen from the Illuminated Rupertsberg Codex*. Armaria Patristica et Mediaevalia. Türnhout: Brepols, 1977.

Newman, Barbara, ed. *The Voice of the Living Light: Hildegard of Bingen and Her World*. Berkeley and Los Angeles: University of California Press, 1998.

Schipperges, Heinrich. *The World of Hildegard of Bingen: Her Life, Times, and Visions*. Translated by John Cumming. Tunbridge Wells: Burns & Oates and Collegeville, MN: Liturgical Press, 1998.

Schroeder, Joy A. "A Fiery Heat: Images of the Holy Spirit in the Writings of Hildegard of Bingen." *Mystics Quarterly* 30, no. 3–4 (2004): 76–95.

3

BONAVENTURE
(CA. 1217–1274)

The symbol of a circle has an esteemed place in Christian iconography, symbolizing the eternity and perfection of the divinity. For St. Bonaventure of Bagnoregio, it also has great significance, for it well symbolizes that dynamic circular movement of exit (*exitus*) and return (*reditus*), the going forth from and returning to the source of all things that is the key to all reality. Indeed, the symbol of a circle also aptly describes Bonaventure's theology and spirituality, so deeply does this notion of circular movement wherein that which is first (*primum*) is last (*ultimum*) pervade his thought. When bringing his *Disputed Questions on the Mystery of the Trinity* to conclusion, for example, he describes eternal life in terms of a circle: "Therefore it follows that eternal life consists in this alone, that the rational spirit, which emanates from the most blessed trinity and is a likeness of the trinity, should return after the matter of a certain intelligible circle—through memory, intelligence and will—to the most blessed trinity by God-conforming glory" (*Disputed Questions* q. 8, ad 7).[1] In his celebrated masterpiece, *The Soul's Journey into God* (*Itinerarium Mentis in Deum*), he describes the being of God in terms of an intelligible circle: "an intelligible sphere whose center is everywhere and whose circumference is nowhere" (*Itin.* 5.8).[2] The order

---

1. Translation will be taken from *Disputed Questions on the Mystery of the Trinity*, trans. Zachary Hayes, vol. 3 of *Works of St. Bonaventure* (New York: The Franciscan Institute, 1979). Hereafter, *Disputed Questions*.

2. Translation will be taken from *Itinerarium Mentis in Deum*, trans. Zachary Hayes, vol. 2 of *Works of St. Bonaventure* (St. Bonaventure, NY: Franciscan Institute Publications, 2002). Hereafter *Itin*. *Itin*. 5.8 refers to chapter 5, part 8.

This is a celebrated axiom of Alan of Lille (d. 1202); see Joseph Ratzinger, *The Theology of History in St. Bonaventure*, trans. Zachary Hayes (Chicago: Franciscan Herald Press, 1971), 144; also G. R. Evans, *Alan of Lille* (Cambridge: Cambridge University Press, 1983).

of Bonaventure's theology is indeed distinctly circular.[3] Even his writing style has a certain circularity about it. Eminent commentator on Bonaventure's thought, Zachary Hayes, OFM, comments: "His [Bonaventure's] vision appears like a tightly drawn circle. Regardless of where one takes hold of it, it reaches out to the trinity and Christology, to creation and man, to metaphysics and epistemology."[4]

Franciscan friar, Master at the University of Paris, seventh minister general of the Order of Friars Minor, a theologian of considerable acumen, the major figure in what is known as the early Franciscan School, cardinal bishop, father of the Council of Lyons, one of the outstanding intellects of the thirteenth century, Bonaventure has an immense reputation in the Christian tradition. Alongside Bernard of Clairvaux, he is rightly esteemed as one of the preeminent mystical teachers of the medieval West.[5] Not only is he deeply formed by the theology of the monastery; he is also a theologian par excellence of the university. He thus brings the logic and skill of the theologian to his mystical consciousness. Admittedly, Bonaventure is renowned for the Christocentrism of his thought, but the architecture of this theology is thoroughly trinitarian. As Bonaventure explains in his *Disputed Questions on the Mystery of the Trinity*, the Trinity is "the foundation of the entire Christian faith" (*Disputed Questions* q. 1, a. 2 concl.). The mystery of the Trinity is the all-encompassing mystery that permeates his understanding of reality, while, at the center of that all-encompassing mystery is Christ, the incarnate Word, who, in his very person, unites both divine and created realms. The result is a remarkably coherent and comprehensive theological vision of cosmic proportions that has rarely been achieved.

Bonaventure died suddenly at the Council of Lyons in 1274. He was declared a saint in 1482. He was honored as a Doctor of the Church and bestowed with the title "Seraphic Doctor," *Doctor Seraphicus*, in 1588. In 1890, Pope Leo XIII extolled Bonaventure and Thomas Aquinas as the two great founders of scholastic theology.[6] John Paul II, in his encyclical

---

3. For an excellent study of the order in Bonaventure's theology, see J. A. Wayne Hellmann, *Divine and Created Order in Bonaventure's Theology*, trans. J. M. Hammond (St. Bonaventure, NY: The Franciscan Institute, 2001).

4. Zachary Hayes, "Introduction," in *Disputed Questions*, 25. Similarly, Hellmann comments: "Bonaventure thinks and writes in a circular and symbolic way" (*Divine and Created Order*, xv).

5. Bernard McGinn, *The Flowering of Mysticism* (New York: Crossroad, 1998), 87.

6. Leo XIII, *Aeterni Patris* §14. The title Seraphic Doctor has its origins in Bonaventure's devotion to Francis and his lifelong probing of Francis's vision of the seraph and, in its wings,

Fides et Ratio (1998), counts Bonaventure among "the great triad" of medieval doctors, alongside Saint Anselm and Saint Thomas Aquinas.[7] John Paul II writes of him: "Let theologians always remember the words of that great master of thought and spirituality, Saint Bonaventure, who in introducing his *Itinerarium Mentis in Deum* invites the reader to recognize the inadequacy of 'reading without repentance, knowledge without devotion, research without the impulse of wonder, prudence without the ability to surrender to joy, action divorced from religion, learning sundered from love, intelligence without humility, study unsustained by divine grace, thought without the wisdom inspired by God.'"[8]

Bonaventure's Life and Times

Little is known of Bonaventure's life outside of the Order.[9] In his vast corpus of writings, only rarely does he make comments about himself. Not even the year of his birth is known with certainty. Some scholars argue that he was born in 1221, while others contend that he was born no later than 1217, with the weight of contemporary scholarship now favoring the earlier date. He was born into an otherwise undistinguished family in Bagnoregio, near Orvieto in Tuscany, Italy. His father was probably a physician by profession, and the boy was baptized with the name Giovanni. He was renamed Bonaventure when he entered the Franciscan Order as a young man. We know little of his childhood, other than the story, which Bonaventure recounted, of his recovery in childhood from a life-threatening illness through his mother's intercession of St. Francis of Assisi.

After his schooling at Bagnoregio, probably under the Franciscan friars, Bonaventure went to the University of Paris. Paris at that time was the lively intellectual center of Christendom. After completing a master's

---

the crucified Jesus. It was that vision that was the source of Bonaventure's *Itinerarium Mentis in Deum*. The seraph, in classical Christian symbolism, is the symbol of love. It is love, the love that is God, that lies at the heart of Bonaventure's theology. Bonaventure himself explains that "the intellect [enlightened by faith] is made to resemble a Seraph, that is, it is enlightened and inflamed through faith, and cries out *Holy* three times" (*Hex* 8.9 in *Collations on the Six Days* [*Collationes in Hexaemeron*], trans. José de Vinck, vol. 5 of *Works of St. Bonaventure* (Paterson, NJ: St. Anthony Guild Press, 1970). Hereafter *Hex.*

7. John Paul II, *Fides et Ratio*, §74.

8. Ibid., §105.

9. For a more detailed introduction to Bonaventure, his life and works, see Zachary Hayes, "Bonaventure: Mystery of the Triune God," in *The History of Franciscan Theology*, Kenan B. Osborne, ed. (St. Bonaventure, NY: The Franciscan Institute, 1994), 39–46.

degree in the arts, around 1243, Bonaventure entered the Franciscan Order (the Order of Friars Minor), which had been founded by Francis of Assisi (1182–1226). Bonaventure proceeded to theological studies under some of the great Franciscan masters of the day, including Alexander of Hales. Within a few years, Bonaventure himself became one of the great masters of early Franciscan theology at the University of Paris and played a significant role in shaping the early Franciscan theological tradition.

After qualifying as a Bachelor of Sacred Scripture, Bonaventure lectured in Scripture. At this stage, Bonaventure wrote several commentaries, of which those on the Gospel of Luke and the Gospel of John are particularly important in attesting to the development of his thought. Bonaventure then progressed to higher degrees in theology. He taught and participated in the theological disputations at the University of Paris. At this stage, by then a Bachelor of Sentences, he wrote his commentaries, eventually four volumes, on the *Sentences* of Peter Lombard, the standard theological textbook at the time. Bonaventure also wrote excurses on disputed questions, including *Disputed Questions on the Mystery of the Trinity*. He eventually became a master of Theology in the school of Friars Minor at the University of Paris.

In 1257, thirty-one years after Francis's death, Bonaventure, although still a young master at the University of Paris, was elected minister general of the Order, its seventh in that role. This election precipitated a radical change in his life. He left university and took up administrative and pastoral responsibilities. He maintained his headquarters in Paris, but his new role involved considerable traveling throughout Europe, visiting the friars of the rapidly growing Order.

Bonaventure was profoundly influenced by St. Francis of Assisi. Indeed it is simply impossible to understand and appreciate Bonaventure's thought without knowing and understanding Francis, *Il Poverello*, Francis of "The Canticle of Brother Sun and Sister Moon." A visit to Mount Alverna in Tuscany in 1259 was especially significant for Bonaventure. It was at Mount Alverna that St. Francis had a vision of "a seraph with six fiery and splendid wings . . . [and] between the wings the figure of a man crucified, with his hands and feet extended in the form of a cross and fastened to a cross" (*The Life of St. Francis* 13.3),[10] after which vision Francis received the stigmata. Bonaventure writes of his own experience at Mount Alverna:

10. See *The Life of St. Francis* (*Legenda Maior*) in *Bonaventure: The Soul's Journey into God, the Tree of Life, the Life of St. Francis,* The Classics of Western Spirituality, trans. Ewert Cousins (New York: Paulist Press, 1978).

> While I was there reflecting on certain ways in which the mind might ascend to God, I recalled, among other things, that miracle which the blessed Francis himself had experienced in this very place, namely the vision of the winged Seraph in the form of the Crucified. As I reflected on this, I saw immediately that this vision pointed not only to the uplifting of our father himself in contemplation but also the road by which one might arrive at this experience. (*Itin.* prol. 2)

This visit to Mount Alverna had an incalculable impact on Bonaventure, moving him to a deeper understanding of St. Francis and his religious experience. It eventually led him to write *The Soul's Journey into God* (*Itinerarium Mentis in Deum*), for whom Francis is the model par excellence, "the example of perfect contemplation" (*Itin.* 7.3).

Bonaventure was deeply involved in the issues of his day. Foremost among them were the tensions in the Order itself, which at this time was sorely afflicted by internal divisions concerning the meaning and purpose of the Franciscan Order, its way of life, its mission, the place of learning in it, and the practice of Francis's ideals, especially in regard to Francis's radical poverty. The issue of evangelical poverty was particularly divisive. Bonaventure played a significant role in the attempt to mediate these divisions.

Theology itself was in transition. In the preceding centuries, theology had been pursued in the context of the monastery, in a way that has come to be known as the monastic style of theology. It was done principally by monks, and it was profoundly formed and shaped by the rhythm of monastic life, prayer, and liturgy, and thus deeply embedded in a monastic way of life. It consisted essentially in commentary on the Scriptures. In the twelfth and thirteenth centuries, however, Europe's centers of learning moved from the monasteries into the towns and universities. There was, first, a move to cathedral schools in the towns, and thence to what became the medieval universities. This relocation prompted the emergence of a professional class of scholars of theology, the secular masters, the so-called seculars. It also prompted a concomitantly profound change in the style of theology, a shift from the monastic toward a more "scholastic" method. Moreover, there was another radically new—and very controversial—influence that found its way into the newly emerging universities, that of the philosophy of Aristotle.

Aristotelian philosophy marked a distinct shift away from the neo-Platonic thought that had prevailed in previous centuries. It offered new concepts and terminology, a new and more critical method, a more rationalist philosophical approach, and a more dialectical style of argument. This new approach was received by church authorities with considerable suspicion, for it was apparently more secular than Platonic thought, and posed a challenge to the inspiration of the Bible and to the monastic theological tradition more generally. For some, this new philosophical movement was distinctly at odds with the Christian worldview and a danger to Christian faith and theology. For others, on the other hand, it offered a self-sufficient vision of reality. A major conflict in worldviews ensued as this new style of theology, together with an increasingly critical and secular culture, took root in the university setting.

A measure of anti-mendicant sentiment also prevailed during Bonaventure's time at the University of Paris, causing considerable tension between the secular and the mendicant masters of the university's faculty.[11] Controversies raged, both within and about the mendicant movement, in what has come to be known as the mendicant-seculars controversy. Aristotelianism captured the imagination of the seculars, and some were particularly enthused by related notions of the self-sufficiency of reason. Bonaventure was an ardent defender of the ideals of mendicancy. He was also a staunch opponent of the more radical Aristotelianism. He had far less confidence in the power of reason than is evident, for example, in the work of his contemporary, Thomas Aquinas. Living in Paris and working at the University of Paris before his election as minister general, a friar of the mendicant Order of Friars Minor, and subsequently its minister general, Bonaventure was thus situated at the heart of the tumult of his times.

In 1273, Bonaventure was named cardinal bishop of Albano. He became involved in the preparations for the Council of Lyons (1274), which sought to reunite the Greek and Latin churches, following the schism in the eleventh century. Bonaventure died quite unexpectedly at the council on July 15, 1274, and was buried that same day.

Bonaventure's Writings

Bonaventure's literary output was vast. His early writings, before his elevation to minister general, include scriptural commentaries, a commentary on the *Sentences* of Peter Lombard, as well as three sets of disputed questions: *On the Knowledge of Christ, On Evangelical Perfection,* and *On the Mystery of the Trinity* (written ca. 1253–1257). *The Commentary on the Sentences of Peter Lombard,* by far the longest of his works, is written in technical rather than literary form, and follows a highly structured schema with divisions

---

11. Alexander Gerken, "Identity and Freedom: Bonaventure's Position and Method," *Greyfriars Review* 4, no. 3 (1990): 95.

and subdivisions, akin to the *Summa* of Thomas Aquinas. Bonaventure's output during his service as minister from 1257 is all the more remarkable, considering his considerable responsibilities in that leadership role and the extensive traveling that it involved. We also have numerous sermons from this time.

The *Breviloquium*, one of his most highly esteemed works, was written in 1257. It is the closest Bonaventure ever comes to a summa, an exposition of the Christian faith. Unlike a summa, however, which is essentially for consultation and reference, the *Breviloquium* is intended for continuous reading. This remarkable work, a masterpiece in its own right, offers a superb compendium of Bonaventure's systematic thought, including his trinitarian theology.

The best known of Bonaventure's many writings—indeed, his preeminent masterpiece—is his *Itinerarium Mentis in Deum, The Soul's Journey into God*, written in 1259. Here, the mystical implications of Bonaventure's trinitarian theology come to the fore. As Bonaventure remarks in his prologue to the text: "I ask . . . that you [the reader] give more attention . . . to the stimulation of affect than to the instruction of the intellect" (*Itin.* prol. 5). The text describes the different ways of seeing God, leading to mystical union with God. Modeled on Francis's vision of the six-winged seraph, it describes six ways of illumination, by which the soul spirals upward in a movement from desire, to indwelling, to union with God, culminating in mystical death, paralleling Francis's reception of the stigmata after his vision of the seraph. Bonaventure concludes this remarkable text with the advice regarding the disposition to prayer that is indispensable to growth in the spiritual life:

> Now if you ask how these things are to come about, ask grace, not doctrine; desire, not intellect; the groaning of prayer and not studious reading; the Spouse, not the master; God, not a human being; darkness, not clarity; not light, but the fire that inflames totally and carries one into God through spiritual fervor and with the most burning affections. (*Itin.* 7.6)

Bonaventure's later works include *Defense of the Mendicants, Soliloquium, The Threefold Way, Tree of Life, Mystical Vine, Five Feasts of the Child Jesus, On the Perfection of Life, Life of St. Francis, Collations on the Ten Commandments*,[12] *Collations on the Gifts of the Holy Spirit*, and *Collations on the Six Days of Creation*

---

12. A collation is something between a sermon and an academic conference.

(*Collationes in Hexaemeron*). The latter, arguably his most mature work, was written in 1273 but left unfinished because of his election to the cardinalate and his work for the Council of Lyons.

While we know little of Bonaventure's own mystical experiences, the profound influence of Francis of Assisi is very clear. Francis is the radi-ant sun around which Bonaventure's thought perennially revolves. For Bonaventure, Francis is the model par excellence of the soul's journey into God. Bonaventure's theology and mysticism is also deeply imbued with Francis's reverence for God as "Most high" and "supreme Good," as is encapsulated in Francis's "Praises to be said at all the Hours": "All power-ful, most holy, most high, supreme God: all good, supreme good, totally good, You who alone are good, may we give you all praise, all glory, all thanks, all honour, all blessing and all good. So be it. So be it. Amen."

True to the scholastic era in which he lived, Bonaventure adopts a philo-sophical style of theology. In terms of philosophical sources, he shows a distinct preference for the Platonic and neo-Platonic rather than the Aristo-telian philosophical tradition that appealed to so many of his contemporaries. Admittedly, he departs from the neo-Platonic schema in some very significant ways, not least in his appreciation of the intrinsic goodness of the created cosmos. But it is essentially the neo-Platonic view, especially in regard to an understanding of reality as a hierarchical dynamic process, the doctrine of emanation and return, and a metaphysics of exemplarity, albeit adapted, that is indelibly etched in Bonaventure's thinking. Images of concentricity, ladders, stages of growth, and ascent and descent abound in his writing. Bonaventure finds support for this understanding of the structure of reality in John 16:28: "I came from the Father and have come into the world; again, I am leaving the world and am going to the Father."

Bonaventure is clearly well acquainted with Aristotle's thought and is in dialogue with it, making hundreds of references to it, demonstrating a sound understanding of it, engaging intelligently and critically with it, and assimilating some aspects of it. Indeed Aristotle's philosophy is never far from his thought. In contradistinction to views with considerable currency in his time, however, particularly those of the more radical Aristotelian persuasion, Bonaventure rejects any notion of philosophy as self-sufficient. He insists that there is a wisdom beyond the power of human reason. He maintains that ultimate reality is decisively revealed, and indeed only able to be known, in the person of Christ.

For Bonaventure, theology, which he describes as a perfect science, indeed the only perfect science, because it alone encompasses all that is, is a reflection on how created reality, having been created by God, returns to God.[13] As he explains, it is "the theologian who considers how the world, made by God, can be returned to Him" (*Hex.* 1.37). Moreover, for Bonaventure, theology is no mere speculation for its own sake, but a practical science, subordinate to and in service of the spiritual life. It is the work of the gift of wisdom that raises the human person to the level of contemplation. Its purpose is to assist human persons to attain their ultimate goal, loving union with God, holiness.

From the theological tradition, Bonaventure draws on Pseudo-Dionysius, particularly for an understanding of goodness as self-diffusive, i.e., that goodness by its very nature communicates itself, and on the Victorines, especially Richard of St. Victor, particularly for an analysis of the nature of interpersonal love and its perfection. Bonaventure also draws on Anselm and Joachim of Fiore.[14] Like all of his era, he is profoundly influenced by Augustine and draws on him most of all. Indeed, Bonaventure is arguably the leading proponent of the Augustinian tradition in the thirteenth century. In key areas of his trinitarian theology, Bonaventure basically follows Augustine. Like Augustine, his trinitarian theology finds its focus in a theology of the trinitarian missions. As for Augustine, the mission is the procession with a temporal effect, whereby it is revealed in history. The trinitarian missions of the Son and Holy Spirit emanate from the inner-trinitarian processions. Incarnation is the mission of the Son, while the mission of the Holy Spirit is sanctification through grace and the church. The visible missions of the Son and Holy Spirit are directed to the invisible missions, the indwelling of the Trinity in the human person, and ever closer likeness to God and union with God. Bonaventure also draws on Augustine's psychological probing of the experience of the human person, made in the image of God, and on Augustine's notion of the deeply symbolic character of creation.

13. *Breviloquium*, trans. Dominic V. Monti, vol. 9 of *Works of St. Bonaventure*, Bonaventure Texts in Translation Series (St. Bonaventure, NY: Franciscan Institute Publications, 2005), 1.1.2. "Theology is the only perfect science, for it begins at the very beginning, which is the First Principle, and continues to the very end, which is the everlasting reward; it proceeds from the summit, which is God Most High, the Creator of all things, and reaches even to the abyss, which is the torment of hell" (*Brevil.* 1.1.2). Bonaventure continues: "Theology is also the only perfect wisdom, for it begins with the supreme cause as the principle of all things that are caused—the very point at which philosophical knowledge ends. But theology goes beyond this, considering that cause as the remedy for sins; and it leads back to it, considering that cause as the reward of meritorious deeds and the goal of [human] desires" (*Brevil.* 1.1.3).

14. For Joachim of Fiore's influence on Bonaventure, see Ratzinger, *The Theology of History in St. Bonaventure*, 104ff.

While Bonaventure's theology is fundamentally Augustinian in character, it is, however, no mere repetition of Augustine. Bonaventure's theological synthesis is uniquely and creatively his own, a genuinely creative and innovative development. This is particularly so in regard to his trinitarian theology. Indeed, it is actually in the field of trinitarian theology that Bonaventure departs most significantly from Augustine and takes a distinctly different tack. He does not take up Augustine's approach by way of the psychological analogy to explicate the trinitarian processions. Instead, he turns to Pseudo-Dionysius and Richard of St. Victor who provide resources for the construction of an alternative explication of the mystery. In all of this, Bonaventure's profound source of inspiration is St. Francis of Assisi and his experience of God.

Bonaventure's Insights into the Mystery of the Trinity

Bonaventure's writings include both deeply spiritual and highly speculative reflections on the mystery of the Trinity. His trinitarian theology permeates his corpus and is evident not only in his theological treatises but in his spiritual and mystical writings, as well as his sermons. The *Disputed Questions on the Mystery of the Trinity* is a highly specialized treatise, in the style of a scholastic disputation, addressing certain specific issues in regard to the Trinity. In contrast to Augustine and Thomas Aquinas who, in their trinitarian treatises, undertake an excursus on the unity and perfections of God prior to and independently of a treatment of the Trinity, Bonaventure instead treats the divine simplicity, infinity, eternity, immutability, and primacy from *within* and *in the course of* his treatment of the mystery of the Trinity. In other words, his treatment of the mystery of the Trinity effectively comprises his treatment of the mystery of God and the divine perfections. As Zachary Hayes comments: "The systematic treatment of the doctrine of the Trinity constitutes the whole of Bonaventure's doctrine about God."[15] This stands in stark contrast to any approach by way of philosophically derived notions of the divine attributes. Certainly, Bonaventure treats God in terms of being, but his theology is thoroughly and consistently from a trinitarian perspective, and it is the love of God, revealed in Scriptures, made manifest in the Crucified One, and communicated directly to loving souls through grace, that captivates Bonaventure.

In his *Commentary on the Sentences of Peter Lombard*, Bonaventure treats the divine processions, relations, persons, properties, notions, and appropriations.

15. Hayes, "Bonaventure: Mystery of the Triune God," 55.

He brings his trinitarian reflections to a new level of synthesis in the *Breviloquium*. There the mystery of the Trinity serves as the foundation of his theological vision. Indeed, he begins the text with the mystery of the Trinity. He writes: "In the beginning, we should understand that sacred doctrine, namely theology, which deals principally with the first Principle—God, three and one—comprises seven topics in all: first, the Trinity of God" (*Brevil.* 1.1.1).

The *Itinerarium*, despite its brevity, is very important, especially chapter 6, which specifically addresses the mystery of the Trinity. Here the profound influence of the Pseudo-Dionysian notion of the good as self-diffusive is strikingly evident.[16] Bonaventure explains: "We understand two modes or levels of contemplating the invisible and eternal qualities of God. . . . The first method fixes our attention primarily and first of all on Being Itself, saying that *The One Who Is* is the first name of God. The second method fixes our attention on the reality of the Good, saying that this is the first name of God" (*Itin.* 5.1-2). Bonaventure proceeds to a consideration of the Trinity by way of reflection on the Good. He explains: "the good is the most basic foundation of our contemplation of the emanations. . . . 'the good is said to be self-diffusive.' The supreme good, therefore, is supremely self-diffusive" (*Itin.* 6.1-2). Bonaventure continues:

> But the highest diffusion does not exist unless it is actual and intrinsic, substantial and personal, natural and voluntary, free and necessary, lacking nothing and perfect. In the supreme good there must be from eternity a production that is actual and consubstantial, and a hypostasis as noble as the producer, and this is the case in production by way of generation and spiration. This is understood to mean that what is of the eternal principle is of the eternal co-producer. In this way there can be both a beloved [*dilectus*] and a co-beloved [*condilectus*], one generated and one spirated, that is, Father, and Son, and Holy Spirit. If this were not the case, it would not be the supreme good since it would not be supremely self-diffusive. (*Itin.* 6.2)

Last but by no means least, Bonaventure's insights into the mystery of the Trinity also figure in the *Hexaemeron*, especially collation 11, in what is Bonaventure's final synthesis, his last testimony, the culmination of his work, left incomplete because of his election to the cardinalate. The first collation, focusing on Christ as "the centre of all knowledge," is programmatic.

16. Pseudo-Dionysius, *The Celestial Hierarchy*, IV.1 and *On the Divine Names*, IV.1, 20, in *Pseudo-Dionysius: The Complete Works*, Classics of Western Spirituality (New York: Paulist Press, 1987).

Three dynamic principles lie at the heart of Bonaventure's understanding of the cosmos: emanation, exemplarity, and consummation. Emanation (*emanatio*) concerns the going forth of all things from God, who is fountain fullness of fecundity, first principle, supreme being, supreme goodness, source of all that is. Exemplarity (*exemplaritas*) concerns how things reflect God by way of likeness to an exemplar or archetypal model, in whose image all things have been created, albeit in various degrees of likeness. Consummation (*consummatio*) concerns how things return to and find eschatological fulfillment in God. Bonaventure himself summarizes his metaphysics: "This is the sum total of our metaphysics: concerned with emanation, exemplarity, and consummation, that is, illumination through spiritual radiations and return to the Supreme Being" (*Hex.* 1.17). Indeed, Bonaventure insists, there is no understanding otherwise: "For no one can have understanding unless he considers where things come from, how they are led back to their end, and how God shines forth in them" (*Hex.* 3.2).

Bonaventure grounds this threefold dynamic in the mystery of the Trinity, finding support for this in Jesus' words in John 16:28: "I came from the Father and have come into the world; again, I am leaving the world and am going to the Father." As Bonaventure explains: "The Word expresses the Father and the things He made, and principally leads us to union with the Father who brings all things together; and in this regard He is the Tree of Life, for by this means we return to the very fountain of life and are revived in it" (*Hex.* 1.17). Here again the symbol of the circle serves to represent the dynamic movement of going forth and return, whereby to arrive at the end is to return to the beginning.

Also fundamental to Bonaventure's vision is the principle of exemplarity, and it operates at two levels in his thinking: trinitarian and christological. In other words, Bonaventure recognizes both a trinitarian exemplarity and a christological exemplarity at work in creation. Trinitarian exemplarity is reflected in all creation, whereby each and every thing in creation reflects its trinitarian maker. Created by God, and ordered to the Trinity as source of all, all reality, at every level, is indelibly stamped with a likeness to its maker, the Trinity. From this perspective, everything in creation is recognized as bearing the mark of its trinitarian creator. The cosmos as a whole is a symbol of the Trinity. Thus Bonaventure describes creation as like a book revealing its trinitarian creator:

> From all that we have said, we may gather that the created world is like a book reflecting, representing, and describing its Maker, the Trinity, at three different levels of expression: as a vestige, as an image,

and as a likeness. The aspect of vestige ['footprint'] is found in every creature; the aspect of image, only in intelligent creatures or rational spirits; the aspect of likeness, only in those spirits that are God-conformed. Through these successive levels, comparable to steps [or the rungs of a ladder], the human intellect is designed to ascend gradually to the supreme Principle which is God. (*Brevil.* 2.12.1)

For Bonaventure, it is precisely the task of theology to read the book of creation, a reading that is beyond the capacity of philosophy: "To read this book is the privilege of the highest contemplatives, not of natural philosophers, for the former alone know the essence of things, and do not consider them only as traces" (*Hex.* 12.15). Moreover, it is in and through the person of Jesus Christ, the incarnate Word, that Christians are able to read the book of creation correctly. He, Bonaventure insists, is "the root of all understanding of all things" (*radix intelligentiae omnium*; *Hex.* 3.4), "the centre of all knowledge" (*Hex.* 1.1). Bonaventure would persuade us: "If, then, you understand the Word, you understand all understandable things" (*Hex.* 3.4).

Bonaventure thus views creation in a profoundly sacramental way. He understands that the whole cosmos, emanating from its trinitarian exemplar, manifests its trinitarian maker in various levels and degrees. He recognizes a hierarchy of likeness of created things to their trinitarian creator: vestige, image, and similitude. Every creature is a vestige representing the Trinity in a distant, shadowy, and unclear way. The image, on the other hand, is found only in intellectual creatures, and particularly in the trinity of powers of memory, intellect, will, which reflects the Trinity in a closer and more distinct way. Bonaventure explains:

> Enter into yourself and recognize that your mind loves itself most fervently. But it cannot love itself if it does not know itself. And it would not know itself unless it remembered itself, for we do not grasp anything with our understanding if it is not present to us in our memory. . . . Now consider the operation of these powers and their relation to each other. Here you can see God through yourself as through an image. And this is to see *through a mirror in an obscure manner*. (*Itin.* 3.1)

The similitude is the most intense likeness and it pertains to the level of grace. It is found in the rational spirit that is conformed to God through grace. God's indwelling presence conforms the human person to the divine image, the trinitarian Exemplar, resulting in a true similitude to the Father, Son, and Holy Spirit. The similitude is effected in the trinity of the human person's powers of memory, intellect, and will. When thus conformed to the divine image, the human person not only knows and loves God, but participates, through grace, in the very love of God and becomes Godlike.

Trinitarian exemplarity finds its fullest expression in the transformation of the trinitarian image to conformity with the eternal Exemplar on the person's journey into God. As Bonaventure explains, when describing the glory that is eternal life, and bringing his treatise on the *Disputed Questions on the Mystery of the Trinity* to conclusion, again employing the symbol of a circle: "Therefore it follows that eternal life consists in this alone, that the rational spirit, which emanates from the most blessed trinity and is a likeness of the trinity, should return after the manner of a certain intelligible circle–through memory, intelligence and will–to the most blessed trinity by God-conforming glory" (*Disputed Questions* q. 8, ad 7). Here too Bonaventure recognizes the image of the Trinity in the trinity of powers (memory, intellect, and will) that is constitutive of the human person.[17]

Bonaventure recognizes that not only the human person but also history reflects the Trinity.[18] Here Bonaventure is influenced, at least in part, by Joachim of Fiore (1135–1202) who had developed a highly innovative–and eventually condemned–theology of history, whereby salvation history has a distinctly trinitarian structure, with history unfolding in three successive stages, each corresponding to a particular divine person.[19]

Furthermore, this exemplarity with which all creation is stamped is not only trinitarian but christological. Indeed, as Bonaventure understands it, this trinitarian exemplarity is effectively concentrated or focused in the person of the Son/Word. The Christocentrism for which Bonaventure is rightly renowned lies precisely here. The exemplar, according to which all things in the cosmos reflect God, is the Word/Son.

Here again Bonaventure's preference for the principles of neo-Platonic philosophy is evident, for Bonaventure, following Augustine, understands the innertrinitarian Word as essentially the divine Idea. He understands the divine ideas to exist eternally in the Word (*Verbum increatum*). In other words, all that actually or potentially exists eternally exists in the Word, the Father's perfect and full self-expression. As the Word incarnate (*Verbum incarnatum*), the Word is exemplar of all created beings in creation, the exemplar of all that is other than the Father, all that is other than God,

---

17. See also *Itin.* 3.5.

18. See Ratzinger, *The Theology of History in St. Bonaventure.*

19. Joachim's attack on Peter Lombard's trinitarian theology was condemned at the Fourth Lateran Council in 1215, as was his own trinitarian doctrine. See DS 803–6; ND 317–20.

and all other relations. As Bonaventure writes: "every creature proclaims the eternal generation [i.e., the eternal inner working of the self-generating Trinity]" (*Hex.* 11.13). It is for this reason that Bonaventure has a distinct preference for the designation Word, rather than Son or Image, for the second person. Word (*Verbum*) is preferable, Bonaventure argues, as it is more suggestive of the second divine person's relationships, both *ad intra* and *ad extra*, as Bonaventure, reflecting on John 1:1-2, explains:

> It has to be said that the word Son only expresses a relationship with the Father while the term Word refers to relationships to the speaker, to what is being said by the word, to the voice that embodies the word, and to the teaching that is learned by another through the medium of the word. And since the Son of Godhead had to be described in these sentences not only in relationship to the Father, from whom he proceeds, but also to creatures, which he made, and to the flesh which he took on, and to the teaching that he communicated, he had to be described in a most excellent and fitting manner with the term Word. For that term relates to all these matters, and a more appropriate term could not be found in the world. (*Commentary on the Gospel of John*, 1, 6, q. 1, resp.)[20]

So, while Bonaventure's theology can rightly be described as Christocentric, it is also thoroughly trinitarian. The Trinity is the foundation that provides the framework within which to interpret the person and the mission of the Word.

When contemplating the innertrinitarian mystery of the divine processions, Bonaventure takes a very different approach compared to Augustine and the psychological analogy. Bonaventure instead begins with the notion of God as good, bringing together Francis of Assisi's profound insight into the mystery of God as good and the New Testament revelation of the divine name as Good: "No one is good but God alone" (Luke 18:19).

Following the Pseudo-Dionysian understanding that goodness, by its very nature, is self-communicative and self-diffusive (*bonum diffusivum sui*), Bonaventure recognizes that this self-diffusiveness explains not only the self-diffusiveness of God *ad extra*, in creation, but the innertrinitarian mystery of the Godhead *ad intra*. Here, Bonaventure's approach is quite different from that of Thomas Aquinas who considers the goodness of God in relation to creation, not in relation per se to the Godhead *ad intra*. In contrast, for Bonaventure, it is the goodness of God that explains the

20. *Commentary on the Gospel of John*, trans. Robert J. Karris, vol. 11 of *Works of St. Bonaventure* (St. Bonaventure, NY: Franciscan Institute Publications, 2007), 62.

plurality of persons within the Godhead and the creativity so extravagantly manifest in creation.

As well as grounding the first emanation in God, the procession of the Word/Son from the first person, the principle that goodness is self-diffusive also grounds Bonaventure's understanding that this first procession proceeds by way of *nature (per modum naturae)*, for it is of the very *nature* of goodness to be self-diffusive. Here too Bonaventure's trinitarian theology stands in distinct contrast to that of Augustine and, following him, Thomas Aquinas who argued by way of analogy with human consciousness and the generation of the "inner word" of understanding, that the procession of the Son, the second person, occurs by way of *intellectual emanation (per modum intellectus)* from the Father.

In regard to the second procession, that of the Holy Spirit, Bonaventure incorporates the argument of Richard of St. Victor, based on an analysis of interpersonal love.[21] Love, Richard recognized, finds its perfection in shared love, in wills united in love for a third *(condilectus)*. Bonaventure thus understands the second innertrinitarian emanation to be grounded in the dynamism and fruitfulness of the will, which necessarily expresses itself in a free self-communication of love. While the Son proceeds from the Father as his proper Image, Word, and Son, *per modum naturae*, the Spirit proceeds from Father and Son as the gift of love, *per modum voluntas* or *per modum liberalitatis*.

In this way, in a synthesis that is uniquely and distinctively his own, Bonaventure supplements the Pseudo-Dionysian notion of the good as self-diffusive, on which basis he grounds the procession of the Son/Word, with Richard of St. Victor's argument for the plurality of persons in God, based on an analysis of the perfection of interpersonal love, the perfection of which requires shared love *(condilectus)*. The second divine person proceeds by way of nature, for goodness naturally diffuses itself, while the third person proceeds by way of the free and generous will.

Bonaventure brings his *Disputed Questions on the Trinity* to a conclusion with the question as to "Whether the trinity can exist together with supreme primacy," to which he responds with an argument that comes as close as that of Richard of St. Victor to near proof of the trinitarian being of God. It is necessary to admit that the first principle includes within itself three hypostases, Bonaventure argues:

21. Richard of St. Victor, *De Trinitate*. In Latin and in French, see *La Trinité*, Richard de Saint-Victor; trans. Gaston Salet (Paris: Cerf, 1999). In English, see "Book 3 of the Trinity," in *Richard of St. Victor: The Twelve Patriarchs; The Mystical Ark; Book Three of the Trinity*, trans. Grover A. Zinn, The Classics of Western Spirituality Series (New York: Paulist Press, 1979).

Supreme primacy in the supreme and highest principle demands the highest actuality, the highest fontality, and the highest fecundity. For the first principle, by virtue of the fact that it is first, is the most perfect in producing, the most fontal in emanating, and the most fecund in germinating. Therefore since the perfect production, emanation and germination is realized only through two intrinsic modes, namely by way of nature and by way of will, that is, by way of the word and by way of love, therefore the highest perfection, fontality and fecundity necessarily demands two kinds of emanation with respect to the two hypostases which are produced and emanate from the first person as from the first producing principle. Therefore, it is necessary to affirm three persons. And since the most perfect production is not realized except with respect to equals, and the most fontal emanation is not realized except with respect to coeternals, and the most fecund germination is not realized except with respect to consubstantial beings, it is necessary to admit that the first principle includes within itself three hypostases that are coequal, coeternal, and consubstantial. (*Disputed Questions*, q. 8, conc.)

A distinctive feature of Bonaventure's trinitarian thought emerges in his treatment of the Father in terms of firstness (*primitas*). Bonaventure writes of the designation of the first person, the Father:

It is proper to the Father to be the one without an originator, the Unbegotten One; the Principle who proceeds from no other; the Father as such. "Unbegottenness" designates him by means of a negation, but this term also implies an affirmation, since unbegottenness posits in the Father a fountain-fullness. The "Principle that proceeds from no other" designates him by an affirmation followed by a negation. "Father" designates him in a proper, complete, and determinate way, by affirmation and the positing of a relation. (*Brevil.* 1.3.7)

Bonaventure gives particular emphasis to the person of the Father as the one without origin, who is ultimate source and origin of all that is, the fountain fullness (*plenitudo fontalis*), fecund source of all, both inside and outside the Godhead. Unlike the Son and Holy Spirit, the Father is not from any other. It is from the Father that the other two divine persons proceed or emanate, as from a font or fountain of fullness. It is by the authority of the Father that the Son and Holy Spirit are sent. There is no suggestion at any point of inequality of persons, however. Bonaventure writes: "Although there is supreme equality among the divine persons, it pertains to the Father alone to send and not to be sent" (*Brevil.* 1.5.1). It is also from the Father that all created reality ultimately emanates.

Here Bonaventure engages the philosophical principle that "the more a being is prior, the more it is the source of others."[22] On this basis, Bonaventure argues for the primacy or firstness (*primitas*) of the Father, as the first person of the Trinity. The Father, who is without origin, is first (*primum*), and it is *because* he is first that fontality (*fontalitas*), fecundity (*fecunditas*), paternity (*paternitas*), and authority (*auctoritas*) are his. It is because the Father is unbegotten (*innascibilitas*), that he is generative. It is because he is without origin that he is fecund source of all. In other words, it is because he is first, that he is fountain fullness (*fontalis plenitudo*), source of all, author of all, with authority over all; it is because he is first that he is Father.

All has its origin in the fountain fullness, goodness, and fecundity of the Father. The innertrinitarian emanations, both necessary and free, proceed from the Father for it is the very nature of goodness to be self-communicative, and the perfection of love gives issue to the third person, by virtue of the sheer munificence of love that finds its fulfillment in shared love of a third (*condilectus*).

While firstness (*primitas*) characterizes the first person and is the reason why the first person is Father, it is being in the center or middle (*medium* or *persona media*) that characterizes the second person and is the reason why the second person is Son, Word, Image, Wisdom, Exemplar, Mediator, and indeed (and here Bonaventure follows Augustine) art of the Father (*ars Patris*; *De Reductio Artium ad Theologiam* 20; also *Hex.* 1.13). Bonaventure recognizes that all of these other designations for the second person are effectively grounded in the order of origin and role of the second person, *qua* second person, center of the Trinity. In *Hexaemeron* he famously describes the Word as "the metaphysical centre":

> The Word expresses the Father and the things He made, and principally leads us to union with the Father who brings all things together.
> . . . Such is the metaphysical Center that leads us back, and this is the sum total of our metaphysics: concerned with emanation, exemplarity, and consummation, that is, illumination through spiritual radiations and return to the Supreme Being. (*Hex.* 1.17)

The centrality of the second divine person derives from a consideration of the *origin* of the three divine persons: one divine person (the first person, the Father) is without origin, the sourceless source; one divine person (the third person, the Holy Spirit) is originated; and one divine person (the

---

22. From Proclus's *Book of Causes*. See *Breviloquium*, vol. 9 of *Works of St. Bonaventure*, Texts in Translation Series, 35 n. 21.

second person, the Son) is both origin and originated, both produced and productive, both receptive and responsive, and, as such, reflecting both the communicativeness of the Father and the receptiveness of the Holy Spirit. Thus, Bonaventure argues: "This [second person], by necessity, must be the central one of the Persons: for if there is one who produces and is not produced and another who is produced and does not produce, there must necessarily be a central one who is produced and produces" (*Hex.* 1.14).

Bonaventure explains the numerous designations for the second person in terms of likeness—expressed, expressing, and personal—and according to form, reason, and nature: "The Son is properly the Image, the Word, and the Son as such. 'Image' designates him as expressed likeness, 'Word' as expressive likeness, and 'Son' as personal likeness. Again, 'Image' designates him as likeness in the order of form, 'Word' as likeness in the order of reason, and 'Son' as likeness in the order of nature" (*Brevil.* 1.3.8).

The Son is not only expressed likeness, perfect Image of the Father, but expressive likeness, exemplar of all subsequent reality.[23] Bonaventure recognizes that the procession of the Son anticipates all that is other than the Father, including the innertrinitarian procession of the Holy Spirit, but also the creation of the world *ad extra*. The Son is thus model, exemplar, structural principle of all that goes forth from the Father. Standing between Father and Holy Spirit, the Son also stands between God and creation. Through the incarnation, he stands at the very center of creation, all things issuing from him, being perfected in him, and returning to God in and through him. For all that comes forth from God, he is Exemplar. In the return of all things to God, he is Mediator, thus "holding the central position in all things" (*Hex.* 1.10). To return to the symbol of the circle: he is at the center of the circle that symbolizes the process of emanation, exemplarity, and consummation that occurs in both the divine and the created realms. All things exist in and through Christ, and all is known in and through Christ. Bonaventure can thus speak of Christ as "the metaphysical centre," because he is truly at the center.

Bonaventure explains that, because the Word is threefold center (*medium*) of all things, in both divine and created realms, a correspondingly threefold understanding is the key to contemplation:

> And so, the key to contemplation is a threefold understanding: of the Uncreated Word by whom all things are brought forth; of the Incarnate Word by whom all things are restored; and the Inspired Word by whom all things are revealed. (*Hex.* 3.2)

23. See Hayes, "Bonaventure: Mystery of the Triune God," 73–79.

As the uncreated Word in the Trinity (*Verbum increatum*), the Word stands at the center of the divine order of persons. As the Word incarnate, the Word made visible in Jesus of Nazareth (*Verbum incarnatum*), the Word descends and enters to the center of the created universe. Third, as *Verbum inspiratum*, the Word resides in our hearts as the Spirit of Christ, who prompts us to recognize Christ and unites us to Christ.

In this way, Bonaventure urges us to recognize that Christ is thus the center of all knowledge (*Hex.* 1), "the central point of all understanding" (*Hex.* 1.11). "[The Father] expresses everything in Him, that is, in the Son or in that very Centre, which so to speak is His Art. Hence this Center is Truth" (*Hex.* 1.13). To know Christ is to know the center, is to know the Trinity, is to know creation. Christ is the ladder, binding the lowest to the highest, through whom we return to God.[24] He is "the way and the door, the stairway and the vehicle" (*Itin.* 7.1).[25]

In a sermon for the second Sunday of Lent, for which the gospel recounts Jesus' transfiguration, Bonaventure powerfully underscores the centrality of Christ. He speaks of the transformation of *everything* in Christ's transfiguration:

> *All things* [are] *transfigured* in the transfiguration of Christ because whatever there was of creation was transfigured: for Christ, as a human being, shares with all creatures; "Indeed he possesses being with rocks, lives among the plants, senses with animals, and understands with angels." Since Christ, as a human being, has something from all of creation, and was transfigured, all is said to be transfigured in him. (*Sunday Sermons*, Sermon 16, Second Sunday in Lent 12[26])

For Bonaventure, the incarnation is "the greatest miracle" (*Hex.* 3.13). It is the center where divine and created orders meet. It closes the circle of emanation and return, descension and ascension. And at the very core of that center is the cross, the greatest testimony to God's goodness and love. As for Francis of Assisi, the cross has a crucial place in Bonaventure's understanding. Bonaventure would leave us in no doubt that mystical union with God is a dying into love. No one can reach those mystical heights of union with God "save through the Crucified," he insists (*Itin.* prol. 3). Ultimately, to know Christ is to be crucified with him, as is epitomized in the

---

24. *Itin.* 1.3; 4.2; 7.1; *Hex* 3.13.

25. See also *Itin.* prol. 3.

26. *The Sunday Sermons of St. Bonaventure*, ed. Timothy J. Johnson, vol. 12 of Bonaventure Texts in Translation series (St. Bonaventure, NY: The Franciscan Institute, 2008), 217.

stigmatized Francis, conformed to Christ crucified, and as such model par excellence of Christian perfection.

At one level, the Holy Spirit has a less prominent place in Bonaventure's trinitarian reflections compared to the Word. There is, however, as Walter Principe has commented, a "richness, warmth and clarity"[27] in Bonaventure's theology of the Holy Spirit. For Bonaventure, the Holy Spirit, as the third and last divine person (*ultimum*), completes and perfects the order of the divine persons. Bonaventure summarizes the order: "The Father is in the order of the originating principle, the Son in the order of the exemplating center, the Holy Spirit in the order of the fulfilling end. These three persons are equal and of equal nobility, for it is of equal nobility for the Holy Spirit to complete the divine persons, for the Father to originate them and for the Son to represent them all" (*Hex.* 1.2). The Holy Spirit brings divine life to its perfection, a perfection that is perfect unity in perfect distinction in a communion of love.

In his commentary on the *Sentences*, Bonaventure describes the dynamic mutual interpenetration of the three, Father, Son, and Holy Spirit, *Primitas*, *Medium*, and *Ultimum*, in terms of *circumincession*, a mutually interpenetrating union in distinction. He writes: "It must be said, that . . . there is among the divine a most high and perfect *circumincession*. And this is called a *circumincession*, by which there is meant, that One is in the Other and vice versa: and this properly and perfectly is in God alone, because circumincession in being [*in essendo*] posits simultaneously a distinction and a unity" (*I Sent.* d. 19, p. 1, a.u., q. 4, conc.).[28] While the Son is the center between Father and Holy Spirit, effecting in person their union in distinction, the Holy Spirit is the bond of unity (*nexus* or *nectens*), proceeding by way of the mutual love of the Father and Son through their loving concord in spirating the Holy Spirit. The Father and Son love each other by the Holy Spirit.[29]

---

27. Walter Principe, "St. Bonaventure's Theology of the Holy Spirit with Reference to the Expression 'Pater et Filius Diligunt se Spiritu Sancto,'" in *S. Bonaventura*, vol. 9 of *Theologia* (Roma: Collegio S. Bonaventura Grottaferrata, 1974), 243–69, at 269.

28. Bonaventure, *I Sent.* d. 19, p.1, a.u., q. 4, conc., online edition, *St. Bonaventure's Commentaries on the Four Books of Sentences of Master Peter Lombard*, The Franciscan Archive, trans. The Franciscan Archive, at http://www.franciscan-archive.org/index2.html (accessed October 25, 2009). See also *Hex.* 21.19, and *Itin.* 6.2 where Bonaventure speaks in terms of the mutual penetration of the divine persons, albeit without the actual use of the term *circumincession*.

29. See Principe, "St. Bonaventure's Theology of the Holy Spirit." Principe commends the "precision and clarity that Bonaventure brings to this question, complicated as it was because it involves so many aspects of the theology of the Holy Spirit" (268).

Bonaventure appropriates goodness and love to the Holy Spirit. He also follows Augustine in preferring the designation Gift for the Holy Spirit. He explains: "The Holy Spirit is properly the Gift, the mutual bond or Love, and the Holy Spirit as such. 'Gift' designates him as one given gratuitously, 'Bond' or 'Love' as one given freely as the gift excelling all others, and 'Holy Spirit' as one given freely as an excelling gift, who is also personal" (*Brevil.* 1.3.9). As Gift, the Holy Spirit is the one in and through whom all other gifts are given (*Itin.* 6.2).[30]

While the return to the Father is effected by the Son/Center/Medium, it is completed and brought to perfection by the Holy Spirit. All comes to completion in the Holy Spirit, *unus nexus*. In the created realm, the role of the Holy Spirit is to draw the human person ever more deeply into conformity with the Word and concomitantly into the Word's relation to the Father. It is by the power of the Holy Spirit that the human person comes to the Son and in and through him to the Father. Here too the Holy Spirit is the *unus nexus*, uniting the soul to God.

The end goal of the spiritual life is a passing over into union with the Trinity. Bonaventure again underscores the role of the Holy Spirit, by whose "fire" one is inflamed "to the very marrow":

> If this passing over is to be perfect, all intellectual activities must be
> given up, and our deepest and total affection must be directed to God
> and transformed into God. But this is mystical and very secret, which
> *no one knows except one who receives it.* And no one receives it except one
> who desires it. And no one desires it but one who is penetrated to the
> very marrow with the fire of the Holy Spirit whom Christ has sent
> into the world. (*Itin.* 7.4)

Here Bonaventure offers a profound insight into the intensely personal journey of the soul to mystical union with God. And here we come full circle in an exploration of his thought, combining, as it does, a penetrating theological vision that is truly cosmic in scope with an equally penetrating insight into the individual human person's journey to union with God, both of which are centered and grounded in the mystery of the Trinity, that sublime mystery "whose center is everywhere and whose circumference is nowhere" (*Itin.* 5.8).

---

30. Bonaventure's extended excurses on the seven gifts of the Holy Spirit, of which the greatest is wisdom, as "experiential knowledge of God," effectively constitutes his teaching on grace.

Conclusion

Bonaventure's theology is renowned for its Christocentrism, and rightly so. Inspired by Francis of Assisi, his theology has Christ, the Word Incarnate and Crucified, at its center. But Christ stands at the center of Bonaventure's theology because, as Bonaventure sees it, Christ is really at the center of all reality. As second person, the Son is center of the Trinity, between Father and Son, Image of the Father, and Exemplar of all that is other than the Father, both *ad intra* and *ad extra*. As Incarnate Word, he is center of the cosmos, its Savior, Mediator between God and creation.

While Christ is undoubtedly at the center of Bonaventure's theology, the architecture of Bonaventure's theology is thoroughly trinitarian. It is the mystery of the Trinity that is the larger frame of reference within which the Christocentrism is grounded. The result is a strikingly coherent and systematic theological vision, wherein a trinitarian exemplarity dovetails with a christological exemplarity. The theological vision is all the more remarkable for its truly cosmic scope.

From Christ as center, Bonaventure works back to the Father, from whom the person of the Son proceeds by way of the self-diffusiveness of the good: not by way of intellectual emanation, as in Augustine's and Aquinas's explication of the first procession, but by way of nature. Bonaventure, again inspired by Francis, holds fast to the notion of God as supreme goodness, a goodness abundantly manifest in the love revealed par excellence in the cross of Christ.

From the procession of the Son from the Father by way of the self-diffusiveness of the good, Bonaventure progresses to the procession of the Holy Spirit whose procession completes the innertrinitarian circle. Bonaventure takes up Richard of St. Victor's explication of the second procession by way of the analogy of interpersonal love, the perfection of which is shared love for a third (*condilectus*).

Unlike Thomas Aquinas, whose theology of the Trinity unfolds in terms of a metaphysics of being, Bonaventure thus fuses the Pseudo-Dionysian metaphysics of the good, the very nature of which is to be self-diffusive, with Richard of St. Victor's reflections on the perfection of interpersonal love. This fusion of insights from Pseudo-Dionysius and Richard of St. Victor enables Bonaventure to develop a powerful and profoundly mystical sense of God as "infinitely rich and fecund mystery whose eternal being is an ecstasy of goodness and love."[31]

31. Hayes, "Introduction," 36.

Christ stands firmly at the center. At one side is the Father who is fecund source of all, fountain fullness of goodness; at the other, the Holy Spirit who is *unus nexus* of Father and Son, and agent of return of all creation to its source, drawing the soul to ever greater conformity to the Son/Word and thus into the relationship between Father and Word.

While not following Augustine's explication of the innertrinitarian emanations in terms of the psychological analogy, Bonaventure does follow Augustine in recognizing an image of the Trinity in the trinity of powers of the human person: memory, intelligence, and will or love. He recognizes everything in creation as bearing the stamp of the Trinity. Bonaventure thus highlights the reality of the whole world as symbol of the Trinity, like a book or a work of art reflecting the artist who created it, trinitarian in form, not only in its structure but also in its historical development. He would thus have us understand the profoundly sacramental character of the cosmos. The result is a coherent trinitarian theology of vast cosmological scope, but also deeply personal in its exploration of the soul's journey to union with the Trinity.

References and Further Reading

Primary Sources

Breviloquium. Translation by Dominic V. Monti. Vol. 9 of *Works of St. Bonaventure.* Bonaventure Texts in Translation Series. Saint Bonaventure, NY: Franciscan Institute Publications, 2005.

Collations on the Six Days. Vol. 5 of *Works of St. Bonaventure.* Translated by José de Vinck. Paterson, NJ: St. Anthony Guild Press, 1970.

Disputed Questions on the Mystery of the Trinity. Vol. 3 of *Works of Saint Bonaventure.* Translation by Zachary Hayes. New York: The Franciscan Institute, 1979.

Itinerarium Mentis in Deum. Translated by Zachary Hayes. Vol. 2 of *Works of St. Bonaventure.* Rev. and exp. ed. Saint Bonaventure, NY: Franciscan Institute Publications, 2002.

The Soul's Journey into God, The Tree of Life, The Life of St. Francis. Translation by Ewert Cousins. The Classics of Western Spirituality Series. New York: Paulist Press, 1978.

Secondary Sources

Cullen, Christopher M. *Bonaventure.* Oxford: Oxford University Press, 2006.
Delio, Ilia. *Bonaventure.* Hyde Park NY: New York City Press, 2001.

Hayes, Zachary. "Bonaventure: Mystery of the Triune God." In *The History of Franciscan Theology*, edited by Kenan B. Osborne, 39–125. St. Bonaventure, NY: The Franciscan Institute Publications, St. Bonaventure University, 1994.

———. "Introduction." In *Disputed Questions on the Mystery of the Trinity*. Edited by George Marcil. Vol. 3 of *Works of Saint Bonaventure*, 13–103. New York: The Franciscan Institute Publications, 1979.

Hellmann, J. A. Wayne. *Divine and Created Order in Bonaventure's Theology*. Translated by J. M. Hammond. St. Bonaventure, NY: The Franciscan Institute Publications, 2001.

Johnson, Timothy, ed. *Bonaventure: Mystic of God's Word*. St. Bonaventure, NY: The Franciscan Institute Publications, St. Bonaventure University, 2006.

McGinn, Bernard. "The Dynamism of the Trinity in Bonaventure and Eckhart." *Eckhart Review* 16 (2007): 46–64. Also *Franciscan Studies* 65 (2007): 137–55.

Monti, Dominic. "Bonaventure's Use of 'The Divine Word' in Academic Theology." In *That Others May Know and Love: Essays in Honor of Zachary Hayes, OFM*, edited by Michael Cusato and Edward Coughlin, 65–88. St. Bonaventure, NY: The Franciscan Institute Publications, 1997.

4

MEISTER ECKHART
(CA. 1260–1328)

In Meister Eckhart, we meet one of the finest scholastic minds of his era. Preacher, teacher, spiritual guide, philosopher, theologian, and mystic; few have been more influential, and few more controversial.

He was a master (meister, magister, master teacher) at the University of Paris, the most distinguished university in medieval Europe, a vibrant and exhilarating intellectual center, where scholars engaged with the thought of Greek philosophers of antiquity, as well as with that of Islamic and Jewish philosophers. Only two theologians, Meister Eckhart and his illustrious predecessor and Dominican confrere, Thomas Aquinas, were appointed *twice* to the prestigious position of Master of the University of Paris. Yet, after a distinguished career as master of the university and meister of the spiritual life, Meister Eckhart was brought to trial for heresy. A year after his death, in 1329, Pope John XXII issued a papal censure that described Eckhart as one "who wished to know more than he should," accused him of leading astray "the hearts of the simple," "especially the uneducated," and condemned twenty-eight articles from Eckhart's work.[1] The taint of suspicion of heresy lingered thereafter over Eckhart's reputation and the orthodoxy of his teaching. In recent decades, however, the tide of opinion has turned in Eckhart's favor. Pope John Paul II, in a speech in 1985 spoke of him with evident approval:

> I think of the marvellous history of Rheno-Flemish mysticism of the thirteenth and especially of the fourteenth centuries. . . . Did not Eckhart teach his disciples: "All that God asks you most pressingly is

---

1. For the bull and some of Eckhart's defense, see *Meister Eckhart: The Essential Sermons, Commentaries, Treatises and Defense*, trans. Edmund Colledge and Bernard McGinn (New York: Paulist Press, 1981), 71–81 (hereafter *Essential Sermons*). Following McGinn, sermons in German are denoted with the Arabic numerals, e.g., Sermon 52, while those in Latin are denoted by Roman numerals, e.g., Sermon XXV.

to go out of yourself . . . and let God be God in you"[2]? One could think that in separating himself from creatures the mystic leaves his brother humanity behind. The same Eckhart affirms that on the contrary the mystic is marvellously present to them on the only level where he can truly reach them, that is, in God.[3]

Thomas Merton, with a similar sense of appreciation, wrote of Eckhart: "Meister Eckhart may have limitations, but I am entranced with him nevertheless. I like the brevity, the incisiveness of his sermons, his way of piercing straight to the heart of the inner life, the awakened spark, the creative and redeeming Word, God born in us."[4] Merton also comments that "Eckhart did not have the kind of mind that wasted time being cautious."[5]

Meister Eckhart's thought is complex and difficult, sometimes very subtle, not always coherent, frequently baffling, sometimes almost impenetrable. Given his predilection for dialectic, it is not easy to locate his position clearly. Nor does his thought yield to any easy synthesis or categorization. His very creative mind resulted in radically new and daring—and at times dangerous, even outrageous—forms of theological discourse. He seemed to delight in exploding traditional forms of discourse, constantly experimenting with language and imagery to express the profound mystery of God that so captivated him. He spoke, for example, in terms of the notion of God beyond God.[6] He urged his congregation: "Let us pray to God that we may be free of 'God'" (Sermon 52, *Essential Sermons*, 200). Alas, his dar-

2. Sermon 5b, in ibid., 184.

3. John Paul II, To Participants in the Convention on *Adrienne von Speyr* (September 28, 1985) §1, at http://www.vatican.va/holy_father/john_paul_ii/speeches/1985/september/documents/hf_jp-ii_spe_19850928_adrienne-von-speyr_fr.html (accessed October 25, 2009).

4. Thomas Merton, *Conjectures of a Guilty Bystander* (London: Burns & Oates, 1968), 54–55. Merton continues: "He is a great man who was pulled down by a lot of little men who thought they could destroy him: who thought they could drag him to Avignon and have him utterly discredited. And indeed he was ruined, after his death in twenty-eight propositions which might doubtless be found somewhere in him, but which had none of his joy, his energy, his freedom. They were not 'his' in the sense that they were not at all what he intended. But they could be made to coincide with words that had been spoken. And I suppose one must take such things into account. Eckhart did not have the kind of mind that wasted time being cautious about every comma: he trusted men to recognize that what he saw was worth seeing because it brought obvious fruits of life and joy. For him, that was what mattered."

5. Ibid.

6. Sermon 48, *Essential Sermons*, 198.

ing inventiveness with language and imagery was to cause him much grief when it aroused the attention and consternation of the Inquisition. But, as for the other mystics in our study, Eckhart's thought is thoroughly trinitarian. Renowned scholar of mystical theology Bernard McGinn writes: "Meister Eckhart is surely to be counted among the more trinitarian Christian mystics."[7]

Eckhart's Life and Times

Eckhart (actually, Eckhart von Hochheim) was born around 1260 in Saxony.[8] We know little of Eckhart's early life, not even his Christian name with certainty. It seems that he was born into a family of the lower aristocracy. Given his renown in Eckhart's own lifetime and the scandal of his inquisitorial trial, it is perhaps even more surprising that neither the date nor the circumstances of his death, nor the place of his burial, is known with certainty. We know only that his death was sometime around April 30, 1328.

Eckhart entered the flourishing Order of Preachers (Dominicans) as a young man. At some stage, he proceeded to higher theological studies at the University of Paris and, as was the usual practice, became a bachelor and teacher of the *Sentences* of Peter Lombard.

Medieval philosophy and theology was in a state of turmoil at this time. In 1277, the bishop of Paris, Stephen Tempier, had, in a syllabus of errors, condemned 219 philosophical and theological propositions then under discussion and dispute in the University of Paris. Given that about twenty of the propositions were clearly in Thomas Aquinas's work, Tempier's syllabus thereby cast a shadow of doubt over the teaching of Eckhart's esteemed Dominican confrere and Master of Paris, who had died just three years previously.

The relationship between philosophy and theology itself was in question. There was bitter controversy over Aristotelian philosophy, with some considering it to be irreconcilable with Christian faith. A certain rivalry between the two sibling mendicant orders, the Franciscans and the Dominicans, and long-standing disputes over such questions as the priority of the will over the intellect, escalated into a dispute regarding the place—if

7. Bernard McGinn, "Prolegomenon to the Role of the Trinity in Meister Eckhart's Mysticism," *Eckhart Review* 6 (1997): 51–61.

8. For an excellent study of Eckhart, see Bernard McGinn, *The Mystical Thought of Meister Eckhart: The Man from whom God Hid Nothing* (New York: Crossroad, 2001).

place at all—of philosophy (other than logic, of course) in the endeavor of theology.[9] Like his Dominican predecessors Albert the Great and Thomas Aquinas who saw no contradiction between philosophy and theology, Eckhart vehemently defended the Dominican understanding that philosophy was a necessary tool for theology (though he would go further than they in his argument).

In 1294, Eckhart was recalled to Saxony and made prior (superior) of his home convent in Erfurt and vicar (local representative of the provincial) of Thuringia. In 1302, Eckhart was recalled to Paris to take up the Dominican chair of theology. He returned to Germany in 1303 to serve as provincial of the newly established province of Saxonia, with responsibility for convents in northern and eastern Germany and in the Low Countries. He proved a capable administrator and leader, as is very evident from the appointments that he was asked to fill. In 1307, he was elected vicar for Bohemia. In 1310, he was elected provincial of the other German Dominican province, Teutonia, a role that he did not take up, on the instruction of the Dominican master general, due to problems at the University of Paris at that time, with increasing conflict with the Franciscans and mounting hostility against the work of Thomas Aquinas.

Eckhart was then posted back to Paris for a second period as magister (1311–1313). During this time, he lived in the same house as the papal Dominican Inquisitor, William of Paris, under whose instructions the Frenchwoman Marguerite Porete had been executed in 1310, having been condemned for her work, *The Mirror of Simple Souls*, and most particularly for failing to preserve the distinction between Creator and created.

Eckhart left Paris in 1313. He went to serve as vicar in Strasbourg in the Rhineland. He left Strasbourg in late 1323 or early 1324 and went to Cologne. No longer a university magister nor a senior official of the Order, he spent the last years of his life preaching and teaching. Cologne was then a lively center of Beguine piety. Beguine mysticism was, however, generally regarded by church authorities with a good measure of suspicion.[10] The Beguines' visionary experiences were considered to be dubious, their

9. This dispute between the Franciscans and the Dominicans, which became known as the *Correctoria Controversy*, concerned the work of Thomas Aquinas. The Franciscans, much to the ire of the Dominicans, claimed to "correct" Aquinas in regard to the nature of Christ.

10. Beguines were devout women, living alone or in communities, who dedicated their lives to God but without taking formal religious vows or becoming members of religious orders, and thus outside of the canonical control and supervision of religious authorities. The extremes of Beguine piety were condemned at the Council of Vienne in 1311–1312.

teachings dangerous, even heretical, and the antiecclesiastical positions that they encouraged unacceptable.

Eckhart's life and work came to a tragic conclusion when the orthodoxy of his work was called into question and he fell afoul of ecclesiastical authorities. An examination of his work by Nicholas of Strasbourg, a member of his Order and a papal visitor to the province at the time, found nothing to censure. Nevertheless, Eckhart was called to appear before a diocesan inquisitorial commission in 1326, conducted under the authority of the Franciscan archbishop of Cologne, Henry of Virneburg, a staunch defender of orthodoxy and church practice and a zealous opponent of heresy.

In the course of his defense, Eckhart submitted a reply to the errors attributed to him. He also protested against the proceeding itself, which was conducted under the jurisdiction of the archbishop's court. He denied the theological competency of the court and appealed to the pope to judge his case, which was then continued at the papal court in Avignon. In the spring of 1327, Eckhart left Cologne for Avignon. The details of this last chapter of his life are not well documented. John XXII established two commissions—one of theologians, one of cardinals—to investigate the charges. Eckhart died in 1328 before the protracted procedure was completed.

Throughout the investigation, Eckhart vehemently insisted that he was not a heretic. As he wrote in his defense: "I can be in error, but I cannot be a heretic," he claimed, "because the first belongs to the intellect, the second to the will."[11] He insisted that he would retract publicly anything found to be erroneous in his preaching or writings, and he appealed to his good intentions in preaching.[12]

Eckhart's defense clearly did not allay the concerns of his inquisitors. In 1329, more than a year after Eckhart's death, John XXII issued a bull of condemnation, "*In agro dominico.*"[13] The bull articulates concerns regarding Eckhart's theology, in both Latin and vernacular writings, noting that: "He presented many things as dogma that were deigned to cloud the true faith in the hearts of many, things which he put forth especially before the uneducated crowd in his sermons and that he also admitted into his writings."[14] The bull specifically condemned twenty-eight articles in his teaching and preaching.

11. See *Essential Sermons*, 72.

12. See ibid., 81.

13. See ibid., 77–81. For recent arguments concerning the papal bull, see Robert E. Lerner, "Meister Eckhart's Specter: Fourteenth-Century Uses of the Bull '*In Agro Dominico*' Including a Newly Discovered Inquisitorial Text of 1337," *Mediaeval Studies* 78 (2008): 115–34.

14. See *Essential Sermons*, 77.

Fifteen propositions were declared to "contain the error or stain of heresy" while another eleven were described as "quite evil-sounding and very rash and suspect of heresy, though with many explanations and additions they might take on or possess a Catholic meaning."[15] A further two articles were also denounced as heretical but, since there was some doubt as to whether Eckhart actually taught them, those articles were handled in a separate category. While the bull's preface castigated Eckhart as someone who "wished to know more than he should," the bull did not actually condemn Eckhart himself as a heretic, and noted that Eckhart had "revoked and also deplored the twenty-six articles, which he admitted that he had preached, and also any others written and taught by him, whether in the schools or in sermons, insofar as they could generate in the minds of the faithful a heretical opinion, or one erroneous and hostile to the true faith."[16]

In spite of the papal condemnation, Eckhart's works continued to be read, especially among German and Dutch readers, for the next century and a half, before falling into obscurity. A resurgence of interest in Eckhart's work then emerged in the nineteenth and twentieth centuries. Indeed, Eckhart set an indelible stamp upon the Rhenish Dominican spiritual movement, along with his two principal disciples, the Dominican masters John Tauler (d. 1361) and Henry Suso (or Seuse, d. 1366), both of whom made use of Eckhart's mystical thought, though with careful qualifications. The tide of opinion eventually turned in Eckhart's favor, and today the question is no longer even one of rehabilitation (the formal process of restoring him to good standing).[17]

Eckhart's trial by the Inquisition remains a complicated and sorry affair.[18] While it was certainly not uncommon for theologians to be investigated and censured for erroneous views, Eckhart's trial for heresy was unprecedented, and it was all the more shocking given his high standing as an esteemed Master of Paris and, no less, his reputation as a pious man. But the times were rife with fears of heresy. There is no doubting that the situation was highly politically charged, and on a range of levels—with the conflict between the secular clergy and the mendicant orders, the struggles between the Avignon papacy and the emperor, the tensions between the

---

15. Ibid., 80.

16. Ibid., 81.

17. See http://www.eckhartsociety.org/eckhart/eckhart-man for a brief description of events since 1980 in regard to Eckhart's "rehabilitation" (accessed October 25, 2009).

18. See Bernard McGinn, "Eckhart's Condemnation Reconsidered," *The Thomist* (1980): 390–414.

teaching magisterium of the church and mystical piety,[19] and, perhaps most perilous of all for Eckhart, the rivalry between the Franciscan and Dominican Orders, and perhaps a certain antagonism for the Meister.

Eckhart's Writings

While there is not yet unanimity regarding the authentic corpus of Eckhart's writings, there is unanimity around the authenticity of a good number of texts, which include scriptural commentaries, a few treatises (in vernacular German as well as in learned Latin), some spiritual works, and numerous sermons by the renowned preacher. What is particularly interesting about Eckhart's corpus of writings is that it includes works in the vernacular German of the people (the High Middle German of the early fourteenth century) and in the Latin of the schools. The Latin works are textually relatively secure, while the sermons, which are the work of those who heard and transcribed them, are clearly less secure, though those deemed to be authentic evince a high level of consistency of thought and imagery.

Eckhart's corpus thus combines two very different registers—technical scholastic works and vernacular sermons and treatises. Eckhart is indeed one of the first of the medieval theologians to venture out of the scholastic Latin of the schools of his era and into the vernacular. In fact, he played a significant role in the development of the use of the vernacular in speculative and mystical theological discourse. McGinn observes "that Meister Eckhart is the *only* major figure in the history of Christian mysticism in whom we can observe the full dynamics of the interplay between Latin mysticism (almost a millennium old by the time he wrote) and the new vernacular theology (still aborning, despite the achievements of the thirteenth century)."[20]

From Eckhart's first period at the University of Paris (1302–1303), there are the *Quaestiones* (*Quaestio Parisiensis*) and the *Sermo die beati Augustini Parisius habitus*, a feast-day sermon in honor of Augustine. Between 1303 and 1310, during a general chapter, Eckhart delivered the *Sermones* on Ecclesiasticus 24:23-27a and 24:27b-31. He commenced the *Opus tripartitum*, his major work, comprising three parts, in 1305, but left much of it incomplete. Of Eckhart's various commentaries, which were written basically for the education and use of preachers, the commentary on the Gospel of John

---

19. See Bernard McGinn, "'Evil-Sounding, Rash, and Suspect of Heresy': Tensions between Mysticism and Magisterium in the History of the Church," *Catholic Historical Review* 20 (2004): 193–212.

20. McGinn, *The Mystical Thought of Meister Eckhart*, 34.

(*Expositio sancti evangelii secundum Iohannem*) is his only extant New Testament commentary.

There are numerous sermons and some treatises from the Strasbourg and Cologne periods, and his most important German sermons come from this period. Sermons IV and 10, as well as his commentary on John's gospel, are significant for their trinitarian insights. While undoubtedly endowed with a powerful intellect and a highly creative mind, Eckhart was also a captivating preacher. His sermons demonstrate a remarkable linguistic virtuosity and considerable rhetorical as well as poetic skill. His move into the vernacular German afforded the opportunity for highly innovative and imaginative use of the language and imagery.

There is nothing in Eckhart's corpus on the scale of Thomas Aquinas's *Summa*, nor a theological handbook like that of Bonaventure's *Breviloquium*. Eckhart was more given to responding to the needs and circumstances of the particular time and occasion, and to preaching on the readings of the day, rather than the composition of lengthy and refined technical treatises. Eckhart is renowned most of all for his sermons, most of which were probably delivered to his fellow Dominicans, but some no doubt to nuns and to lay audiences, including Beguines. Indeed, Eckhart considered himself to be first and foremost a preacher, and, only after that, a teacher and scholar. In this, he was deeply imbued with a sense of the charism of the Order of Preachers to which he belonged, for whom preaching is the core mission. He was, nonetheless, a highly trained and skilled scholastic theologian. His writing attests to his mastery of the methods, technical language and concepts of scholastic theology. Eckhart's theology is based essentially on Western sources, especially Augustine, Peter Lombard, and Thomas Aquinas, but also on Pseudo-Dionysius and Bonaventure. He is also clearly familiar with the work of Plato and Aristotle and demonstrates a profound command of the philosophical sources, as would be expected of a Master of Paris.

There is no doubt that the teachings of the Beguine mystics also had a strong influence on Eckhart's thought, including his vernacular teaching in the latter years of his life. The influence of Marguerite Porete is especially evident and it is almost certain that he knew her work, *Mirror of Simple Souls*. Eckhart appears also to be influenced by the German Beguine, Mechthild of Magdeburg (d. 1280), author of *The Flowing Light of the Godhead*, and it is probable that he knew her work.[21]

21. See Bernard McGinn, ed., *Meister Eckhart and the Beguine Mystics: Hadewijch of Brabant, Mechthild of Magdeburg, and Marguerite Porete* (New York: Continuum, 1994).

Eckhart does not speak of himself or of his own mystical experience, but his sermons and writings are suggestive, albeit indirectly, of his own mystical experience, a profound experience of encounter with God that takes place in silence and stillness and that is radically beyond language. In Sermon 69, for example, he writes, "Know that God loves the soul so powerfully that it staggers the mind" (*Teacher and Preacher*, 312). In Sermon 71, in reference it would seem to himself, he describes "a man as though in a dream." He writes, "When the soul comes into the One and there enters into a pure rejection of itself, it finds God as in a nothing. It seemed to a man as though in a dream—it was a waking dream—that he became pregnant with nothing as a woman does with a child, and in this nothing God was born; he was the fruit of the nothing. God was born in the nothing" (*Teacher and Preacher*, 323). In Sermon 2, he writes, "If you could look upon this with my heart, you would well understand what I say, for it is true, and it is Truth's own self that says it" (*Essential Sermons*, 181).

Eckhart, with great daring, breaks out of a number of the traditional categories of scholastic theology and engages highly innovative language and images. His work abounds in seeming contradictions, paradox, hyperbole, wordplays, imagery, simile, and metaphor.[22] He speaks, for example, of the groundless ground (*gruntlôs grunt*) and the groundless Godhead (*gruntlôsen gottheit*). While clearly following his esteemed Dominican predecessor, Thomas Aquinas, in many respects, he also departs from him in notable ways. Eckhart has a metaphysical-theological style that is distinctively his own. He effectively reverses the strategy of analogy, as it is normally applied, and argues that what is formally predicated of creatures cannot, by definition, be predicated of God, and vice versa. Instead of the analogical discourse, used to such great effect by Thomas Aquinas, Eckhart opts for a highly dialectical style of theological discourse. He seems to delight in deconstructing all forms of knowing into unknowing. He speaks as though deliberately intent on confounding his audience, as if to shock his hearers out of any sense of familiarity, and thus to waken them to a radically new understanding. It is almost as if the medium—his very style of theology—is itself the message, or at least integral to it: the message of the impenetrable, ineffable mystery of God. "He [God] is above all love and loveableness" (Sermon 83, *Essential Sermons*, 208). Here is the key to his thought: the sheer ineffability and infinity of the holy mystery that is God. As he says in one of his sermons, "The brightness of the divine

22. See Frank Tobin, "Master of Language," chap. 5 in *Meister Eckhart: Thought and Language* (Philadelphia: University of Pennsylvania Press, 1986), 147–83.

nature is beyond words. God is a word, a word unspoken" (Sermon 53, *Essential Sermons*, 203).

Eckhart's Insights into the Mystery of the Trinity

Eckhart's treatment of the Trinity is one of the most complex and confounding aspects of his thought. His most revealing—and audacious—passages are to be found in his sermons, both vernacular and Latin. The pulpit afforded him the occasion to indulge his exuberance and his liking for linguistic experimentation. It seems that he sensed the radical inadequacy of scholastic theology, for all its sophisticated technicalities and subtle refinements, to express the sheer mystery of God, and so constantly struggled to convey that utterly unutterably profound mystery of God and of the soul's union with God, pressing ever further to ever new and daring expressions.

In spite of the fact that it is virtually impossible to present a unified, coherent, and consistent depiction of Eckhart's trinitarian theology, for he offers no single clear exposition of the mystery, a few themes and motifs are central to his thought: (1) a metaphysics of flow and the metaphor of *bullitio* (boiling); (2) the one simple silent ground of divine and human being and the notion of union without distinction; and (3) the birth of the Word in the soul. These themes are inextricably interconnected and together give structural coherence to Eckhart's thought.

As would be expected of a magister of the University of Paris, Eckhart is deeply informed by the Greek philosophies of antiquity as well as classical Christian thought. He stands firmly within the broad tradition of Christian Platonism, and the neo-Platonist metaphysics of *exitus-reditus* pervades his thought.[23] As Bernard McGinn explains, Eckhart's metaphysics can aptly be described as a metaphysics of flow.[24] Eckhart himself says, "I have often said, God's going-out is his going-in" (Sermon 53, *Essential Sermons*, 204). When speaking of grace, Eckhart employs the same metaphor when he says, "The first grace [grace freely given] consists in a type of flowing out, a departure from God; the second [saving grace] consists in a type of flowing back, a return to God himself" (Sermon XXV, §259, *Teacher and Preacher*, 218).

---

23. *Exitus:* flowing out, *emanatio, effluxus, ausfliessen; reditus*: flowing back, *restoratio, refluxus, ingang, durchbrechen.*

24. See McGinn, *The Mystical Thought of Meister Eckhart*, 71–113.

In articulating this dynamic of emanation and return that is fundamental to his understanding of reality, Eckhart uses a variety of Latin and German expressions, engaging such motifs as boiling, boiling over, swelling up, bursting forth, and breaking through. In describing the emanation of the Son, for example, Eckhart explains, "The image [the Word/Son as Image of the Father] is an emanation from the depths in silence, excluding everything that comes from without. It is a form of life, as if you were to imagine something swelling up from itself and in itself and then inwardly boiling without 'boiling over' yet understood" (Sermon XLIX, §511, *Teacher and Preacher*, 236). In a remarkable exegesis on the text "I am who I am" (Exod 3:14), Eckhart explains in a similar vein that "the repetition (namely, that it says 'I am who am') . . . indicates a 'boiling' or giving birth to itself–glowing in itself, and melting and boiling in and into itself, light that totally forces its whole being in light and into light and that is everywhere totally turned back and reflected upon itself" (Commentary on Exodus, §16, *Teacher and Preacher*, 46).

Images of boiling and of boiling over also feature in his discussion of grace. Eckhart writes, for example: "God as good is the principle of the 'boiling over' on the outside; as personal notion he is the principle of the 'boiling within himself,' which is the cause and exemplar of the 'boiling over'" (Sermon XXV, §258, *Teacher and Preacher*, 218). Eckhart understands that our *exitus* takes place through God's creative "boiling over" outside the divine nature, while our *reditus*, our deification, takes place through the trinitarian "boiling" in itself that is grace.

The metaphor of *bullitio*, boiling, figures particularly strongly in his explication of the stages of *exitus/emanatio* of existence. He speaks in terms of (1) a *bullitio*, an "inner boiling" or breaking-out or bubbling, by which he refers to the trinitarian boiling, the principle of which emanation, following Pseudo-Dionysius, is that goodness diffuses itself; and (2) an *ebullitio*, a "boiling over" outside the divine nature, which results in the production of something out of nothing by way of "creating" (*creatio*), or a making (*factio*) of something out of something else. As Eckhart explains:

> There are three stages in the production of existence. The first . . .
> is that by which something from itself, out of itself, and in itself produces a pure nature, pouring it forth formally without the cooperation of the will, but rather with its concomitant activity. This is the way the Good diffuses itself. This is also how the power of willing can be a principle even if the end is not yet grasped. The second stage is like the "boiling over" in the manner of an efficient cause and with a view toward an end by which something produces something else that is

> from itself, but not out of itself. This production is either out of some other thing (and then it is called "making"), or it is out of nothing (and then it is the third stage of production which is called "creating"). (Sermon XLIX, §511, *Teacher and Preacher*, 237)

Eckhart in this way distinguishes between a trinitarian *bullitio*, which refers to the emanation of the divine persons, and a creative *ebullitio*, which refers to the creation of the world.[25] The two are intrinsically related, however, with the creative *ebullitio* having its source in the trinitarian *bullitio* by which the Father generates the Son and by which the Love that is the Holy Spirit emanates from the two persons, Father and Son, together as one principle. In other words, God's inner *bullitio*, boiling, is the ground, source, and exemplar of the "boiling over," *ebullitio*, that is creation. Moreover, the *creatio* and *factio*—the creating and making of things that is the *ebullitio*—express the same trinitarian mode and structure of action as the *bullitio*. In both cases, there is something generating (Father), something generated (Son), and the mutual love of what generates and what is generated (Holy Spirit). On this basis, Eckhart recognizes a trinitarian structure in *all* activity in the cosmos, for as he explains: "Every action of nature, morality, and art in its wholeness possesses three things: something generating, something generated, and the love of what generates for what is generated and vice versa" (Commentary on Wisdom, §28, *Teacher and Preacher*, 150). While Augustine of Hippo and Thomas Aquinas had recognized trinitarian vestiges in everything in creation, and Bonaventure the trinitarian structure in everything in creation, Eckhart presses further and articulates an understanding of *all activity* as essentially trinitarian in its structure and dynamism.

The notion of the ground (*grunt* or *grund*, in German) is another distinctive feature of Eckhart's vernacular thought. He uses the term and its derivatives repeatedly. Indeed Bernard McGinn has suggested that the description "mysticism of the ground" provides "a helpful prism for understanding the special character of the mysticism of Eckhart and those influenced by him."[26] Admittedly, Eckhart is not alone in employing this notion of *grunt*. Mechthild of Magdeburg and Hadewijch, for example, had used it before him, and the term was emerging as an important mystical term in the German vernacular at this time. But Eckhart's development of it is

25. With the notion that both *bullitio* and *ebullitio* were coeternal, Eckhart comes very close to teaching that creation is eternal, a teaching condemned in the papal bull *In agro domini*.

26. McGinn, *The Mystical Thought of Meister Eckhart*, 37.

uniquely and distinctively his own. Ground, McGinn explains, "is a deceptively simple word, but as used by Eckhart, its complexity, creativity, and power are truly remarkable."[27] McGinn describes it in terms of "a master metaphor" at the center of Eckhart's mysticism. There is no Latin equivalent that captures the richness and subtlety of the vernacular *grunt*, although it has some similarity with *unum* (unity, oneness).[28] It is important to note that ground (*grunt*) is not used with the sense of cause. It connotes a deeper and more profound meaning than simply cause, and a greater richness and dynamism than such Latin notions as *essentia, deitas,* and *divinitas.* Indeed, in Eckhart's hands, the notion of *grunt* points *beyond* the three persons and their common essence. Eckhart uses the metaphors of ocean and of desert, wilderness, and wasteland to express the unfathomably vast and radically unknowable expanse of this supratrinitarian ground.[29]

Eckhart frequently speaks in rather startling terms of the unity and identity of God's ground and the human person's ground: "God's ground and the soul's ground are/is one ground" (e.g., Sermon 15, *Essential Sermons,* 192). He means that, in their deepest reality, both God and the soul are grounded in the one same ground, in other words, not one grounded in the other, but both grounded, in a fused identity, in the *one* ground. As Eckhart explains: "Here God's ground is my ground, and my ground is God's ground. Here I live from what is my own, as God lives from what is his own" (Sermon 5b, *Essential Sermons,* 184). Eckhart means, even more, that in the hidden innermost depth or abyss, the soul and God are one and identical. In this way, he explains, "God's existence must be my existence and God's is-ness is my is-ness." (Sermon 6, *Essential Sermons,* 187). In a similar way, he speaks of "the just soul" as "equal with God and close beside [God], equal beside him, not beneath or above" (Sermon 6, *Essential Sermons,* 187).[30]

---

27. Ibid.

28. Ibid., 43.

29. See, for example, Sermon 10, *Meister Eckhart: Teacher and Preacher,* ed. Bernard McGinn, Classics of Western Spirituality (New York: Paulist Press, 1986), 265. See Bernard McGinn, "Ocean and Desert as Symbols of Mystical Absorption in the Christian Tradition," *Journal of Religion* 74 (1994): 155–81, esp. 167–72.

30. Eckhart argues that the procession of the Son from the Father is imaged well in the justice of the just man, *insofar as* (*inquantum*) he is just. The just person, *insofar as* he or she is just, is born of justice (*iustitia*) as the Son is born of the Father, and is no different from the Son. See Commentary on John §14, *Essential Sermons,* 126. Eckhart often employs his now famous "*inquantum*" (insofar as) principle, whereby an analogy of attribution applies "insofar as," as in this example. See *Essential Sermons,* 113–14, and 126–29.

Eckhart finds scriptural warrant for this notion of the mystical identity of God's ground and the soul's ground, this fusion of the two in the oneness of the groundless ground, in various Johannine texts, including John 17:21 (Christ's prayer that all who believe in him "that they may all be one. As you, Father, are in me and I am in you, may they also be in us"). Eckhart would also have us understand that this identity of the divine ground with the ground of the soul is a profoundly dynamic one.

Admittedly, Eckhart also sometimes speaks of God as penetrating and being in the soul's ground,[31] but the unity of which he speaks is, at the deepest level, one of *fused identity*. Similarly, and somewhat confusingly, at times Eckhart seems to identify the ground with the Father, but again, at its deepest level, *grunt* lies deeper even than the Trinity, beyond–strange though it might seem–the distinctions of the three divine persons, beyond the divine essence. Eckhart explains, adding "I will say more, surprising though this is":

> [The spark in the soul] wants nothing but its naked God, as he is in himself. It is not content with the Father or the Son or the Holy Spirit, or with the three Persons so far as each of them persists in his properties . . . this same light is not content with the simple divine essence in its repose . . . it wants to know the source of this essence, it wants to go to the simple ground, into the quiet desert, into which distinction never gazed, not the Father, nor the Son, nor the Holy Spirit. (Sermon 48, *Essential Sermons*, 198)

In a similarly perplexing vein, Eckhart sometimes distinguishes between God and the Godhead, "God beyond God." He explains:

> I say "one Godhead" because here nothing is yet flowing out, nor is it touched at all or thought. By negating something of God–say, I negate goodness of him (of course, I cannot really negate anything of him)–by negating something of God, I catch hold of something that he is *not*. It is precisely this that has to be removed. God is one, he is a negation of negation. (Sermon 21, *Teacher and Preacher*, 281)

Eckhart thus distinguishes between the personal trinitarian God and the nameless, distinctionless, supratrinitarian ground or Godhead that transcends this. "Then how should I love him?" Eckhart asks, to which he replies:

> You should love him as he is a non-God, a nonspirit, a nonperson, a nonimage, but as he is a pure, unmixed, bright "One," separated from

31. See, for example, Sermon 10, *Teacher and Preacher*, 261.

all duality; and in that One we should eternally sink down, out of "something" into "nothing." (Sermon 83, *Essential Sermons*, 208)

There is thus in Eckhart's thought an absolute unity or oneness that is somehow above and beyond the Trinity, a supratrinitarian unity, so to speak, and it has a certain undeniable priority in Eckhart's understanding. In another sermon, Eckhart elaborates on the distinction between God and the Godhead (*Gottheit*), where "God unbecomes":

> God and Godhead are as different as heaven and earth. . . . Everything that is in the Godhead is one, and of that there is nothing to be said. God works, the Godhead does no work: there is nothing for it to do, there is no activity in it. It never peeped at any work. God and Godhead are distinguished by working and not-working. When I return to God, if I do not remain there, my breakthrough will be far nobler than my outflowing. . . . When I enter the ground, the bottom, the river and fount of the Godhead, none will ask me whence I came or where I have been. No one missed me, for there God *unbecomes*. (Sermon 56, Walshe, vol. 2, 80–82)[32]

It seems that, for Eckhart, the Godhead is the silent, simple, unchanging One, without movement, without number, beyond the plurality of persons, a prior inner ground, primal source. It is pure potentiality, pregnant with possibility, and, as such, the ground for the possibility of all emanation and activity, even the divine *bullitio* itself. Eckhart strains to describe it, employing such metaphors as ocean, desert, wasteland, and abyss. He understands that the Trinity emanates from this desert-like emptiness in a process analogous to a boiling up and over (*bullitio*) of the One into itself of the trinitarian God.

Closely related to the notion of *grunt* and the fused identity of God and the soul is Eckhart's notion, similarly somewhat baffling, of a "unity of indistinction" or a "union without distinction or difference," that applies both within the Trinity itself and in regard to the soul in union with the Trinity. Eckhart's commentary on Wisdom 7:27 ("Although she is but one, she can do all things"), another particularly significant text for him, offers an insight into this notion of indistinction in God. Indeed, Eckhart insists that the unity and infinity of God *demands* a certain indistinction:

> We must understand that the term "one" is the same as indistinct, for all distinct things are two or more, but all indistinct things are one.

---

32. *Meister Eckhart: Sermons and Treatises*, trans. M. O'C. Walshe, 3 vols. (London and Dulverton: Watkins, 1979–1987).

Furthermore, there is an indistinction that concerns God's nature, both because he is infinite, and also because he is not determined by the confines or limits of any genera or beings. (Commentary on Wisdom, §144, *Teacher and Preacher*, 166)

For Eckhart, it necessarily follows from the fact that God is infinite and beyond numeration that the Trinity of divine persons exists in divine indistinction, absolutely identical. God is absolutely One, hence there can be no distinction in God, he reasons. Eckhart thus speaks in terms of a dialectic of indistinction in the essence and distinction of persons in the Trinity. He offers an explanation:

I once said in a Latin sermon on the Feast of the Trinity: The difference comes from the oneness, that is, the difference in the Trinity. The oneness is the difference and the difference is the oneness. The greater the difference, the greater the unity, because this is difference beyond difference. Even if there were a thousand persons, there would be nothing but oneness. (Sermon 10, *Teacher and Preacher*, 265)

This text well demonstrates the priority that Eckhart gives to the notion of the One (*unum/unitas*), in other words, the absolute oneness of God, a oneness without distinction or difference, a oneness that is utter simplicity and unity. This is also exemplified, in even more radical terms, in the text from the treatise, The Book of Benedictus, where Eckhart writes:

In the One, "God-Father-Son-and-Holy Spirit" are stripped of every distinction and property, and are one. And the One makes us blessed, and the further we are away from the One, the less we are sons and the Son, and the less perfectly does the Holy Spirit spring up in us and flow out from us. (The Book of Benedictus, *Essential Sermons*, 227)

But notice the dialectic that Eckhart brings to bear here: the closer one is to the One, the closer one is to the Three. There is ever in Eckhart's thought a dialectical relationship between God as One and the Trinity of divine persons. Despite that certain undeniable priority of the One in his thought, Eckhart is no unitarian. To the contrary, he is profoundly trinitarian. In the twentieth century, the Swiss theologian Hans Urs von Balthasar will echo Eckhart when he describes the divine reality in terms of the one "event" that is God, the event whereby God is Trinity.

Admittedly, Eckhart presses the notion of indistinction to dangerous limits when he strains to express a reality seemingly beyond the Trinity, coming terribly close to compromising, if not actually negating, the Trinity *qua* ultimate reality. In a sermon, for example, he explains: "The One is primal source of the first emanation, namely of the Son and of the Holy Spirit from the Father by way of eternal procession. The Good is the source of the second, as we may say, the temporal production of the creature" (Commentary on John, §564, *Teacher and Preacher*, 188).

No less audacious is Eckhart's notion of the soul in unity with God, a unity that is a union without distinction. His teaching stands in contrast with the more common monastic approach (for example, that of the Cistercians, such as William of St. Thierry, and the Victorines), which expressed the soul's union with God in terms of a unity *in distinction*, a *unitas spiritus* (as per 1 Cor 6:17), in which the distinction of substances, Creator and created, is carefully preserved.[33] But, as Eckhart describes it, in the state of union of the soul with God, an *indistinct* identity, a union of identity, is attained. Eckhart will sometimes speak in terms of "breaking through" (*durchbrechen*) to this one ground wherein the soul's identity is fused with God, in a ground that has no ground. In another sermon, for example, Eckhart exhorts his congregation:

> Understand, all our perfection and all our bliss depends on our traversing and transcending all creatureliness, all being and getting into the ground that is groundless. We pray to our dear Lord God that we may be one and indwelling, and may God help us into the ground. Amen. (Sermon 80, Walshe, Vol. 2, 238)

For Eckhart, this "break-through" (*durchbruch*) to a unity of indistinction, an indistinct oneness with the Godhead, is indeed the summit of the mystical life. He explains:

> "I," says our Lord through the prophet Osee [Hosea], "will lead the noble soul out into a desert, and there I will speak to her heart" (Os. 2:14), one with One, one from One, one in One, and in One, one everlastingly. (The Book of Benedictus, *Essential Sermons*, 247)

Again Eckhart indicates that this mystical union wherein the soul enters into a fused identity with God is a union of identity, a union of indistinction. Eckhart does, however, contrast this fused identity of the soul and God with that of the three divine persons in the Trinity: "Concerning the three Persons in God: There are three of them without number, but they are a multiplicity. Between man and God, however, there is not only no

---

33. Bernard McGinn notes that Eckhart's disciples, John Tauler and Henry Suso (or Seuse), introduce a number of qualifications compared to their master. See McGinn, "The Problems of Mystical Union in Eckhart, Seuse, and Tauler," in *Meister Eckhart in Erfurt*, ed. Andreas Speer (Berlin: Walter de Gruyter & Co., 2005), 538–53, at 553.

distinction, there is no multiplicity either. There is nothing but one" (Sermon 40, *Teacher and Preacher*, 301).

Eckhart's notions of the *grunt* and the fused identity of the soul in mystical union with God culminate in what has been called "the birth mysticism" that is so strong and distinctive a feature of his thought. Here we come to the sublime heights of Eckhart's mysticism. Again, his striking imagery figures most prominently in his vernacular preaching. Now this birth mysticism is certainly not new or original to Eckhart. It has deep roots in the history of Christian mysticism, going back at least as far as Origen, who envisaged a threefold birth of the Son/Word from the Father, in the incarnation, and in the soul. But, again, Eckhart gives it a unique complexion. The birth of the Word/Son in the soul is expressed particularly clearly, for example, in Sermon 6 where Eckhart exclaims "yet I say more" and then expounds:

> The Father gives birth to his Son in eternity, equal to himself. "The Word was with God, and God was the Word" (Jn 1:1); it was the same in the same nature. Yet I say more: He has given birth to him in my soul. Not only is the soul with him, and he equal with it, but he is in it, and the Father gives his Son birth in the soul in the same way as he gives him birth in eternity, and not otherwise. He must do it whether he likes it or not. The Father gives birth to his Son without ceasing. (Sermon 6, *Essential Sermons*, 187)

Recognizing that the Son's birth takes place not only "in eternity" (i.e., in God *ad intra*) but also in the human person's soul, Eckhart proceeds to a startling summary of his understanding of the unity and identity of the soul and the Son. In Sermon 6, Eckhart continues:

> And I say more: He gives me birth, me, his Son and the same Son. I say more: He gives birth not only to me, his Son, but he gives birth to me as himself and himself as me and to me as his being and nature. In the innermost source, there I spring out in the Holy Spirit, where there is one life and one being and one work. Everything God performs is one; therefore he gives me, his Son, birth without any distinction. . . . What is changed into something else becomes one with it. I am so changed into him that he produces his being in me as one, not just similar. By the living God, this is true! There is no distinction. (Sermon 6, *Essential Sermons*, 187–88)

But this is no rare moment of rhetorical hyperbole for Eckhart. He frequently stresses that there is no distinction, no difference, between the only-begotten Son and the soul. For example, as he explains:

> Everything that pleases God pleases him in his only-begotten Son; everything that God loves he loves in his only-begotten Son. Now man should so live that he is one with the only-begotten Son and that he *is* the only-begotten Son. Between the only-begotten Son and the soul there is no difference. (Sermon 10, *Teacher and Preacher*, 264)

While arguing for the identity of the soul and the Son, Eckhart does, however, acknowledge a difference between them: "Where the Father gives birth to his Son in me, there I am the same Son and not a different one. We are, of course, different with respect to our humanity, but there I am the same Son and not a different one" (Sermon 4, *Teacher and Preacher*, 251).

The birth of the Son in the soul has distinctly trinitarian connotations for Eckhart. It means that the soul is identical with the Son in being born, but also with the Father in his begetting of the Son, and with the Holy Spirit in being spirated from the Father and the Son. It is a matter of "God being God" in the human person. Here, as John Paul II recognized, is the full force of Eckhart's exhortation, "Let God be God in you":

> Where the creature stops, there God begins to be. Now God wants no more from you than that you should in creaturely fashion go out of yourself, and let God be God in you. The smallest creaturely image that ever forms in you is as great as God is great. . . . Go completely out of yourself for God's love, and God comes completely out of himself for love of you. And when these two have gone out, what remains there is a simplified One. In this One the Father brings his Son to birth in the innermost source. Then the Holy Spirit blossoms forth, and then there springs up in God a will that belongs to the soul. (Sermon 5b, *Essential Sermons*, 184)

For Eckhart, here precisely is the very reason for the incarnation: it is for God to give birth to the soul as his Son. Eckhart explains:

> People imagine that God only became man there [in Palestine]. This is not true. God has just as much become man here [in the soul] as there, and he has become man so that he might give birth to you, his only-begotten Son, and nothing less. (Sermon 30, *Teacher and Preacher*, 293)

But, for Eckhart, the still deeper reason for the incarnation and for the begetting of the Son in the human soul is *revelation*, the revelation that "we are this same Son":

> The Father can do nothing but give birth; the Son can do nothing but be born. All that the Father has and is, the abyss of the divine being and divine nature, all this he brings forth completely in his

only-begotten Son. What the Son hears from the Father he has revealed to us: That we are this same Son. All that the Son has he had
from his Father: being and nature, so that we might be this same
only-begotten Son. (Sermon 29, *Teacher and Preacher*, 289)

Here lies the profound significance of Eckhart's birth mysticism. The
birth of the Son in the soul is *revelation*, for it is to the Son that the Father
reveals himself. The begetting of the Son in the soul is revelation of the
divine image in the human soul *and* "its shining forth in him," "as God's
revealing self":

When a person uncovers and lays bare the divine image that God
created in him in creating his nature, then the image of God becomes
visible. Giving birth is to be taken here as God's revealing self. That
the Son is said to be born of the Father is due to the fact that the Father,
as a father, is revealing to him his secrets. And so, the more and the
more clearly a person lays bare the image of God in himself, the more
clearly God is born in him. And thus God's continual giving birth is
to be taken to mean that the Father uncovers completely the image
and is shining forth in him. (Sermon 40, *Teacher and Preacher*, 301)

This giving birth of the Son in the soul is God's delight and joy. For the
human person, it is his or her entry into the utter abyss of God, in the fullness
of divine being and nature, and into God's knowing and God's love, into
"nothing other than what God is himself." Eckhart speaks in very evocative
terms of the passion and urgency with which "God hastens to make it all
ours just as it is his" for "in this fullness God has delight and joy":

In the eternal Word, that which hears is the same as that which is heard.
Everything which the eternal Father teaches is his being, his nature, and
his total divinity. All this he reveals to us completely in his only-begotten
Son and teaches us that we are this same Son. . . . God works all his
works so that we might be the only-begotten Son. When God sees that
we are the only-begotten Son, he is very quick to pursue us and acts as
though his divine being were going to burst and completely vanish, so
that he might reveal to us the utter abyss of his divinity and the fullness
of his being and his nature. God hastens to make it all ours just as it is
his. Here in this fullness God has delight and joy. Such a person stands
in God's knowing and in God's love and becomes nothing other than
what God is himself. (Sermon 12, *Teacher and Preacher*, 267–68)

Eckhart's notion of the *grunt*, and the fused identity of the soul in a union
of indistinction with God in the *grunt*, thus comes to a climax in his penetrat-

ing insight into the Father's begetting of the Son *in the soul*. Now this follows logically in Eckhart's thought: since the Father's begetting of the Son takes place in the *grunt*, and by virtue of the soul's union of indistinction (in a place that Eckhart variously refers to as "the spark" or "the castle" or the peak of the soul), the Father's begetting of the Son takes place in the soul. But the ramifications are radical: Eckhart recognizes that the soul is thus one with the *bullitio*, the inner boiling, that is innertrinitarian life. Between the only-begotten Son and the soul, Eckhart therefore insists, there is no difference.

The birth of the Son in the soul serves as entry point and linchpin for Eckhart's understanding of the Trinity of the three divine persons. Admittedly, the person of the Son figures most prominently in his work, but Father and Holy Spirit are by no means eclipsed. Where the Son is, there also is the Father who, with eternal delight, gives birth to the Son, and there too the Spirit who blossoms forth from them. Eckhart explains:

> I was once asked what the Father does in heaven. I answered: He gives birth to his Son and this activity pleases him so much and is such a delight to him that he never does anything else but give birth to his Son, and the two of them cause the Holy Spirit to blossom forth. (Sermon 4, *Teacher and Preacher*, 251)

The fontality and primordiality, the primacy and fecundity of the Father figure strongly in Eckhart's thinking. While the ground is the potentiality for all emanation, the Father is *principium*, primordial fullness, the source of all things, both within and outside the Trinity. The Father is also the goal, the goal that suffices. In this, another Johannine text, "show us the Father, and we will be satisfied" (John 14:8), is particularly important for Eckhart.[34]

The Holy Spirit is also never far from Eckhart's thought. Where the Son is, there is necessarily also the Holy Spirit, as Eckhart recognizes in the analogy of the activity of production:

> Each and every form of production cannot be understood without the mutual pleasure and love that is the bond of the producer and the thing produced and is of the same nature with them, as was shown above. From this it follows that where equality proceeds from unity, the Son from the Father, by that very fact necessarily and immediately there is the Holy Spirit, the bond of the Father and Son. (Commentary on John, §556, *Teacher and Preacher*, 185)

---

34. See Eckhart's Commentary on John, *Teacher and Preacher*, §546–76.

Particularly in his sermons, Eckhart speaks with warmth and exuberance of the Holy Spirit, describing, for example, "my catching fire in him [the Holy Spirit] and becoming totally melted and becoming simply love":

> Whenever the Son appears in the soul, the love of the Holy Spirit also appears. Therefore, I say: The Father's being consists in giving birth to the Son; the Son's being consists in my being born in him and like him; the Holy Spirit's being lies in my catching fire in him and becoming totally melted and becoming simply love. (Sermon XXXIX, *Teacher and Preacher*, 298)

Eckhart follows the traditional understanding in the West that the Holy Spirit proceeds from the Father and the Son by way of love:

> We attribute likeness in the divinity to the Son, heat and love to the Holy Spirit. . . . It is the nature of love that it flows and springs up out of two as one. One as one does not produce love; two as two does not produce love; two as one perforce produces natural, consenting, fiery love. (The Book of Benedictus, *Essential Sermons*, 221)

Eckhart departs from Thomas Aquinas,[35] however, and follows Peter Lombard in arguing in both his Latin and vernacular works that the Holy Spirit *is* the love by which God loves us and we love God.

In regard to the procession of the Son/Word, Eckhart follows Augustine and Aquinas and understands that procession in terms of intellectual emanation. Intellect has a certain prominence in the Meister's thought, as indeed it enjoys in the Dominican tradition wherein understanding is considered to have priority over the will.

In Eckhart's Latin sermon, Sermon IV, preached on the feast of the Trinity, he preaches on another of the texts of particular significance for him, Romans 11:36 ("For from him and through him and to him are all things"). The sermon is particularly revealing of Eckhart's trinitarian thought, including his understanding of the Holy Spirit as nexus or bond of Father and Son *in* which is the ground for our return to the source. In this sermon, Eckhart explains: "Note that these three terms (from, through, and in) seem to be not only appropriated, but proper to the divine Persons" (Sermon IV, §21, *Teacher and Preacher*, 207). Eckhart presses further than mere appropriation of roles and traits to the three divine persons, and recognizes the terms (from, through, and in) as *proper* to the three divine persons, respectively: "from him" as proper to the Father, "through him" to the Son, and "in him" to the Holy Spirit. Having said so much about

---

35. Thomas Aquinas, *Summa theologiae* IIaIIae, q. 23, a. 2.

the Trinity of persons, Eckhart then concludes Sermon IV in a rather surprising way, as if deconstructing his own thought:

> In summary, note that everything that is said or written about the Holy Trinity is in no way really so or true. First, [this follows] from the nature of the distinction of terms, especially between the distinct and the indistinct, between temporal and eternal beings, between the sensible and the intellectual heaven, between the material body and the spiritual body. Second, [it follows] that since God is inexpressible in and of his nature, what we say he is, surely is not in him. (Sermon IV, §30, *Teacher and Preacher*, 210)

Almost by way of aside, Eckhart adds a short concessionary note: "It is true, of course, that there is something in God corresponding to the Trinity we speak of and to other similar things" (Sermon IV, §30, *Teacher and Preacher*, 210).

Conclusion

On reflection, one cannot but note that Meister Eckhart shows little apparent interest in the actual events of salvation history as such when articulating his insights into the mystery of the Trinity. Jesus' paschal mystery, for example, receives little attention in his teaching and preaching. Instead, at the heart of Meister Eckhart's thought is a profound sense of the absolute unity and oneness of God. He understands that the divine persons of the Trinity are ultimately indistinct within the silent, simple, unchanging One. The Trinity emanates from this desert-like emptiness in a process somewhat analogous to *bullitio*, boiling. It is a boiling up of the One into a Trinity of divine persons, Father, Son, and Holy Spirit, while remaining unchanged and absolutely One. So it is that Meister Eckhart can say: "But as he is simply one, without any manner and properties, he is not Father or Son or Holy Spirit, and yet he is a something that is neither this nor that" (Sermon 2, *Essential Sermons*, 181).

The inner boiling, *bullitio*, is the source of the *ebullitio*, the boiling over of the Trinity in the creation of the cosmos, and with it the trinitarian structure of creation and all activity within it. For Eckhart, created reality is thoroughly trinitarian not only in its structure, but in all action, for in every action there is something generating (Father), something generated (Son), and the mutual love of what generates and what is generated (Holy Spirit).

The insight at the epicenter of his distinctly trinitarian—as distinct from his supratrinitarian—thought, with profound ramifications for Christian life, is Eckhart's notion of the Father's begetting of the Son and the procession of the Holy Spirit in the very soul of the human person. No matter, it seems for Eckhart, that this blurs the distinction between the immanent and economic Trinity, the action of the Trinity *ad intra* and *ad extra*. What captivates him is rather the goal of the spiritual life, which is not just union but fused identity with God in that groundless ground, God beyond God, that one simple ground that knows no distinction, the *grunt*.

The close connection between *bullitio* (the inner boiling that is the innertrinitarian emanations) and *ebullitio* (the boiling over that is the emanation of the cosmos from God) affords a strong structural coherence to Eckhart's thought, in spite of his daring linguistic experimentation. Eckhart's insistence on the silent groundless ground, however, gives his theology a distinctly and determinedly apophatic complexion. McGinn comments, moreover, that Eckhart "is not only speculatively apophatic in his approach to God, but also pragmatically so."[36] His strongly dialectical language and mode of thought intensifies the sense of unutterable mystery, at the same time sorely challenging the classical expressions of trinitarian theology.

The strongest challenge of Eckhart's thought is that he practically dissolves—certainly muddies—the trinitarian and christological distinctions so carefully enunciated and protected in the theological tradition. His notion of the union of *indistinction*, both within the divine nature and in the soul's union with God, also stands in considerable tension with classical thinking, which would speak rather in terms of a union of *distinction*.

While the weight of scholarly opinion now questions the integrity of the inquisitorial trial and papal censure of the Master of Paris, the papal bull was not entirely unreasonable in expressing concern for the possibility of confusion and error for simple and uneducated folk. One could well imagine that his hearers might be baffled, confused, even shocked. But one could also well imagine that his hearers might also have been profoundly moved in response to the Meister's call to "Let God be God in you," his many striking images, and the freshness, ardor, and vigor of his preaching and his vision. He held aloft before them, as he continues to do now, the sheer wonder and glory of the mystery of the emanation of the Word and birth of the Son in one's very soul. Of all the mystics whose work we have examined, Meister Eckhart, most of all, reminds us of the radical inadequacy of all of our language about God, that the mystery of the unity and Trinity of God and indeed of our union with God is beyond words.

36. Bernard McGinn, "The Language of Inner Experience in Christian Mysticism," *Spiritus* 1, no. 2 (2001): 166.

References and Further Reading

Primary Sources

Meister Eckhart: The Essential Sermons, Commentaries, Treatises and Defense. Translation by Edmund Colledge and Bernard McGinn. New York: Paulist Press, 1981.

Meister Eckhart: Teacher and Preacher. Edited by Bernard McGinn. Latin sermons translated by Bernard McGinn and German sermons translated by Frank Tobin. The Classics of Western Spirituality. New York: Paulist Press, 1986.

Meister Eckhart: Sermons and Treatises. Translated and edited by M. O'C. Walshe. 3 vols. London and Dulverton: Watkins, 1979–1987.

Secondary Sources

Hollywood, Amy. *The Soul as Virgin Wife: Mechthild of Magdeburg, Marguerite Porete, and Meister Eckhart.* The Classics of Western Spirituality. Notre Dame, IN, and London: University of Notre Dame Press, 1995.

International Eckhart Society. Website at http://www.eckhartsociety.org (accessed August 22, 2009).

McGinn, Bernard. "The Dynamism of the Trinity in Bonaventure and Eckhart." *Eckhart Review* 16 (2007): 46–64. Also *Franciscan Studies* 65 (2007): 137–55.

———. "God Beyond God: Theology and Mysticism in the Thought of Meister Eckhart." *Journal of Religion* 61 (1981): 1–19.

———, ed. *Meister Eckhart and the Beguine Mystics: Hadewijch of Brabant, Mechthild of Magdeburg, and Marguerite Porete.* New York: Continuum, 1994.

———. *The Mystical Thought of Meister Eckhart: The Man from whom God Hid Nothing.* New York: Crossroad, 2001.

———. "A Prolegomenon to the Role of the Trinity in Meister Eckhart's Mysticism." *Eckhart Review* 6 (1997): 51–61.

Schürmann, Reiner. *Meister Eckhart: Mystic and Philosopher.* Bloomington: Indiana University Press, 1978.

Tobin, Frank. *Meister Eckhart: Thought and Language.* Philadelphia: University of Pennsylvania Press, 1986.

5

JULIAN OF NORWICH
(1342/3–CA. 1416)

Very few medieval men or women match the popularity of Julian of Norwich in the modern English-speaking world. Her readership includes such distinguished literati as William Butler Yeats, Aldous Huxley, Dorothy Day, and Iris Murdoch. T. S. Eliot quotes from her in "Little Gidding," in the *Four Quartets*.[1] Thomas Merton is particularly effusive in praise of her: "There can be no doubt that Lady Julian is the greatest of the English mystics. Not only that, but she is one of the greatest English theologians. . . . Actually, in Julian of Norwich, we find an admirable synthesis of mystical experience and theological reflection. . . . In a word, Julian of Norwich gives a coherent and indeed systematically constructed corpus of doctrine, which has only recently begun to be studied as it deserves."[2] In another place, Merton writes: "She is a true theologian with greater clarity, depth, and order than St. Theresa [Teresa]: she really elaborates, theologically, the content of her revelations. She first experienced, then thought, and the thoughtful deepening of experience worked it back into her life, deeper and deeper, until her whole life as a recluse at Norwich was simply a matter of getting completely saturated in the light she had

---

1. "And all shall be well and / All manner of thing shall be well / When the tongues of flame are in-folded / Into the crowned knot of fire / And the fire and the rose are one" (T. S. Eliot, "Little Gidding"). Eliot's words—"We shall not cease from exploration / And the end of all our exploring / Will be to arrive where we started / And know the place for the first time" ("Little Gidding")—are also in close accord with Julian's understanding.

2. Thomas Merton, "The English Mystics," in *Mystics and Zen Masters* (New York: Dell, 1961), 140–41. In a letter quoted by Robert Llewelyn, Merton writes that "Julian is without doubt one of the most wonderful of all Christian voices. She gets greater and greater in my eyes as I grow older. . . . I think that Julian of Norwich is with Newman the greatest English theologian" (*All Shall Be Well: The Spirituality of Julian of Norwich for Today* [New York: Paulist Press, 1982], 137 n.1).

received all at once, in the 'shewings,' when she thought she was about to die."[3]

Julian's popularity in modern times is all the more astonishing given her relative obscurity in her own lifetime and the scarcity of biographical data that we have about her. While she herself eludes us, and apparently determinedly so, she is nevertheless no work of fiction. There is no doubting her historicity. But even her writings are few, with just a short version and a long version of her account of the visions, which she received in the space of a few hours over two days when she was thirty and a half years old. It is however these writings that we have, few though they are, that have prompted the remarkable affection and admiration that she now enjoys.

Julian's corpus—the work of a layperson, a woman indeed, in vernacular English in the late Middle Ages—is extraordinary in its own right and constitutes a remarkable literary as well as theological achievement. But what has particularly captivated and enthralled her modern readership is her insight into the profound depths of God's love and compassion for the human person and Julian's image of Jesus as Mother, an image that, while having a long and respected history in the Christian tradition, is developed by Julian with redoubtable originality, precision, and creativity.

Julian's Life and Times

Born into fourteenth-century late medieval England, a contemporary of Geoffrey Chaucer, William Langland, Margery Kempe, and John Wyclif, Julian lived in troubled times. From 1337, England and France were at war, in the tragedy that would become the Hundred Years' War. In 1381, the Peasant Uprising spread throughout East Anglia before it was brutally crushed. The Black Death (bubonic plague) recurred several times during the century, wreaking havoc and misery with each episode, and with devastating effects on the cultural and economic fabric of society. Norwich was afflicted by the plague five times between 1348 and 1406. To add to

---

3. Thomas Merton, *Conjectures of a Guilty Bystander* (London: Burns & Oates, 1968), 191–92. Merton continues, "One of her most telling and central convictions is her orientation to what one might call *an eschatological secret*, the hidden dynamism which is at work already and by which 'all manner of thing shall be well.' . . . She must indeed believe and accept the fact that there is a hell, yet also at the same time, impossibly one would think, she believes even more firmly that 'the word of Christ shall be saved in all things' and 'all manner of thing shall be well.' This is, for her, the heart of theology: not solving the contradiction, but remaining in the midst of it, in peace, knowing that it is fully solved but that the solution is secret, and will never be guessed until it is revealed" (192).

the distress and consternation of the times, some monastic writers and priests ascribed the cause of the plague to God as punishment for the sinfulness of the people. It was a bleak period indeed, a time of disease and distress, social disorder and instability.

It was also a time of schism and discord in the church. The strong and confident leadership of the post–Fourth Lateran Council (1215) period was long dissipated, as was the church's vigor and sense of mission. To add to the confusion and disquiet of the times, from 1378 to 1417, there was the scandal of a divided papacy, with three popes claiming papal authority at one stage.

The church in England was under particular strain. The stringently antipapal statutes promulgated by the English parliament in the second half of the fourteenth century were indicative of the stress. The Oxford professor John Wyclif (1330–1384), a forerunner of the Reformation who would in due course be declared a heretic, further intensified the tensions in the English church, sorely challenging the authority of the church in matters of both doctrine and practice. At the same time, the Inquisition was gathering momentum on the continent, determined to suppress heresy and root out any challenge to church authority. In England, as well as on the continent, it was a particularly dangerous time for anyone deemed not to be orthodox.

In terms of popular piety, a devotion to the suffering and passion of Christ was particularly strong at this stage of medieval culture. Christian visual art of the period attests to the popularity of images depicting the Man of Sorrows, the Suffering Christ, his body scourged, his head crowned with thorns, his face sorrowful. Meanwhile, in English literature, the vernacular was in the process of reemerging as a literary language, as is demonstrated in the writings of Chaucer and the author of the *Cloud of Unknowing*.

This, then, is the context in which Julian received her visions and wrote about them. What is surprising is that in these very troubled times she writes not in a spirit of doom and gloom but with hope and optimism. One of the most tender and touching images that Julian evokes in her writings is that of all creation akin to a hazelnut, small and vulnerable, yet full of life and potential, and so loved by God, its creator, and so lovingly supported and sustained by God in its very being. Julian's catch cry, "all will be well," resounds like a refrain in her writings, as if to reassure and to reassert the height and the depth and the breadth of God's ongoing tender loving care for creation, like a mother for her child, a love so tangibly revealed in Christ's redeeming work and the Trinity's manifest commitment to the restoration and salvation of the world.

The details of Julian's life elude us and she remains an enigmatic figure, about whom we know singularly little with any certainty. She was born in late 1342 or early 1343 and the introductory heading of the shorter version of "her shewings [i.e., showings]," as she herself often called them, states that she was still living in 1413. A will in 1416 designates a recluse by the name of Julian of Norwich as a beneficiary, and this would seem to indicate that she may have still been alive in that year, if indeed the will refers to her, though this is not entirely certain. We do not know from where she originally came, nor anything about her family, her upbringing and education, her social standing, nor how it came to pass that she became an anchoress attached to the church of St. Julian in Conisford in Norwich, nor indeed how or when she died. We do not even know her baptismal name with certainty.[4] It is as anchoress of the church of St. Julian that she is known as Julian, or Juliana, or Dame Juliana of Norwich. Her effacement would seem to be deliberate. She remains apparently intentionally behind the text, determinedly in obscurity, insistent that we who are disposed to learn from her might not be distracted in any way from the wonder and the glory of the divine mystery of love that was revealed to her and that her writings describe for us.

One thing we do know without any doubt is that Julian was an anchoress. An anchoress was a woman who, like a hermit, withdrew from society in order to devote herself to an enclosed life of contemplative solitude, penance, asceticism, and prayer. Unlike hermits who lived in desert or remote places, however, an anchoress lived in a populated area. An anchoress could be either a professed member of a religious order or a solitary woman. An anchorhold in fact offered a more accessible form of religious life compared to entry into religious orders for which dowries were required. Solitary women could thus dedicate their lives to God and live simple and basically unregulated contemplative lives, in seclusion and detachment from the world. With the permission of the appropriate ecclesiastical authority, an anchoress would live in a permanent enclosure (called an anchorage or anchorhold), which was attached to or part of a church or religious foundation. Enclosure was sometimes marked with a ceremony akin to a funeral, symbolizing the anchoress's complete renunciation of

---

4. E. A. Jones argues against the commonly accepted view that Julian was not her baptismal name, principally on the basis of rites of enclosure: "There is, in fact, nowhere in any of the extant rites for the enclosure of an anchorite where a changing of name is stated or implied" (See E. A. Jones, "A Mystic by Any Other Name: Julian(?) of Norwich," *Mystics Quarterly* 33, no. 3 [2007]: 1–17).

earthly things and her death to the world. After enclosure, the anchoress would remain, normally for the rest of her life, in the one location. While having only very limited contact with the outside world, visitors would call on her for counsel. We know, for example, that Margery Kempe (born ca. 1373) of nearby Lynn sought Julian's counsel sometime in 1415, which suggests that Julian enjoyed at least some renown as a spiritual counselor in the local area.

At some stage, date unknown, be it before or after "her showings," Julian took up residence in an anchorhold, adjacent to the church of St. Julian in Conisford in Norwich. Julian's anchorhold actually belonged to the Benedictine nuns at nearby Carrow. It is thanks to Benedictine and Brigittine convents in England and on the continent that Julian's writings were saved from the destruction that was the fate of so many books in the period of the Protestant Reformation and preserved for posterity, eventually to be printed, first in 1670, about three hundred years after her death.

The church of St. Julian still stands in Norwich, though not the actual anchorhold in which Julian lived. Standing in the graveyard, nestled against the church of St. Julian, the anchorhold would have had three small windows. Through one window, Julian would see into the church, observe the celebration of the Eucharist and, most important of all, the consecration, the most sacred moment of the Mass in medieval piety, and receive Communion. Through another window, opening onto the street, Julian would consult with people who came to seek her advice and guidance. Through another, she would communicate with her maidservants, who tended to Julian's needs, assisting, for example, with shopping and errands. We know of two of her servants, as they are named as beneficiaries of wills at the time.

Norwich was a bustling city, second in all England only to London in population and in prosperity. It boasted one of the best libraries in medieval England and several highly respected institutions of learning and their libraries, including communities of the Franciscan, Dominican, Augustinian, Benedictine, and Carmelite Orders. An Augustinian friary was located opposite the church of St. Julian. Norwich's superb cathedral, dedicated to the Trinity, was rebuilt in Gothic style in Julian's lifetime. Norwich also had about fifty parish churches. Julian thus lived in a culturally refined, theologically rich, spiritually attuned, and intellectually stimulating environment.

Julian's writings exhibit a certain Franciscan influence, in particular in regard to her devotion to Jesus' passion. Her writings also manifest a certain Benedictine-like quality. But here too Julian remains as elusive as ever. Although Margery Kempe gives Julian the title of "Dame," which is customary for nuns at the time, it is not clear whether Julian was a professed member of a religious community, Benedictine or otherwise. What is clear from her writings is that Julian was well educated in Latin and in the spiritual classics. She was by no means illiterate, despite her own assertion in the introduction that the revelations came to her as a "simple creature that cowde [knew] no letter." Lynn Staley explains: "By describing herself as unlettered—and thus ascribing the Long Text to inward teaching and prayer—Julian deliberately fashioned a miniature of the mystic as divinely inspired writer that served as an insignia of spiritual authority."[5] She writes lucidly and coherently and with considerable rhetorical and poetic skill. Her writings abound with scriptural allusions and indicate a proficiency in the knowledge and use of the Latin Vulgate biblical text. She appears also to have a sound grounding in the classical spiritual writings of the time. She seems to know the work of William of St. Thierry particularly well, especially his treatise, *Golden Epistle,* and his writing on God as Mother. She also appears to know at least some Hebrew, and expatiates, for example, on the meaning of Adam (as representative of the human person, see Long Text 51.270, 274), and on God's "I am, I am it [he]" (Exod 3; see LT 26.223 and 59.295–96). Her maxim, spoken to her by Christ, "all shall be well" effectively translates the Hebrew *shalom.*

She is clearly a learned woman, though she wears her scholarship lightly. Her writings attest to her intelligence and imagination, good humor and compassion. She is also clearly a woman of prayer, with a remarkable depth of insight and understanding born of prayerful reflection over many years. She skillfully combines speculative effort with an eminently practical approach. Though she herself remains elusive, her writing exudes a confidence and an air of almost magisterial authority.

Julian's Writings

In her description of her showings, Julian explains that, in May 1373 in Norwich at the age of thirty and a half, she was gravely ill with "a bodily sickness." After seven days and nights of illness, and with her mother at

5. Lynn Staley, "Julian of Norwich and the Later Fourteenth-Century Crisis of Authority," in *The Powers of the Holy: Religion, Politics and Gender in Later Medieval English Culture,* ed. David Aers (University Park: Pennsylvania State University, 1996), 107–78, at 109. Staley adds: "Her self-characterization also had a political point, for she placed contemplation, rather than authorial strategy, in the foreground, affording herself the screen she needed to explore alternatives to contemporary views about subjectivity, about sin, and about the divine nature."

her bedside, it seemed that she was at death's door. As death approached, a priest held a crucifix before Julian's eyes to comfort her. It was at this point that Julian had a profound religious experience. It was as if the crucifix became animated before her very eyes, covered in blood, and she entered into an experience of participating in Jesus' death and resurrection. She writes:

> And at this, suddenly I saw the red blood trickling down from under the crown, all hot, flowing freely and copiously, a living stream, just as it seemed to me that it was at the time when the crown of thorns was thrust down upon his blessed head. (Short Text 3:129[6])

According to Julian's account of this remarkable experience, she received fifteen showings that day, which were confirmed with a sixteenth vision on the evening of the next day. In what seemed a miraculous intervention, Julian then recovered from her illness, and lived to old age as an anchoress. It is this intense spiritual experience that occurred in May 1373 in Norwich that Julian describes in *The Shewings of Julian of Norwich.*

Julian left two accounts of the showings or revelations. At some stage after her showings, though precisely when is not clear as there is no evidence of the date of composition, Julian wrote what is now referred to as the Short Text of her account of her experience. We have only one version of the Short Text (ST).[7] Many years later, after sustained and prayerful reflection on her experience and plumbing of its theological meaning and significance, Julian wrote a longer manuscript, a version about six times longer, which is now known as the Long Text (LT).[8] She writes: "For twenty years after the time of the revelation except three months, I received an inward instruction" (LT 51.270). We have three extant complete versions of the Long Text, none of them earlier than the seventeenth century, and manifesting

6. Unless otherwise indicated, quotations are taken from Edmund Colledge and James Walsh, *Julian of Norwich Showings*, The Classics of Western Spirituality Series (New York: Paulist Press, 1978). We will cite the chapter number and the page reference, for example, 3.129 means a quotation from chapter 3 on page 129 of the Colledge and Walsh 1978 Paulist edition. For the full critical edition, with extensive notes, in 2 vols., Edmund Colledge and James Walsh eds., *A Book of Showings to the Anchoress Julian of Norwich*, Studies and Texts 35 (Toronto: Pontifical Institute of Mediaeval Studies, 1978).

7. London, British Library MS Additional 37790, fols. 97–115.

8. For a helpful comparison of the two texts, see Barry Windeatt, "Julian's Second Thoughts: The Long Text Tradition," in *A Companion to Julian of Norwich*, ed. Liz Herbert McAvoy (Cambridge: D. S. Brewer, 2008), 101–15.

significant linguistic differences between them. Scholars are not in agreement as to the authentic authoritative version of her Long Text.[9]

Despite linguistic differences between the three versions of the LT, there is a high level of concordance between them.[10] Both the ST and the LT would appear to be designed as communal rather than private texts. Unlike the ST, which is more of a report on rather than an analysis of her visionary experience and focuses primarily on the visions themselves, the LT is manifestly a very different undertaking and is distinctly theological in its focus. Written some years after the ST, the LT demonstrates a more integrated understanding of her showings in their entirety, a considerable development in her grasp of their theological import, and a deeper penetration of the mysteries of the incarnation and the Trinity in particular.

In describing her own personal experience, Julian writes in the first person. Both texts are written in the vernacular Middle English, northeastern dialect, of Julian's times, which poses some difficulties in rendering them in modern English, with inevitable losses in translation. The style of Julian's writing is uniquely and idiosyncratically her own, combining the personal and the theological, the autobiographical with the speculative, the meditative with the practical and pastoral. Julian herself insists that her text is neither a guidebook for contemplatives nor a theological treatise. Nevertheless, Julian treats in some depth the mysteries of the Trinity, Christ, the reason for the incarnation, the nature of sin and the mystery of grace, creation and providence, the church and the sacraments, and the human person in relation to self, to neighbor, and to God. At the core, from which all else radiates, is a profound insight into the divine and distinctly trinitarian love, "the endless love" with which God beholds and unites the human person to Godself in an indivisible "oneing" or unity.

In this survey of Julian's trinitarian insights, we will mainly focus on the later Long Text, which includes sections that are not included in the Short Text, such as those on Jesus Christ as Mother and on the Allegory of the Lord and the Servant.

---

9. London, British Library MS Sloane 2499; London, British Library MS Sloane 3705; and Paris, Bibliothèque Nationale MS Fonds Anglais 40. Two manuscripts of excerpts also exist: London, Westminster Cathedral Treasury MS 4, fols. 72v–112v; and Upholland, Lancashire, The Upholland Anthology, fols. 114r–117v.

10. For a discussion of the textual issues, see Marion Glasscoe, "Visions and Revisions: A Further Look at the Manuscripts of Julian of Norwich," *Studies in Bibliography* 42 (1989): 103–20.

Julian's Insights into the Mystery of the Trinity

After many years of prayerful probing of the meaning of her sixteen visions, all of which occurred in a matter of hours in May 1373, Julian concludes her final account of the import and significance of her visions with a sublime reflection on God's love:

> And from that time that it was revealed, I desired many times to know in what was our Lord's meaning. And fifteen years later and more, I was answered in spiritual understanding, and it was said: What, do you wish to know your Lord's meaning in this thing? Know it well, love was his meaning. Who reveals it to you? Love. What did he reveal to you? Love. Why does he reveal it to you? For love. Remain in this, and you will know more of the same. But you will never know different, without end. So I was taught that love is our Lord's meaning. (LT 86.342)

Julian then elaborates on the meaning of her revelations, a meaning that is all the more compelling, given the historical context of social distress in which she writes:

> And I saw very certainly in this and in everything that before God made us he loved us, which love was never abated and never will be. And in this love he has done all his works, and in this love he has made all things profitable to us, and in this love our life is everlasting. In our creation we had beginning, but the love in which he created us was in him from without beginning. In this love we have our beginning, and all this shall we see in God without end. (LT 86.342–43)

Love was God's meaning, she realizes, an endless love, for all eternity, a spacious love that makes "all things profitable to us." She will frequently use the word "endless" to describe the unutterable love of God. And Julian stresses that this was *God's* meaning, not her own construction or interpretation. Having desired greatly through those years after her visions to learn what was their meaning, she had now been taught their meaning and taught that their meaning is love.

So ends the later and longer version of her account of her visions. If we now turn to Julian's words of introduction to this longer account of her showings, there Julian also casts a very wide ambit and a distinctly trinitarian one. All subsequent revelations, she stresses, are founded and grounded and "*oned*" (another of Julian's favorite words) in her very first revelation. In a way that is redolent of the role of the prologue in John's gospel as embryonic of all that unfolds in the gospel that follows, Julian's first showing or revelation is embryonic of all that is revealed in her subsequent showings, the setting in which it is all "grounded and oned."[11] Julian explains:

> This is a revelation of love that Jesus Christ, our endless bliss, made in sixteen showings, of which the first is about his precious crowning with thorns; and in this was contained and specified the blessed Trinity, with the Incarnation and the union between God and man's soul, with many fair revelations and teachings of endless wisdom and love, in which all the revelations which follow are founded and connected. (LT 1.175)

Though the first vision is of Jesus' passion, specifically his crowning with thorns, in it, Julian explains, is "contained and specified the blessed Trinity." Thus, right from the very beginning of her long account, Julian situates her showings in an unmistakably and profoundly trinitarian context. We notice too in these opening lines that Julian alludes to the Augustinian psychological analogy and its operations of wisdom and love, when she speaks of her "many fair shewings of endless wisdom and teachings of love."

What Julian would have us understand, right from the start, is that the mystery of the Trinity is the foundational reality within which the work of Christ's suffering and death is located. The Son is thus always comprehended in relation to the Father and to the Spirit. As Julian explains, "for where Jesus appears the blessed Trinity is understood, as I see it" (LT 4.181).

Moreover, and perhaps rather strangely, at least at first glance—for in the classical theological tradition, it has not been the *locus* for trinitarian theology—it is preeminently in the passion of Christ that God's trinitarian love is manifest so clearly. But, for Julian, the Trinity—its endless might, endless goodness, and endless wisdom—is revealed most excellently in the crucified and risen Christ. As she explains: "All the Trinity worked in Christ's Passion, administering abundant virtues and plentiful grace to us by him; but only the virgin's Son suffered, in which all the blessed Trinity rejoice" (LT 23.219).

In the first and programmatic vision of Jesus crowned with thorns, "red blood running down from under the crown, hot and running freely and copiously" (LT 4.181), Julian comprehends—with great joy—the great love of the Trinity, a love that creates, sustains, and protects:

11. See Colledge and Walsh who also make this comparison (*Julian of Norwich Showings*, 27).

> And in the same revelation, suddenly the Trinity filled my heart full
> of the greatest joy, and I understood that it will be so in heaven with-
> out end to all who will come there. For the Trinity is God, God is the
> Trinity. The Trinity is our maker, the Trinity is our protector, the
> Trinity is our everlasting lover, the Trinity is our endless joy and our
> bliss, by our Lord Jesus Christ and in our Lord Jesus Christ. And this
> was revealed in the first vision and in them all, for where Jesus appears
> the blessed Trinity is understood, as I see it. (LT 4.181)

In this way, and always for Julian, the mystery of the Trinity functions
to ground and encompass her account of her showings. While a palpable
sense of the suffering Christ is Julian's point of departure, this leads her
directly and immediately to the mystery of Trinity. The nexus, the precise
point of interconnection, is the mystery of God's love. With utter clarity,
Julian perceives that the passion of Christ is the manifestation par excellence of God's triune love. Love is the meaning!

It is also in this first of sixteen revelations that Julian sees something
small, no bigger than a hazelnut, as she describes it, and, wondering how
something so small and fragile could last, she is answered: "It lasts and
always will, because God loves it; and thus everything has being through
the love of God" (LT 5.183). The image of the hazelnut, "this little thing,"
is emblematic of the Trinity's work of creation, conservation, and love. The
revelation of the love with which it is held by God leads Julian to comprehend the threefoldness of God's love, those same properties of divine love—
God as maker, keeper or preserver, and lover of all that is in the economy
of God's creation—that she perceives in the sight of Jesus' passion. She
writes: "In this little thing I saw three properties. The first is that God made
it, the second is that God loves it, the third is that God preserves it. But
what did I see in it? It is that God is the Creator and the protector and the
lover" (LT 5.183). In both passages, the trinitarian resonances are unmistakable: Father as Creator, Son as Lover, and Spirit as Sustainer.

Here too, in this first revelation, Julian perceives the sheer goodness
and closeness—even coziness—of God's love, so close and so cozy that it is
as if we were clad in it. For Julian, the homeliness of God's love and goodness is like the familiarity or homeliness of the very clothes that cover and
shelter, comfort and protect us. She writes: "He is our clothing, who wraps
and enfolds us for love, embraces us and shelters us, surrounds us for his
love, which is so tender that he may never desert us" (LT 5.183). Later,
she elaborates further:

> For as the body is clad in the cloth, and the flesh in the skin, and the
> bones in the flesh, and the heart in the trunk, so are we, soul and

body, clad and enclosed in the goodness of God. Yes, and more closely, for all these vanish and waste away; the goodness of God is always complete, and closer to us, beyond any comparison. For truly our lover desires the soul to adhere to him with all its power, and us always to adhere to his goodness. For of all things that the heart can think, this pleases God most and soonest profits the soul. (LT 6.186)

Here too we see an instance of another frequently recurring theme in Julian's writing: God wants us to know, wants us to understand. When describing God's love, Julian often speaks in terms of God's love as homely and courteous.[12] She writes, for example:

> I saw our Lord God as a lord in his own house, who has called all his friends to a splendid feast. Then I did not see him seated anywhere in his own house; but I saw him reign in his house as a king and fill it with joy and mirth, gladdening and consoling his dear friends with himself, very familiarly [homely] and courteously, with wonderful melody in endless love in his own fair blissful countenance, which glorious countenance fills all heaven full of the joy and bliss of the divinity. (LT 14.203)

Homeliness connotes the intimacy and comfortableness, constancy and familiarity, the safety and security of God's love for us. Moreover, this notion of the homeliness of God's love, which is so strong in Julian's comprehension, is no mere wordplay. Julian would have us understand, again stressing that "[God] wants us to know," that God is our very home, where we are "treasured and hidden," "preciously knitted to him," and "by a knot so subtle and so mighty" (LT 53.284). Knitting is another privileged metaphor in Julian's writing, for which the term "joining" hardly does justice. By knitting, Julian means a dynamic interpenetration, a thorough intermingling, a blending or fusion, a "oneing" (as in at-one-ment[13]). Julian's use of "knitting" and "knot" thus connotes a dynamic mutual indwelling, a reciprocal enclosure, wherein God is our home and we God's home. As she explains:

> Greatly ought we to rejoice that God dwells in our soul; and more greatly ought we to rejoice that our soul dwells in God. Our soul is created to be God's dwelling place, and the dwelling of our soul is

---

12. For a helpful description of the notions of homeliness and courtesy in Julian's apprehension of God's love, see Joan M. Nuth, *Wisdom's Daughter: The Theology of Julian of Norwich* (New York: Crossroad, 1991), 73–79. See also Mary Olson, "God's Inappropriate Grace: Images of Courtesy in Julian of Norwich's Showings" *Mystics Quarterly* 20 (1994): 47–59. Colledge and Walsh translate "homely" as "familiar."

13. See Brant Pelphrey, *Christ Our Mother: Julian of Norwich*, Way of Christian Mystics 7 (Wilmington, DE: Michael Glazier, 1989), 42.

God, who is uncreated. . . . We are enclosed in the Father, and we
are enclosed in the Son, and we are enclosed in the Holy Spirit. And
the Father is enclosed in us, and the Son is enclosed in us, and the
Holy Spirit is enclosed in us, almighty, all wisdom and all goodness,
one God, one Lord. (LT 54.285)

In tandem with the homeliness of God's love, and often figuring as a
complement to it, is courtesy. Julian explains: "For our Lord himself is
supreme familiarity, and he is as courteous as he is familiar [homely], for
his is true courtesy" (LT 77.311; see also LT 10.196). Courtesy speaks of
the gentleness and tenderness, the thoughtfulness and kindness, hospitality
and steadfastness, and of God's desire to give pleasure in God's dealings
with us. It also has a certain magnanimity and nobility about it. The
courtesy of God's love is particularly well illustrated in Julian's description
of the qualities of "the cheerful giver," whose joy and delight is the pleasure
and comfort of the one whom he loves and to whom he gives the gift:

And in this he brought to my mind the qualities of a cheerful giver.
Always a cheerful giver pays only little attention to the thing which
he is giving, but all his desire and all his intention is to please and
comfort the one to whom he is giving it. And if the receiver accept
the gift gladly and gratefully, then the courteous giver counts as nothing all his expense and all his labour, because of the joy and the delight
that he has because he has pleased and comforted the one whom he
loves. (LT 23.219–20)

Perhaps nowhere in Julian's writing are the homeliness and courtesy of
God's love evoked more strikingly that in the parable or allegory of a Lord
and a Servant, which Julian recounts in chapter 51, the longest chapter by
far in her LT account. The parable effectively serves as a theological linchpin in Julian's explication of her showings in the LT, and yet it does not
appear at all in the ST, perhaps because it was only after years of reflection
on it that Julian comprehended its meaning and significance.

In this parable, Julian describes two persons. One, the lord, "sits in
state, in rest and in peace." The lord looks on his servant "very lovingly
and sweetly and mildly." The servant stands before his lord, "respectfully,
ready to do his lord's will." The lord then sends his servant to do his will,
and the servant hurries away willingly, greatly desiring to do the lord's
will. But the servant falls and, seriously injured and in pain, is incapaci-
tated. The lord, with no hint of anger or blame, looks tenderly on his
injured servant, "very meekly and kindly, with great compassion and pity."
Then, with great and gracious magnanimity, "this courteous lord" says:

See my loved servant, what harm and injuries he has had and accepted in my service for my love, yes, and for his good will. Is it not reasonable that I should reward him for his fright and his fear, his hurt and his injuries and all his woe? And, furthermore, is it not proper for me to give him a gift, better for him and more honourable than his own health could have been? Otherwise, it seems to me that I should be ungracious. (LT 51.268–69)

Julian provides a very detailed explanation of the meaning of the allegory, an explanation apparently wrought only after much pondering. The allegory is clearly replete with resonances with the suffering servant in the servant songs of the book of Isaiah. What emerges, with singular clarity, however, is the "courteous" character of the lord, as meek and mild, compassionate and merciful, and the utter steadfastness, tenderness, and homeliness of his love for his servant.

The lord also recognizes that, having fallen, the servant neither sees clearly his loving lord nor indeed himself as his lord sees him. "[The servant] neither sees clearly his loving lord . . . nor does he truly see what he himself is in the sight of his loving lord" (LT 51.270-71). In this Julian's account is reminiscent of Augustine's understanding of sin and the distortion of our vision, our will, our reason, and our love that it occasions.

What is particularly touching is that the lord has no anger or wrath that his will has not been accomplished. Nor is there threat of punishment or rebuke for the servant's noncompliance. Indeed, Julian explains: "I saw that only pain blames and punishes, and our courteous Lord comforts and succours, and always he is kindly disposed to the soul, loving and longing to bring us to his bliss" (LT 51.271). The lord's attitude is not one of criticism or reproach, but of love and concern for his servant and for the harm and distress that the servant has suffered in the lord's service. Rather than condemnation or displeasure, the lord responds with a gift for his servant.[14]

Julian comprehends that the servant is both the second person of the Trinity and Adam (in other words, every person, all people). The Adam/Christ typology figures strongly in Julian's thought. But, in her expressly trinitarian explanation of the parable, the lord is the Father, first person of the Trinity, and the servant is the Son, second person of the Trinity. The Son is equal in divinity with the Father, and sits at the right hand of the Father, true God and true man, while the Holy Spirit is the love that is in them both (LT 51.274). The Son's reward, the Father's gift, is "a rich and

---

14. Julian notes that the color of the Lord's clothing was "azure blue" (51.271) and that "the blueness of the clothing signifies his steadfastness" (51.272).

precious crown upon his head" (LT 51.278), a head that was once crowned of thorns. Julian comprehends that now "we be his crown, which crown is the Father's joy, the Son's honour, the Holy Spirit's delight" (LT 51.278).[15] Julian's explication of the parable concludes with a vision of the blessed Trinity which she describes in terms reminiscent of the classical understanding of the trinitarian perichoresis whereby the divine persons mutually and dynamically indwell each other: "and the Father in the Son, and the Holy Spirit in the Father and in the Son" (LT 51.278).

In her descriptions of the Blessed Trinity, a mystery implicated, as she explains, in every one of her visions, Julian shows a great fondness, that is characteristic of her times, for triads, and she makes use of a variety of them, engaging them with a certain fluidity. Indeed, triads abound in her descriptions of divine love, divine action in the world, and the nature and destiny of the human person.

In her vision of the "little thing" no bigger than a hazelnut, Julian comprehends that God is maker, preserver or keeper, and lover of all creation. As she explains: "The first is that God made it, the second is that God loves it, the third, that God preserves it. But what did I see in it? It is that God is the Creator and the protector and the lover" (LT 5.183). Julian provides further insight, when just a little later, she writes: "For he is everlastingness, and he made us only for himself, and restored us by his precious Passion and always preserves us in his blessed love; and all this is of his goodness" (LT 5.184). The lover is clearly the one who "restored us by his precious Passion."

Julian frequently refers to God in terms of the traditional divine traits of power (or might), wisdom, and goodness (or love). For example, she writes: "for as truly as we have our being from the endless power of God and from his endless wisdom and from his endless goodness, just as truly we have our preservation in the endless power of God and in his endless wisdom and in his endless goodness" (LT 49.264). Julian is undoubtedly well acquainted with the traditional theological strategy of appropriation that recognizes that the divine traits apply, properly speaking, to the Godhead, but that appropriates the divine traits to the different divine persons on the basis of a certain propriety or aptness that is grounded in the origin

15. Later, in a similar vein, Julian writes of *us as his crown, us as the gift*: "And so Christ is our way, safely leading us in his laws, and Christ in his body mightily bears us up into heaven; for I saw that Christ, having us all in him who shall be saved by him, honourably presents his Father in heaven with us, which present his Father most thankfully receives, and courteously gives to his Son Jesus Christ. This gift and operation is joy to the Father and bliss to the Son and delight to the Holy Spirit" (LT 55.286).

and mission of the particular divine person. While recognizing that all traits properly refer to the one God—as she explains: "all [is] one God, one Lord" (LT 58.293)—Julian appropriates the divine traits of power (or might), wisdom, and goodness (or love) to the Father, Son, and Holy Spirit respectively. For example, she writes: "For before he made us he loved us, and when we were made we loved him; and this is made only of the natural substantial goodness of the Holy Spirit, mighty by reason of the might of the Father, wise in mind of the wisdom of the Son. And so is man's soul made by God, and in the same moment joined [knit] to God" (LT 53.283–84).

Julian describes the human person in terms of the triad of human memory, reason, and will, here too following Augustine in his explorations of the mystery of the Trinity by means of the psychological analogy. The Augustinian resonances are particularly strong, as in the following text:

> Truth sees God, and wisdom contemplates God, and of these two comes the third, and that is a marvellous delight in God, which is love. Where truth and wisdom are, truly there is love, truly coming from them both, and all are of God's making. For God is endless supreme truth, endless supreme wisdom, endless supreme love, uncreated; and a man's soul is a creature in God which has the same properties created. (LT 44.256)

Even Julian's understanding of prayer is articulated in expressly trinitarian terms. She explains, for example: "Beseeching is a true and gracious, enduring will of the soul, united [*oned*] and joined [knitted, *fastenyd*] to our Lord's will by the sweet secret operation of the Holy Spirit" (LT 41.249). She understands that it is the Father who "ones and fastens" the will of the soul to the will of the incarnate Son by "the sweet secret operation" of the Holy Spirit.

Julian also follows conventional theological wisdom when, while comprehending the trinitarian perichoresis whereby each divine person abides in and works through the other, she appropriates the triad of works of the Trinity *ad extra*—creation, reconciliation, and sanctification—to the particular divine persons: Father as source of all being, the Son as redeemer, and Holy Spirit as sanctifier.

Joy, bliss, and delight is another of Julian's triads, and here she appropriates joy to the Father, bliss to the Son, and delight to the Holy Spirit. So she writes:

> It is a joy, a bliss and an endless delight to me, there were shown to me three heavens, and in this way. By "joy" I understood that the Father was pleased, and by "bliss" that the Son was honoured, and by "endless

delight" the Holy Spirit. The Father is pleased, the Son is honoured, the Holy Spirit takes delight. (LT 23.218; see also LT 55.286)

In effect, the triad of joy/pleasure, bliss/honor, and delight manifests the triad of might, wisdom, and goodness.

Nature, mercy, and grace is another very important triad in Julian's understanding of the divine mystery, and she aligns it with humanity's being, increase, fulfillment. In what serves as a lapidary summary of her trinitarian theology, she explains: "For all our life consists of three: In the first we have our being, and in the second we have our increasing, and in the third we have our fulfillment. The first is nature, the second is mercy and the third is grace" (LT 58.294). Here too she applies the strategy of appropriation. The works of the Trinity—nature, mercy, and grace—and the effect that each achieves in the human person—our being, increase, fulfillment—are appropriated respectively to the Father, Son, and Holy Spirit. The *nature* of the Father is creative of our very being, God's mercy is reflected in the Son's redemption of us, while God's love for us is expressed in the *grace* of the Holy Spirit. Again, as for the triads of might, wisdom, and goodness, and of maker, preserver or keeper, and lover, Julian's frame of reference is the economy of salvation history, God *ad extra*, the economic Trinity as distinct from God *ad intra*. In fact, she shows little interest in pondering the Godhead *ad intra* per se.

Julian comprehends that, through the action of God's wisdom and love, God's mercy and grace, the human person, having been created in the image of God, is progressively transformed into God's image and likeness. Again, the resonances with Augustine's articulation of the invisible missions of the Son and Spirit, the divine Wisdom and Love, conforming the human person to the divine image, are very evident.

In her sixteenth and final showing, Julian comprehends the mystery of the Trinity in even more depth and in her description of it she engages yet another triad to describe the "touchings" of the Trinity: life, love, and light. As she explains, she sees these three properties: "In this matter I had touching, sight and feeling of three properties of God, in which consist the strength and the effect of all the revelation. . . . The properties are these: life, love and light. In life is wonderful familiarity, in love is gentle courtesy, and in light is endless nature" (LT 83.339). Here she would seem to be aligning the Trinity of the three divine persons, Father, Son, and Holy Spirit with the triad of light, life, and love.

She then engages another triad in the description of this revelation: "I had three kinds of understanding in this light of charity. The first is uncreated [unmade] charity, the second is created charity, and the third is given charity" (LT 84.341). This too would seem to be a reference to the Father, Son, and Holy Spirit: the Father as uncreated charity, unoriginated love; the Son as created charity, incarnate love; and the Holy Spirit as the gift of charity, the love that is given to us.

With the triad of fatherhood, motherhood, and lordship, we come to Julian's most famous image, that of divine motherhood, and the wealth of theological insight that, for Julian, culminates in it. Julian describes our making in expressly trinitarian terms:

> And so in our making, God almighty is our loving Father, and God all wisdom is our loving Mother, with the love and the goodness of the Holy Spirit, which is all one God, one Lord. (LT 58.293)

Julian here aligns the triads of fatherhood, motherhood, and lordship with might, wisdom, and goodness, and Father, Son, and Holy Spirit. The New Testament image—particularly strong in the Johannine and Pauline writings—of Jesus Christ as the Wisdom of God, the feminine Sophia of the Wisdom literature of the Old Testament, is thus expanded by Julian to include the motherhood of the Son. For Julian, the image of divine motherhood, in reference both to creation and incarnation, applies primarily and indeed properly, to Christ, but, true to the strategy of appropriation, she recognizes that the whole Trinity is implicated in and works as one in the motherhood of Christ, as in all things.

The notion of the divine motherhood is by no means original to Julian. It was actually quite common in medieval devotion, though admittedly more common in private devotion than in more formal and speculative theological discourse. The image in fact has strong roots in the biblical tradition.[16] It also figures strongly in the patristic and mystical tradition, and can be found, for example, in the writings of Ambrose, Augustine, and Anselm, and, among others, in the early Cistercians.[17] What is unique to Julian, and arguably unparalleled in the Christian tradition, is that Julian

16. There are biblical precedents in both the Old Testament and the New Testament that speak of God as a mother. For example, "Shall I open the womb and not deliver? says the LORD; shall I, the one who delivers, shut the womb? says your God" (Isa 66:9); "How often have I desired to gather your children together as a hen gathers her brood under her wings, and you were not willing" (Matt 23:37).

17. See Caroline Walker Bynum, *Jesus as Mother: Studies in the Spirituality of the High Middle Ages* (Los Angeles and London: University of California Press, 1982), 110–69. See also Kerrie Hide, "The Deep Wisdom of Christ our Mother: Echoes in Augustine and Julian of Norwich," *Australasian Catholic Record* 4 (1997): 432–44.

applies this image to the Trinity, and with remarkable sophistication and coherence. In a particularly striking passage, with unmistakable trinitarian references, and also with evident allusions to God's revelation and self-naming, recounted in Exodus 3, Julian speaks in terms of the fatherhood, motherhood, and lordship of God:

> As truly as God is our Father, so truly is God our Mother, and he revealed that in everything, and especially in these sweet words where he says: I am he; that is to say: I am he, the power and goodness of fatherhood; I am he, the wisdom and the lovingness of motherhood; I am he, the light and grace which is all blessed love; I am he, the Trinity; I am he, the unity; I am he, the great supreme goodness of every kind of thing; I am he who makes you to love; I am he who makes you to long; I am he, the endless fulfilling of all true desires. (LT 59.295–96; see also LT 26.223)

Julian further explains that it is the Father who wills and the Holy Spirit who confirms that the second person is our Mother:

> Our great Father, almighty God, who is being, knows us and loved us before time began. Out of this knowledge, in his most wonderful deep love, by the prescient eternal counsel of all the blessed Trinity, he wanted the second person to become our Mother, our brother and our saviour. From this it follows that as truly as God is our Father, so truly is God our Mother. Our Father wills, our Mother works, our good Lord the Holy Spirit confirms. And therefore it is our part to love our God in whom we have our being, reverently thanking and praising him for our creation, mightily praying to our Mother for mercy and pity, and to our Lord the Holy Spirit for help and grace. (LT 59.296)

Thus, Julian explains, Jesus is our very mother, as willed by the Father and confirmed by the Holy Spirit, and he is our mother both "in nature" and "in grace":

> And so Jesus is our true Mother in nature by our first creation, and he is our true Mother in grace by his taking our created nature. All the lovely works and all the sweet loving offices of beloved motherhood are appropriated to the second person, for in him we have this godly will, whole and safe forever, both in nature and in grace, from his own goodness, proper to him. (LT 59.296–97)

Julian then describes three "manners of beholding" or movements in Jesus' motherhood, at the same time clearly underscoring Christ's unique role as mediator of salvation and grace:

I understood three manners of contemplating motherhood in God. The first is the foundation of our nature's creation; the second is his taking of our nature, where the motherhood of grace begins; the third is motherhood at work. And in that, by the same grace, everything is penetrated, in length and in breadth, in height and in depth without end; and it is all one love. (LT 59.297)

In her elaboration of the different manners or movements in the Son's motherhood, Julian begins with the motherhood of our first creation or making. The motherhood of grace constitutes the second manner or movement and refers to the motherhood of our redemption. It is initiated with the Son "taking of our nature" and culminates in the hard labor of Jesus' passion and death. Here Julian employs the popular medieval image of Jesus' suffering and death on the cross in terms of the mother's travail in giving birth. But Jesus' labor is a giving birth not to pain and death but to joy and endless bliss. As Julian explains: "We know that all our mothers bear us for pain and for death. O, what is that? But our true Mother Jesus, he alone bears us for joy and for endless life, blessed may he be" (LT 60.297–98).[18]

The motherhood of grace includes not only our spiritual bringing to birth and new life but our nurture, through the sacraments, and our nourishment, especially in the Eucharist. Julian continues, with allusions to the eucharistic symbol of the pelican that feeds its young with its own flesh, and again speaking in terms of the courtesy and tenderness:

The mother can give her child to suck of her milk, but our precious Mother Jesus can feed us with himself, and does, most courteously and most tenderly, with the blessed sacrament, which is the precious food of true life; and with all the sweet sacraments he sustains us most mercifully and graciously. (LT 60.298)[19]

18. Julian's writing is here reminiscent of Jesus' words in John's gospel: "'Very truly, I tell you, no one can see the kingdom of God without being born from above.' Nicodemus said to him, 'How can anyone be born after having grown old? Can one enter a second time into the mother's womb and be born?' Jesus answered, 'Very truly, I tell you, no one can enter the kingdom of God without being born of water and Spirit'" (John 3:3-5). And, of the woman in labor: "When a woman is in labor, she has pain, because her hour has come. But when her child is born, she no longer remembers the anguish because of the joy of having brought a human being into the world" (John 16:21).

19. Bynum also notes that in Julian's time, the High Middle Ages, it was thought that mother's breast milk was processed blood, in which case the allusion to the Eucharist is even stronger. See Bynum, *Jesus as Mother*, 132.

The third movement of the Son's motherhood is his motherhood in working. Here Julian speaks of the motherhood of our sanctification. She comprehends that Jesus is mother to us, not just in bringing us to birth and sustaining us, but in motherly attention to the care, guidance, and discipline—even chastisement—of her child, in order "to make the child receive virtues and grace" (LT 60.299) and ultimately eternal life.

It is not that Julian wishes to substitute the notion of motherhood for that of the fatherhood of God. The images of motherhood and fatherhood are complementary, not opposed or mutually exclusive. For Julian, a true rendering of the tender and steadfast love of God necessitates an under-standing of what she calls the property of the fatherhood, the property of the motherhood, and the property of the lordship in the one God. She recognizes the qualities of both motherhood and fatherhood in the God-head. Here too her much-loved notions of "knitting" and of "oneing" are relevant. For Julian, both fatherhood and motherhood, along with lordship, effectively coinhere in the Godhead.

While Julian's approach is strongly Christocentric, grounded in her visions of Christ's sufferings, the mystery of the Trinity is Julian's larger frame of reference, constantly implied and signified in her writing. It is this larger and all-pervasive trinitarian setting that in fact allows for the person of the Holy Spirit to emerge with vitality in Julian's writing. Her treatment of the Holy Spirit is always firmly situated in relationship to the Father and the Son, their roles and proper functions. Julian's image of "the cheerful giver" (chap. 23) casts particular light on the person of the Holy Spirit. The Father is the cheerful giver. The Son receives the gift of the Father's love, along with the gift of his humanity, and, himself a courteous giver, returns the gift of love to the Father. The Holy Spirit is in the gift, the joy, and the delight of their mutual love and of their love for us, a love that pleases and comforts.

Julian refers to both Son and Holy Spirit as Lord. The Holy Spirit is equal in nature, dignity, and majesty to the Father and the Son, cocreator with them and source of love and grace. While our being or creation is appropriated to the Father and our increasing—through mercy—to the Son, our fulfillment—in grace—is appropriated to the Holy Spirit (LT 58.294). For Julian, the Holy Spirit is primarily a source of grace. Mercy and grace work together, as "two ways of operating in one love" (LT 48.262).

The Holy Spirit teaches, renews, leads, animates, inspires contrition, reconciles the soul to God, protects, and brings peace and comfort to the soul.[20] It is by the sweet inward work, "the sweet secret operation" (LT

20. See especially LT chaps. 13, 14, 17, 30, 39, 40, 48, 56, 57, 58, 59, 74, 77.

41.249) of the Holy Spirit, that the soul's will is fastened to the will of the Son, Jesus Christ. It is through the Holy Spirit that Father and Son give themselves to the human person. It is in the gift of the Holy Spirit that "we have our reward and our gift for our living and our labour" (LT 58.294).

The Holy Spirit is given to the church and works through the church. Indeed, the church shares in the mission of the Holy Spirit. We are drawn, counseled, and taught outwardly by the church, inwardly by Holy Spirit (LT 30.228).

What is perhaps most arresting in Julian's comprehension of the Holy Spirit is the very palpable sense she evokes of what she describes as "the touch of the Holy Spirit" (LT 5.184), the "touching of his grace" (LT 52.279), "the blessed touching of the Holy Spirit" (LT 74.324). By "touching," Julian would have us understand "being directly affected and moved by the Holy Spirit to experience the reality of God."[21]

Conclusion

Julian's writings exude an indomitable spirit of hope and optimism that is all the more amazing in the light of the social trauma of her time, a trauma no doubt exacerbated by the suggestion that the plague was God's punishment for the sinfulness of the people. Instead of wrath and punishment, Julian confidently proclaims the unutterable goodness and love of God, and the goodness of creation as created by God. She would have us understand that there is no blame in God, that God does not desert us, that God's love will prevail and "all will be well" (ST 15.151). She highlights God's unfailing homeliness and courtesy and the abiding mutual enclosure of God and the human person. Indeed, at the very heart of her insights is the notion of the mutual indwelling of God and the soul, our being closed and enclosed in the immense love that is the Trinity. She stresses the radical transformation that grace achieves in us, a transformation so great and so wonderful that, again, "all will be well" (ST 15.151). Indeed, in an age ablaze with zeal to root out heresy, Julian comes very close to the notion of universal salvation, that all shall indeed be saved. It is a bold, albeit carefully tempered, theological vision that Julian puts before us.

Julian's reflections of God's love and goodness, so manifest in Jesus' suffering and death, lead her to the mystery of the Trinity. For Julian, "the Trinity is God, and God is the Trinity. The Trinity is our maker, our protector, our everlasting lover, our endless joy and our bliss, from our

---

21. See Colledge and Walsh, *Julian of Norwich Showings*, 289 n. 267.

Lord Jesus Christ and in our Lord Jesus Christ" (LT 4.181). It is the Trinity that is the all-pervading frame of reference of her thought, because it is the Trinity that is the all-embracing love, love unmade, made, and given, in which we and all creation are closed and enclosed, knitted and oned.

Though she is clearly by no means incompetent in speculative thought or averse to contemplation of the Trinity *in se*, the Trinity in itself, God *ad intra*, it is God's work in the world that is the focus of Julian's attention, and in a world so much in need of reassurance of the divine presence and involvement. Julian's trinitarian reflections almost invariably pertain to God in relation to the economy, to God's working *ad extra*. She comprehends with remarkable clarity that God's work in the world, the Trinity's operations *ad extra*, are preeminently manifest in the incarnate Word/Son. The second person of the Trinity, the Word made flesh, the Son incarnate, Wisdom among us, crucified for us, is the linchpin of her theology. But she recognizes in Jesus Christ the redemptive activity of the whole Trinity, whose joy and delight is the incarnation (LT 23.218; 55.286). Julian thus maintains a dual theological focus—on incarnation and on Trinity.

Julian has no one privileged image of the Trinity. Indeed she enjoys a certain fluidity in her triadic imagery. It is interesting to note that, in her reflections on the divine love, Julian does not privilege spousal imagery. When she does speak in terms of the spousal relationship between the soul and God, her reference is to the familial and domestic, not to the ardent engagement of lovers. Julian favors the more familiar and homely metaphors. By means of images of mother and child, clothing, homeliness, courtesy, knitting, and oneing, keeping and protecting, cleaving and enclosing, she consistently evokes and underscores the personal, homely, intimate, and familial. This imagery culminates in her comprehension of the motherhood of God.

In her reflections on the mystery of the Three, Julian clearly maintains the distinct personhood of each and their distinct roles. But no less clearly she recognizes that to speak of one divine person is to signify and imply all Three. In her understanding of the divine Three and their relations, there is no sense at all of a hierarchical ordering of the Three. No one is ranked above the others. While genuinely original in her thought, she is thoroughly orthodox in her trinitarian theology; her fundamental message is the abundant, unfailing, and sustaining love of God, whereby "all will be well."

References and Further Reading

Primary Sources

Edmund Colledge and James Walsh, eds. *Julian of Norwich: A Book of Showings*. 2 vols. Toronto: Pontifical Institute of Mediaeval Studies, 1978.
———. *Julian of Norwich Showings*. The Classics of Western Spirituality Series. New York: Paulist Press, 1978.

Secondary Sources

Hide, Kerrie. *Gifted Origins to Graced Fulfillment: The Soteriology of Julian of Norwich*. Collegeville, MN: Liturgical Press, 2001.
Jantzen, Grace. *Julian of Norwich: Mystic and Theologian*. London: SPCK, 1987.
Nuth, Joan M. *Wisdom's Daughter: The Theology of Julian of Norwich*. New York: Crossroad, 1991.
———. "The Theologian: Julian of Norwich." In *God's Lovers in an Age of Anxiety: The Medieval English Mystics*. 99–120. London: Dartman, Longman and Todd, 2001.

6

TERESA OF AVILA
(1515–1582)

On her death, the prodigious and prolific Spanish baroque playwright and poet Lope de Vega Carpio extolled the Spanish Madre Teresa de Jesús, Teresa of Avila, as "*sol de España, y luz del mundo*," "the Sun of Spain and light of the world."[1] Centuries later, she continues to be one of the most loved and esteemed mystics in Christian history.

She lived in a particularly tempestuous time for the church. Protestantism was sweeping across Europe. Images of Christ and the saints were being destroyed.[2] She wrote: "May this ship, which is the church, not always have to journey in a tempest like this" (*The Way* 35.5[3]). In response to the Protestant Reformation, the church embarked on a Catholic Counter-Reformation and convened the Council of Trent (1545–1563). It would prove to be one of the most important councils in the history of the church. Protestant heresies were condemned, church doctrines defined, decrees on matters of faith and reform promulgated, and a major program of reform

1. R. A. Herrera, *Silent Music: The Life, Work, and Thought of St. John of the Cross* (Grand Rapids, MI: Eerdmans, 2004), 32, quoting Efrén de la Madre de Dios, *Teresa de Jesús* (Madrid: BAC, 1981), 246. See Cuatro Soliloquios De Lope de Vega Carpio, at http://www.cervantesvirtual.com/servlet/SirveObras/09256281966850128810046/028765_0096.pdf (accessed October 25, 2009).

2. The use of religious images was a particularly contentious issue in the Protestant Reformation. Teresa however had a great appreciation of the efficacy of religious images. As she explained: "I shouldn't renounce anything that awakened my love; nor should I take such a thing away from my nuns" (*Spiritual Testimonies*, 26).

3. All translations are taken from *The Collected Works of St. Teresa of Avila*, trans. Kieran Kavanaugh and Otilio Rodriguez, 3 vols. (Washington, DC: Institute of Carmelite Studies, 1976–1985). We shall use the following abbreviations in the footnotes: *The Book of Her Life* (hereafter, *Her Life*); *Spiritual Testimonies; The Way of Perfection* (hereafter, *The Way*); *Meditations on the Song of Songs* (hereafter, *Song of Songs*); *The Interior Castle* (hereafter, *Interior Castle*). For *Interior Castle* citations, IV.3.6 means Fourth Dwelling Place, chapter 3, paragraph 6. For Teresa's other works, the numbers provided indicate the chapter and paragraph numbers.

initiated. Trent's reforms would, however, be implemented very unevenly across Catholic Europe. In particular, the church in Spain would adopt a very idiosyncratic and harsh approach to the reforms.

The Inquisition in the Spanish church, first established in 1478 to deal with the threat of Jews and Moors to Christendom, was especially repressive. Its censures extended far and wide in Spanish society. A mistrust of women in particular was widespread (e.g., *The Way* 21.2), and the restrictions imposed on their education and their freedom of expression were severe.[4] A general climate of mistrust and suspicion prevailed, especially in regard to religious experience. Any form of mental prayer was regarded with suspicion, for mental prayer—as distinct from vocal prayer (using authorized words and devotional forms)—ran the risk of an overinflated confidence in oneself and in the authority of the individual, over and against the authority of the church and its sacramental mediation of grace. Therein, as church authorities saw it, was the very seed of Protestantism. The Inquisition's censures included the prohibition of books thought to be harmful to simple souls. An index of forbidden books, published in 1559 by the supreme inquisitor and archbishop of Seville, Fernando Valdés, included many popular books in the vernacular on Scripture and prayer. This index impacted seriously Teresa and her nuns, who, "unlettered," could not read Latin, thus prompting Teresa to fill the void and write her own books on prayer for her sisters.

Teresa's Life and Times

Teresa de Cepeda y Ahumada was born on March 28, 1515, in Spain under the reign of the Catholic monarchs, Ferdinand of Aragon and Isabella of Castille, whose marriage achieved the union of kingdoms that would become modern Spain. It was a time of imperial expansion. Spain was rising to preeminence and power on the world stage. The New World had recently been discovered in 1492, bringing power and prestige to Spain but oppression and exploitation to the Americas at the hands of the conquistadors. In that same year, 1492, Isabella and Ferdinand had decreed the expulsion of the Jews from Spain.

---

4. See Alison Weber, *Teresa of Avila and the Rhetoric of Femininity* (Princeton, NJ: Princeton University Press, 1990), 17–41; Antonio Perez-Romero, *Subversion and Liberation in the Writings of St. Teresa of Avila* (Amsterdam and Atlanta, GA: Éditions Rodopi B.V., 1996); Gillian T. W. Ahlgren, *Teresa of Avila and the Politics of Sanctity* (Ithaca, NY, and London: Cornell University Press, 1996).

She was a Christian of Jewish descent. Her grandfather, a Toledan cloth merchant, was a *converso*, a Jewish convert to Catholicism, and, as such, marginal to society. In a society where honor and dignity were paramount, he suffered great dishonor when, accused of Judaizing, he was forced by inquisitorial authorities to submit to an *auto-da-fe* and wear the humiliating *sanbenito* (a penitential scapulary garment[5]) for seven Fridays in public penance for his offense. The family later moved from Toledo to Avila, but the shame and dishonor of that experience would not be so easily etched from the family's memory. Teresa would be highly critical of this obsession with honor and nobility that was pervasive throughout Spanish society. She would emphasize virtue, not blood, humility, not pride.[6]

Her father was a merchant. He lived as an honorable Christian with a bogus aristocratic identity. Teresa was the first of ten children of his second marriage, following the death of his first wife, from which marriage there were two children. By all accounts, Teresa was friendly, cheerful, intelligent, and vivacious, a good conversationalist with a great gift for friendship. At recreation in community, for example, she would sometimes begin to dance, turning around and clapping her hands.

Although pious and fervent in childhood, she, according to her own account, became flighty and vain in adolescence. Her father sent her to the convent school of Augustinian nuns in Avila. Teresa became ill and had to leave the school. A visit during convalescence to her devout hermit uncle, Don Pedro de Cepeda, who introduced her to some spiritual writings, proved decisive. She decided to enter religious life. Without her father's consent, Teresa entered the Carmelite monastery of the Incarnation in Avila. Her father later resigned himself to her decision and provided a generous dowry.

Religious life at Incarnation followed the so-called Mitigated Rule. It was fairly austere with a strict regime of fasting, silence, and the Divine Office. There was, however, no emphasis on or time for private or mental prayer. There was great suspicion of mental prayer in the church at this time, particularly if practiced by women. The Aristotelian view that women were a mistake of nature, an aberration, and that they were guided by passion rather than intellect prevailed among scholastic theologians of the time.

5. See Francisco de Goya's painting, *Inquisition Scene* (reproduction available at Art Resource, http://www.artres.com/c/htm/Home.aspx, Image reference ART146039 [accessed October 25, 2008]).

6. My thanks to Greg Burke, OCD, of Varroville NSW for drawing my attention to the significance of Teresa's *converse* origins and their influence on her experience and on her social and ecclesial critique.

Teresa enjoyed religious life, but about two years after her entry, when she was in her twenties, she fell seriously ill. Her father arranged for her to go away for special treatment. Her first breakthrough in prayer occurred during this time away from the Incarnation Monastery. In convalescence once again at her uncle's home, she read *The Third Spiritual Alphabet* by the distinguished spiritual writer and Franciscan, Fray Francisco de Osuna (ca. 1492–1540). Osuna described three stages of prayer: (1) vocal prayer, (2) reflective and meditative prayer, and (3) mental and spiritual prayer, when one moves beyond words and ultimately to union with God. Teresa was particularly taken by Osuna's writing about "the prayer of recollection"[7] and began to practice Osuna's method. She writes, "I did not know how to proceed in prayer or how to be recollected. And so I was very happy with this book and resolved to follow that path [the path of the prayer of recollection] with all my strength" (*Her Life* 4.7).

She returned to Avila, but in very poor health. She remained an invalid for three years after which, through the intercession of St. Joseph, she could walk again, although she was to suffer poor health for the rest of her life. In spite of her efforts to follow Osuna's method, however, Teresa then suffered enormous difficulties with prayer, which she endured for the next eighteen years. She writes: "And very often, for some years, I was more anxious that the hour I had determined to spend in prayer be over than I was to remain there, and more anxious to listen for the striking of the clock than to attend to other good things" (*Her Life* 8.7).

Then, after years of struggle and aridity in her spiritual life, she had two remarkable mystical experiences. One occurred in Lent 1554. Seeing the statue of the wounded Christ (Man of Sorrows, *Ecce Homo*), she was moved to tears (*Her Life* 9.1). She discovered that, if she concentrated her attention on those scenes in Christ's life when he was alone and in need, she could habitually recollect herself. She found herself able to relate to God in prayer as an intimate sharing among friends. This indeed was how she then defined mental prayer: "an intimate sharing between friends" (*Her Life* 8.5). She recognized a correspondence between her own experience and that of St. Augustine, recounted in his *Confessions*: "As I began to read the *Confessions*, it seemed to me I saw myself in them. I began to commend myself very much to this glorious saint" (*Her Life* 9.8).

7. "Recollection" is a term that would become central to Teresa's Carmelite spirituality and to the order she founded. It refers to one's effort to withdraw from or acquit oneself of anything and everything, in order to interiorly dispose oneself, or to present oneself, or to open oneself to penetration by God, and thus to find God at the center of one's soul.

Teresa began to experience the very presence of God in her soul, sublime experiences that were given to her, not through her own efforts, but through the favor of grace.[8] She found that, on those occasions when the favor of grace in prayer was given by God, she reached a higher level of prayer, a state of suspension in the soul, when her soul seemed to be quite outside itself. Teresa also began to experience very unusual mystical phenomena, locutions (of which she distinguished three kinds[9]), levitations, visions (of which she also distinguished three kinds[10]), raptures, transports, ecstasies, religious favors, and mystical union. Her renowned experience of transverberation occurred in 1559, when Teresa had a vision of an angel plunging a large golden dart several times into her heart and felt the angel carrying off the deepest part of her, leaving her in great pain and "all on fire with great love of God,"[11] an experience now famously depicted in sculpture by the Renaissance artist Giovanni Lorenzo Bernini.[12] So unusual were her experiences that she herself felt a measure of fear as to whether these were illusions or delusions from the devil, diabolical in nature. In addition to the fear of women's religious experience in sixteenth-century Spain, fear of the devil and of the devil's powers and wiles was rife. She writes: "Since at that time other women had fallen into serious illusions and deceptions caused by the devil, I began to be afraid. . . . I began to fear and wonder whether the devil, making me think the experience was good, wanted me to suspect the intellect so that he could draw me away from mental prayer and so that I might not think upon the Passion or benefit from the use of the intellect, which seemed to me a great loss because I didn't understand this prayer" (*Her Life* 23.2). Teresa therefore sought spiritual direction from learned confessors. The first confessors whom she consulted concluded that her experiences were from the devil (*Her Life* 23.14). Teresa sought further advice. The Jesuit, Francis Borgia, reassured her that her experience was indeed from God (*Her Life* 24.3).

8. Teresa uses the word "soul" rather freely and flexibly, variously meaning person, or the self, or the whole person, or the subject of religious experience, or the writer herself, or sometimes the reader, as the experience to which all are called.

9. See *Collected Works*, vol. 1, 480 n. 6.

10. In describing her experiences, Teresa, following Augustine (*De Genesi ad litteram*, 1. XII, vii, n. 16), distinguishes three kinds of visions: intellectual, in other words, nonimaginative (see *Her Life* 27.3); imaginative, perceived with what Teresa would describe in terms of the eyes of the soul, i.e., the imagination (see *Her Life* 28.4); and corporeal, seen with one's eyes, which Teresa reported never to have experienced (see *Her Life* 28.4).

11. *Her Life* 29.10 and 29.13.

12. In the Church of Santa Maria della Vittoria in Rome.

Another remarkable mystical experience, a vision of a different kind,[13] came a few years later. "Being in prayer on the feastday of the glorious St. Peter, I saw or, to put it better, I felt Christ beside me; I saw nothing with my bodily eyes or with my soul, but it seemed to me that Christ was at my side—I saw that it was He, in my opinion, who was speaking to me" (*Her Life* 27.2). This experience left her with an abiding sense "that Jesus Christ was always present at my side" (*Her Life* 27.2). Teresa explains that, in this kind of locution, this intellectual vision, "this heavenly gift," "the soul sees that in an instant it is wise; the mystery of the Blessed Trinity and other sublime things are so explained that there is no theologian with whom it would not dispute in favor of the truth of these grandeurs" (*Her Life* 27.9). Teresa continues: "It [the soul] is left full of amazement; one of these favors is enough to change a soul completely, free it from the love of things, and make it love Him who it sees makes it capable, without any effort of its own, of blessings so great, who communicates secrets to it and treats it with such friendship and love that one cannot describe this in writing" (*Her Life* 27.9).

In due course, and after some prompting from friends, Teresa determined to establish a new form of Carmelite community, one living in closer and more accord with the original austere Carmelite rule, the so-called Primitive Rule of the Carmelites, the observances of the ancient Order of Our Lady of Mount Carmel, which dated back to the twelfth century. A similar reform had taken place in both male and female branches of the Franciscan Order. Teresa's new form of life would include fasting, abstinence from red meat, and wearing a coarse habit, together with vows of enclosure, seclusion, and silence. The first new house, dedicated to St. Joseph, was established in Avila in 1562. By the time of Teresa's death in October 1582, she had personally founded fourteen more houses, and, in total, seventeen Carmels for women had been established. In 1568, the first male house following Teresa's new form of life was established in Duruelo, the beginning of the male branch of the new order. A second foundation for men was founded in Pastrana in 1569. Eventually, the so-called reformed order, the Order of Discalced Carmelites—discalced because of their shoeless, sandal-shod feet, the sandals and simpler habits symbolizing their new way of life—was formally separated from the

---

13. It was what Teresa describes as an intellectual vision. Teresa explains that "when it comes, I say that we neither act nor do anything; all seems to be the work of the Lord. . . . in the case of these locutions, the intellect does know, yet it doesn't know how the locution got there" (*Her Life* 27.7).

so-called unreformed order. A groundswell of support for her canonization gathered after her death. She had been denounced to the Inquisition and scrutinized by it several times during her lifetime, and a doctrinal investigation of her writings was undertaken soon after her death, which determined that they were orthodox.[14] She was canonized in 1622, just forty years after her death. In 1972, Teresa, together with Catherine of Siena, was proclaimed a Doctor of the Church, the first women to be so honored.

Teresa's Writings

The proclamation by the supreme inquisitor and archbishop of Seville, Fernando Valdés, in 1559 of an index of forbidden books thought to be harmful to simple souls was no merely academic matter of little import to the faithful.[15] The 1559 index included many popular Spanish spiritual books on prayer and mysticism, including some by contemporary Spanish writers such as Francis Borgia, John of Avila, and Francisco de Osuna, many of them Teresa's favorites. Moreover, Scripture in Teresa's time was available only in Latin, not in the vernacular. Indeed, the Spanish Inquisition expressly prohibited vernacular versions of the Bible.[16] But Teresa, like most women of her time, had little by way of formal education and virtually none in Latin or in the Scriptures. She, along with her sisters in religious life, therefore relied on spiritual books written in the vernacular for spiritual nourishment. In response to a lack of spiritual books on prayer in the vernacular, which resulted from their prohibition by the Inquisition, Teresa began to write her own expositions on prayer for use by her sisters in religious life, in order to counsel and teach them about the spiritual way to union with God.[17]

Teresa's writings are expressly intended for the education in mystical theology of her sisters. They are not systematic in expression and language. Rather, they flow directly from Teresa's own mystical experiences and interior life and combine testimony and teaching. Spanning some twenty

14. See Gillian T. W. Ahlgren, "Preter Naturam? Posthumous Debates on Teresa's Orthodoxy," in *Teresa of Avila and the Politics of Sanctity* (Ithaca, NY, and London: Cornell University Press, 1996), 114–44.

15. Valdés' first printed index of forbidden books was in 1551.

16. The Council of Trent, in its fourth session in April 1546, prescribed the Latin Vulgate as the authoritative text of the Bible. The translation of the Bible into the vernacular was debated, but without reaching agreement, hence no promulgation was made on the issue. Luther had completed a German translation of the Bible in 1534.

17. See *Her Life* 26.5.

years of her life, they show the development in her thought. She variously refers to the writings of Jerome, Augustine, John Cassian, Gregory, Francis of Assisi, Anthony of Padua, Bernard of Clairvaux, and Catherine of Siena, and at times draws on their terminology and concepts.

The Book of Her Life (1562–1565) was written as she was approaching fifty years old, at the request of one of her spiritual advisors. It is not an autobiography as such, nor a diary, but rather an account of her interior life, a testimony to her spiritual experiences and the abundance of graces that she had received in her spiritual journey. The work abounds with evocative metaphors and analogies in the effort to give an adequate account of the mystical favors that Teresa had experienced.[18]

The Way of Perfection (1566–1569?) was written a year or so later, after the prohibition on circulation of *The Book of Her Life* among her nuns. They pressed her to write such a book for them, as they were eager to learn about contemplation (*The Way* prol.). In response to their request, in this book Teresa offers a practical book of advice and guidance about prayer.

Teresa's *Meditations on the Song of Songs* (1566–1575?) are an excursus on the love between Christ and the soul. Given that the publication and the reading of the Bible in the vernacular were forbidden in Spain at this time, Teresa did not have access to the full vernacular text of the *Song of Songs*. She was, however, familiar with a number of texts, having heard them in Latin or read them in translation in spiritual books.

Interior Castle (1577), her last and her most celebrated work, is about prayer and its stages. It was begun on the feast of the Trinity in 1577. In it, Teresa outlines a cartography of the soul, which includes seven dwelling places, with prayer the gate of entry to the castle, and with God's dwelling place at the center of all. The first three of these several dwelling places are achievable by human effort, the latter four only by divine grace. *The Interior Castle* gives a description of her own mystical experience.

Spiritual Testimonies (1560–1581) complement *The Book of Her Life*. These comprise about sixty short spiritual testimonies, which Teresa wrote in the form of a diary. *The Book of Her Foundations* (1573–1574) records the first years of the reform. We also have numerous letters that Teresa wrote. Written with candor and spontaneity, they describe her trials and triumphs, her sorrows and joys, and evince her indefatigable effort, indomitable spirit, and reforming zeal.

18. See the long list under "Figures of Speech" in the indexes of *Collected Works*, vol. 1, 509 and vol. 2, 515.

What first emerges very clearly in Teresa's writings is her very practical and balanced common sense. She writes, for example: "The important thing is not to think much but to love much" (*Interior Castle* IV.1.7). In speaking of prayer, she explains: "the time of prayer should be shortened, however delightful the prayer may be, when it is seen that the bodily energies are failing or that the head might suffer harm. Discretion is very necessary in all" (*The Way* 19.13). She is realistic as well as sensible in her advice: "I heard . . . be patient, for as long as you live, a wandering mind cannot be avoided" (*Spiritual Testimonies* 39). She instructs her sisters, "the Lord asks of us only two things: love of His Majesty and love of our neighbor" (*Interior Castle* V.3.7). She urges them, "the more advanced you are in the love for your neighbour the more advanced you will be in the love of God" (*Interior Castle* V.3.8). She warns them, "if we fail in love of neighbour we are lost" (*Interior Castle* V.3.12). She counsels them, "Suffering is the way of truth" (*Spiritual Testimonies* 32). Drawing *The Interior Castle* to a conclusion, having described the supreme heights of mystical union, she writes with simplicity: "The Lord doesn't look so much at the greatness of our works as at the love with which they are done. And if we do what we can, His Majesty will enable us each day to do more and more, provided that we do not quickly tire" (*Interior Castle* VII.4.15). She offers an example from her own experience: "One day while I was anxiously desiring to help the order, the Lord told me: 'Do what lies in your power; surrender yourself to me, and do not be disturbed about everything; rejoice in the good that has been given you, for it is very great; my Father takes His delight in you, and the Holy Spirit loves you'" (*Spiritual Testimonies* 10).

Her understanding of prayer has an exquisite simplicity. As she explains, prayer is "an intimate sharing between friends . . . taking time frequently to be alone with Him who we know loves us" (*Her Life* 8.5). Herein lies Teresa's way to perfection: as friends who love each other and share their feelings and thoughts. She recognized that friendship with God is energized and intensified by continuing growth in prayer *and* charity. She warns her sisters that "prayer and comfortable living are incompatible" (*The Way* 4.2). Again, she is also very practical in her advice to her sisters: "to get used to solitude is a great help for prayer" (*The Way* 4.9).

In contrast to the notion of honor, so esteemed in contemporary Spanish society (*The Way* 12.8), Teresa places great emphasis on humility. She explains that "a great deal of humility . . . is an important aspect of prayer and indispensable for all persons who practice it" (*The Way* 17.1). She stresses: "The truly humble person always walks in doubt about his own virtues" (*The Way* 38.9). She warns: "Without it [humility] everything goes wrong" (*Interior Castle* I.2.8). For Teresa, humility is important not only as corrective to society's ill-founded stress on honor, but as a means of detachment from the world and attachment to God. She would have her sisters understand what she herself had been taught: "This is true humility: to know what you can do and what I [God] can do" (*Spiritual Testimonies* 24). ✔

Similarly, she recognizes that deep prayer and union is not just for an elite few, but for all, given by God. Indeed, this is one of her key insights—that *everyone* is called to the summit of the mountain, where God abides in divine glory. However, total surrender to God and determination to persevere are required. But it is not that all are called to follow the same path. "There are different paths along which God leads souls" (*The Way* 6.5), she explains. "God doesn't lead all by the same path" (*The Way* 17.2; 24.1).

Her method of prayer is one of recollection, a gentle drawing inward of the faculties, a withdrawal from exterior things into the inner spiritual, and of presence, being fully present to God and opening ourselves to God's presence to us. She compares the prayer of recollection with "a hedgehog curling up or a turtle drawing into its shell" (*Interior Castle* IV.3.3). It is recollection because, as Teresa explains, "the soul collects its faculties together and enters within itself to be with its God" (*The Way* 28.4). It "is not a silence of the faculties; it is an enclosure of the faculties in the soul" (*The Way* 29.4). She stresses: "I'm not asking you to do anything more than look at Him" (*The Way* 26.3). The Eucharist is a time of very special importance to her. Most of the great experiences of union she reports as having occurred during or shortly after reception of the Eucharist.

She compares Martha and Mary Magdalene, who, for Teresa, represent not only the active and contemplative life, but the outer/exterior and the inner/interior parts of the soul.[19] She insists: "what difference does it make whether we serve in the one way or the other" (*The Way* 17.6). She explains: "this is not a matter of our choosing but the Lord's" (*The Way* 17.7). For Teresa, the joining of the active and contemplative is analogous to the union of the two natures in Christ.[20]

Teresa does not employ the technical terminology and refined conceptuality of scholastic theology. Indeed, it is plausible that she deliberately

19. This distinction between the interior and exterior parts of the soul is a vital element in Teresa's anthropology.

20. See Edward Howells, *John of the Cross and Teresa of Avila: Mystical Knowing and Selfhood* (New York: Crossroad, 2002), 78–80; see also 83–92. Howells suggests that Teresa uses the roles of Mary and Martha rather than the scholastic terminology of Christology because of her lack of formal education in the area, but perhaps also in order not to draw unwanted attention from the authorities.

avoids them in order not to attract the attention or to incur the wrath of the Inquisition.[21] Instead, Teresa engages many varied and richly evocative analogies and metaphors to describe the soul's experience of prayer, the structure of the soul and the nature of mystical—as distinct from ordinary—knowledge.[22]

Given Teresa's own great gift for friendship and conversation, it is not surprising that Teresa understands prayer in terms of friendship. Human friendship is a powerful image for her. The image of friendship is intensified when Teresa describes the innermost dwelling places of the Interior Castle, when Teresa uses the analogy of betrothal (*Interior Castle* VI) and of marriage (*Interior Castle* VII) for the mystical union of the soul and God. In these advanced stages, mystical graces are like jewels that the spouse gives to the beloved bride (*Interior Castle* VI.5.11).

Describing the four ways of prayer and the inflow of grace that is the fruit of prayer, she employs the analogy of watering a garden: (1) manually, by use of a bucket to draw water from a well, which corresponds to beginners in prayer, the stage of meditation; (2) with less labor, by means of a water wheel and by aqueducts, which compares to the prayer of recollection; (3) by water flowing from a river or spring, through irrigation channels, equivalent to what Teresa calls "the sleep of the faculties" (*Her Life* 16.1); and finally (4) rainfall, which soaks and saturates the entire garden, which is the equivalent of the prayer of union.[23]

She also describes the soul in a state of union with God as like an infant nursing at its mother's breast (*The Way* 31.9-10). Without requiring the babe's effort to suckle, the mother puts the milk in its mouth in order to give it delight. Similarly, the soul is given milk, without its effort, and without understanding how.

At another point, she describes the soul in terms of "a brightly polished mirror" (*Her Life* 40.5; also *Interior Castle* VII.8). In its center is Christ. She sees him clearly in every part of her soul, as though in a mirror, a mirror that is engraved on the Lord. As she describes it: "And this mirror also—I don't know how to explain it—was completely engraved upon the Lord Himself by means of a very loving communication I wouldn't know how

---

21. In *Teresa of Avila and the Rhetoric of Femininity*, Alison Weber argues that Teresa successfully used a "rhetoric of female subordination" to make her writings acceptable to the inquisitorial authorities.

22. Again, see the long list under "Figures of Speech" in the indexes of *Collected Works*, vol. 1, 509 and vol. 2, 515.

23. See *Her Life* 11–22.

to describe" (*Her Life* 40.5). In looking in the mirror of union, the soul sees God *and* itself.[24] The analogy of the mirror thus highlights the awareness and understanding of self as well as that of God.

Her most famous analogy is explored in *The Interior Castle*, where she describes the soul as like a castle, a palace, an interior mansion in which there are many rooms (just as in heaven there are many dwelling places; John 14:2), the innermost one being where one finds God.[25] The castle is made entirely out of diamond or very clear crystal. The sun, which is in the innermost royal chamber, shines in all parts. A great king, "He who would fill a thousand worlds and many more with His grandeur," is the soul's guest, adapting himself to the soul's size. Teresa explains: "since He loves us He adapts Himself to its [the soul's] size," enlarging it little by little until it has the capacity to receive what he will place within it (*The Way* 28.11-12). "The soul is capable of much more than we can imagine" (*Interior Castle* I.2.8), Teresa explains. "The door of entry to this castle is prayer" (*Interior Castle* II.1.11). "Once you get used to enjoying this castle, you will find rest in all things" (*Interior Castle* epilogue.2).

In *The Interior Castle*, when reflecting on the text from Colossians, "you have died, and your life is hidden with Christ in God" (Col 3:3), she famously invokes the image of the soul as a silkworm. Just as the silkworm builds a cocoon, buries itself within it, and in due course emerges as a beautiful butterfly, so does the soul bury itself in Christ (*Interior Castle* V.II). The cocoon is Christ, within whom the soul dies, thus becoming conformed to Christ by dying with Christ. "Let it die; let this silkworm die, as it does in completing what it was created to do! And you will see how we see God, as well as ourselves placed inside His greatness, as is this little silkworm within its cocoon" (*Interior Castle* V.2.6). The goal, she stresses, is to make us Christlike. The silkworm dies when it has built its cocoon, similarly the soul when it is conformed to and within Christ. Then, when the silkworm is truly dead to the world, the butterfly emerges. So too the soul is transformed, having been placed, through this prayer, within the greatness of God. Later, there is a second death. The butterfly dies (*Interior Castle* VII.3), dies into the mystery of union with Christ, permanently united to Christ. It is in and through this union with Christ that the soul enters into the mystery of the Trinity.

24. Teresa compares mortal sin with the "clouding of this mirror with mist and leaving it black; and thus this Lord cannot be revealed or seen, even though He is always present giving us being" (*Her Life* 40.5).

25. It is not that there are just seven dwelling places; there are many others.

Teresa's Insights into the Mystery of the Trinity

At the heart of Teresa's mystical insights is the profoundly trinitarian shape and character of the soul's union with God. She doesn't have the technical terminology of scholastic theology and philosophy at her disposal, nor formal training in Scriptures to bring to her interpretation of her experiences. But she brings a remarkable knowledge of the Scriptures and a wide reading of the spiritual classics. She writes with great confidence, "a strange certitude" (*Spiritual Testimonies* 59.21), which is born of her personal experience and the infused knowledge that comes with it. She recounts: "Once while reciting the psalm *Quicumque vult*, I was given so clear an understanding of how there is only one God and three Persons that I was amazed and greatly consoled. . . . When I think about or discuss the Blessed Trinity, it seems I understand how it is possible; and this gives me great happiness" (*Her Life* 39.25). She insists: "The mystery of the Blessed Trinity and other sublime things are so explained that there is no theologian with whom it [the soul] would not dispute in favor of the truth of these grandeurs" (*Her Life* 27.9).

In *The Interior Castle*, Teresa describes the highest state of union of soul with the Trinity, which occurs in the most interior place in the soul, where God alone dwells. Here God removes "the scales from the soul's eyes" (*Interior Castle* VII.1.6) and lets it see and understand. Teresa stresses that "there is a great difference between all the previous visions and those of this dwelling place" (*Interior Castle* VII.2.2). Teresa describes her intellectual vision and "the admirable knowledge" of the trinitarian indwelling that is then given to the soul:

> When the soul is brought into the seventh dwelling place, the Most Blessed Trinity, all three Persons, through an intellectual vision, is revealed to it through a certain representation of the truth. . . . [T]hese Persons are distinct, and through an admirable knowledge the soul understands as a most profound truth that all three Persons are one substance and one power and one knowledge and one God alone. . . . Here all three Persons communicate themselves to it, speak to it, and explain those words of the Lord in the Gospel: that He and the Father and the Holy Spirit will come to dwell with the soul that loves Him and keeps His commandments. (*Interior Castle* VII.1.6)

There is first the illumination that these three persons are distinct, and then, "as a profound truth," that they are one in substance, power, and divinity. She sees that the three divine persons communicate themselves to the soul and speak to it. But more than this, they explain the abiding interior indwelling of the Trinity in the soul. Moreover, now the three divine persons never seem to leave the soul. The divine company of the Three dwells permanently in the soul. As Teresa explains:

> How different is hearing and believing these words from understanding their truth in this way! Each day this soul becomes more amazed, for these Persons never seem to leave it any more, but it clearly beholds that they are within it. In the extreme interior, in some place very deep within itself, the nature of which it doesn't know how to explain, because of a lack of learning, it perceives this divine company. (*Interior Castle* VII.1.7)

Lastly, this awareness of the presence of the trinitarian indwelling leads the blessed soul not away from the world but outwards and to service. It brings with it not only an intellectual clarity regarding this divine company but also a clarity in regard to "everything pertaining to the service of God." The soul is now more focused on and more occupied with God's will, and God's will, Teresa is very clear, is always the life of practical charity in community. Moreover, she apprehends that faithfulness in service to God will be matched by God clearly making known the indwelling presence to the soul, as Teresa explains:

> You may think that as a result the soul will be outside itself and so absorbed that it will be unable to be occupied with anything else. On the contrary, the soul is much more occupied than before with everything pertaining to the service of God; and once its duties are over it remains with that enjoyable company. If the soul does not fail God, He will never fail, in my opinion, to make His presence clearly known to it. (*Interior Castle* VII.1.8)

This then is no passing vision, but a habitual awareness of the distinctness and the mutuality of the indwelling divine persons and their relations. The soul is now in a new relation with God, and with this new relation comes a new and distinctly trinitarian understanding of God. Teresa explains: "It's like the experience of two persons here on earth who love each other deeply and understand each other well; even without signs, just by a glance, it seems, they understand each other" (*Her Life* 27.10). This, as Teresa sees it, is the ultimate mystical knowing. There are no further visions or revelations. There is also a very deep peace that comes with this mystical knowing. Teresa suggests that this experience is rather like the appearance to the disciples of the risen Lord, through a closed door, when the Lord says, "Peace be with you" (*Interior Castle* VII.2.3).

As Teresa had earlier stressed to her sisters, it is through participation in Christ that the soul enters into this innertrinitarian company. In her exposition on the Our Father prayer (*The Way* 27–42),[26] she explained that, in the first stage of recollection, the soul represents the Son in his passion and offers him to the Father (*The Way* 28.4), and that, in the Eucharist, the Father gives Jesus to us (*The Way* 33.5), so that "He is in our house" (*The Way* 34.8). Teresa elaborates on the significance of Communion: "Receiving Communion is not like picturing with the imagination, as when we reflect upon the Lord on the cross or in other episodes of the Passion. . . . In Communion the event is happening now, and it is entirely true" (*The Way* 34.8). In one of the *Spiritual Testimonies*, Teresa describes how "Once after receiving Communion I was given understanding of how the Father receives within our soul the most holy Body of Christ, and of how I know and have seen that these divine Persons are present, and of how pleasing to the Father this offering of his Son is, because He delights and rejoices with Him here–let us say–on earth" (*Spiritual Testimonies* 52).

Teresa's *Spiritual Testimonies* reveal the deepening of her understanding of the relationship between the soul and God in union. She describes two visions that she experienced in May and June 1571. In an intellectual vision of the Blessed Trinity, she came to an understanding of the three divine persons such that all three persons were represented in clear distinction from each other:

> My soul began to enkindle, and it seemed to me I knew clearly in an intellectual vision that the entire Blessed Trinity was present. In this state my soul understood by a certain kind of representation (like an illustration of the truth), in such a way that my dullness could perceive, how God is three and one. And so it seemed to me that all three Persons were represented distinctly in my soul and that they spoke to me, telling me that from this day I would see an improvement in myself in respect to three things and that each one of these Persons would grant me a favor: one, the favor of charity; another, the favor of being able to suffer gladly; and the third, the favor of experiencing this charity with an enkindling in the soul. I understood those words the Lord spoke, that the three divine Persons would be with the soul in grace, for I saw from within myself in the way described. . . . It seems those three Persons, being only one God, were so fixed within my soul that I saw that were such divine company to continue it would be impossible not to be recollected. (*Spiritual Testimonies* 13)

26. See Rowan Williams' exploration of Teresa's reflections on the Our Father, *Teresa of Avila*, Outstanding Christian Thinkers Series (London: Cassell Publishers, 1991), 88–102.

In this vision, Teresa comes to an understanding of the mutual but distinct activity of the three divine persons—with each person speaking to her, and each granting a favor to her, with the gifts reflecting the givers: the Father the gift of charity; the Son the ability to suffer gladly; and the Holy Spirit the experience of "enkindling."

"Enkindling" is a vital metaphor for Teresa in describing the Holy Spirit. In *The Way of Perfection*, Teresa writes, "The Holy Spirit must be present between such a Son and such a Father, and He will enkindle your will and bind it with a very great love" (*The Way* 27.7). In *Soliloquy* 7, Teresa uses the metaphor again: "Consider the great delight and great love that Father has in knowing His Son and the Son in knowing His Father; and the enkindling love with which the Holy Spirit is joined with them; and how no one of them is able to be separate from this love and knowledge, because they are one. These sovereign Persons know each other, love each other, and delight in each other." In a similar vein, in *Meditations on the Song of Songs*, she writes, "It seems to me that the Holy Spirit must be the mediator between the soul and God, the One who moves it with such ardent desires, for He enkindles it in a supreme fire, which is so near" (*Song of Songs* 5.5). Enkindling effectively signifies the soul's entry into the trinitarian communion, wherein the Holy Spirit is the bond of love between Father and Son.

In another spiritual testimony, Teresa describes "the divine company" in terms of an abiding indwelling, in which the three divine persons are "so fixed within her soul," "very habitually present." On this occasion, she sees her soul as saturated to overflowing with the divinity, like a sponge absorbing and being saturated to overflowing by water, and the soul "in a certain way rejoicing within itself and possessing the three Persons":

> I have experienced this presence of the three Persons. . . . They are very habitually present in my soul. Since I was accustomed to experience only the presence of Jesus, it always seemed to me there was some obstacle to my seeing three Persons, although I understand there is only one God. And the Lord told me today while I was reflecting upon this that I was mistaken in thinking of things of the soul through comparison with corporeal things, that I should know that these spiritual things are very different and that the soul is capable of great rejoicing. It seemed to me there came the thought of how a sponge absorbs and is saturated with water; so, I thought, was my soul which was overflowing with that divinity and in a certain way rejoicing within itself and possessing the three Persons. (*Spiritual Testimonies* 14)

Teresa explains that, in this state of union, one's knowledge of these spiritual things is very different from one's knowledge of corporeal things:

God is not known here *through* created things; rather there is a direct or unmediated knowledge of God that is given to her. In other words, God is known first, and created things subsequently. This mystical knowing is thus not analogous to natural knowing. In this mystical knowing, the cause is not known through its effects, but rather the effects are known through their cause.

The words that Teresa then hears occasion a radical about-turn of perspective and a correspondingly radical transformation in her understanding of the indwelling:

> I also heard the words: "Don't try to hold Me within yourself, but try to hold yourself within Me." It seemed to me that from within my soul—where I saw these three Persons present—these persons were communicating themselves to all creation without fail, nor did they fail to be with me. (*Spiritual Testimonies* 14)

She now sees that it is more truly a matter of *herself dwelling within the Trinity*, rather than *the Trinity dwelling within her*. The image is reminiscent of the silkworm that dies in the cocoon and is placed "inside His greatness" (*Interior Castle* V.2.6). Moreover, Teresa now sees clearly the three divine persons and their overflowing self-communication not just to her, but to all creation, and without fail.[27]

In another vision, she describes the infused knowledge of the distinction of the three divine persons in the Trinity, a distinction so real that "we can behold and speak to each one," a distinction much greater than that conveyed by artistic representations of the Trinity in the form of one person with three faces:

> One day, after the feast of St. Matthew, being in the state I'm usually in since I've seen the vision of the Blessed Trinity and how it dwells in a soul in the state of grace, a very clear understanding of this mystery was granted to me so that in certain ways and through comparisons I beheld it in an imaginative vision. Although at other times knowledge of the Blessed Trinity was given me through an intellectual

---

27. Note that her reference to "from within her soul" is ambiguous: Does she mean simply that it is from within her soul that she perceives the communication of the divine persons to all creation? Or does she mean something more, i.e., that it is from within her soul that the three persons are communicating themselves to all creation? In other words, does she here recognize that the soul is located at the source of the trinitarian communication to creation? Such an interpretation is possible and plausible, for it is not out of tune with her developing understanding.

vision, the truth, after a few days, no longer remained with me so that I could think about it and find consolation in it, as I can now. . . . To us ignorant people it appears that all three Persons of the Blessed Trinity are—as represented in paintings—in one Person, as when three faces are painted on one body.[28] . . . What was represented to me were three distinct Persons, for we can behold and speak to each one. Afterward I reflected that only the Son took human flesh, through which this truth of the Trinity was seen. These Persons love, communicate with, and know each other. Well, if each one is by Himself, how is it that we say all three are one essence, and believe it? And this is a very great truth for which I would die a thousand deaths. In all three Persons there is no more than one will, one power, and one dominion, in such a way that one cannot do anything without the others. . . . [T]here is only one all-powerful God . . . . [A]nyone who pleases one of these three divine Persons, pleases all three, and the same goes for anyone who might offend one. . . . [T]he essence is one; and where one is, all three are, for they cannot be separated. Well, how do we see that the three Persons are separate, and how did the Son take on human flesh and not the Father or the Holy Spirit? This I haven't understood. (*Spiritual Testimonies* 29)

In this vision, Teresa again sees the divine persons in their clear distinction from each other, and this time she sees them loving, communicating with, and knowing *each other* (whereas in *Spiritual Testimonies* 13 Teresa speaks of them communicating *with her*). Here then, it is their mutuality and innertrinitarian relationality that is highlighted and their inseparable unity in this distinction. Together, she insists, the Three constitute the one essence, one will, one power, one dominion, of the one all-powerful Godhead. Indeed, she asserts that this is "a very great truth for which [she] would die a thousand deaths." As Teresa again explains in a later testimony: "Although knowledge is given in a strange manner that these Persons are distinct, the soul understands there is only one God" (*Spiritual Testimonies* 59.23).

Teresa again stresses the habitual indwelling of the divine Three and their inseparable unity when describing another vision. This time the habitual indwelling is expressed in terms of being *imprinted* in the soul. She writes:

28. Teresa here refers to the tricephalous image of the Trinity—a three-headed figure or a three-faced head—which was apparently particularly popular in Spain and subsequently in the New World of South America and Latin America under the Spanish Conquest. As a depiction of the Trinity, it was first officially condemned after the Counter-Reformation by Pope Urban VIII in 1628, though its use prevailed for some time. It can be seen, for example, in St. Peter's in Rome in the tomb for Pope Sixtus IV (1484), the work of artist Pollaiuolo.

Having received Communion on the feast of St. Augustine, I understood—I'm unable to say how—and almost saw (although it was something intellectual and passed quickly) how the three Persons of the Blessed Trinity, which I bear imprinted in my soul, are one. By means of the strangest painting and a very clear light, I was given an understanding that was an activity very different from merely holding this truth by faith. As a result, I haven't been able to think of any of the three divine Persons without thinking of all three. Thus I was reflecting today upon how, since they were so united, the Son alone could have taken human flesh; and the Lord gave me understanding of how although they are united they are distinct. These are grandeurs which make the soul again desire to be free from this body that hinders their enjoyment. For although it seems our lowliness was not meant for understanding anything about them, the soul, without knowing how, received incomparably greater benefit from this understanding, even though it lasts only a moment—than from many years of meditation. (*Spiritual Testimonies* 42)

The notion of the Trinity's imprint in the soul is very significant in Teresa's thought. She similarly uses the analogy of impressing a seal in wax to describe the soul in disposing itself to union with God: "For indeed the soul does no more in this union than does the wax when another impresses a seal on it" (*Interior Castle* V.2.12). Akin to this is the notion of engraving, of which she speaks in *The Book of Her Life*, when describing the soul as "like a brightly polished mirror," a mirror "completely engraved upon the Lord Himself by means of a very loving communication I wouldn't know how to describe" (*Her Life* 40.5). In the seventh dwelling place of *The Interior Castle*, Teresa picks up on this image of the mirror and bemoans "not see[ing] ourselves in this mirror that we contemplate, where our image is engraved" (*Interior Castle* VII.2.8). The metaphor of the mirror highlights the simultaneity of seeing ourselves *and* seeing the Trinity, the interconnection between entering into the inner dynamism of the three divine persons of the Trinity and authentic knowledge of ourselves.

The vision recounted in *Spiritual Testimonies* 42 appears to afford yet a new depth of understanding of the mystery of the Trinity, their unity and distinction. Her understanding is now from *within the mystery*, not from outside it, as it were, when "merely holding this truth by faith." In this new stage of illumination, Teresa finds it *impossible* to think of *any* of the Three without thinking of *all* Three. In perceiving their unity and distinction, she also perceives herself in union with and yet distinct from God. The soul thus knows God and differentiates between the three persons and, at the same time, it distinguishes itself from God.

A further clarity of understanding and indeed awareness emerges in the last of her spiritual testimonies, written in 1581, toward the end of her life. Here Teresa describes "the interior peace" (*Spiritual Testimonies* 65.9), the understanding of the indwelling Trinity, and the conformity to God's will that the soul attains at its most developed level. She writes:

> The presence of the three Persons is so impossible to doubt that it seems one experiences what St. John says [John 14:23], that they will make their abode in the soul. God does this not only by grace but also by His presence, because He wants to give the experience of this presence. It brings with it an abundance of indescribable blessings, especially the blessing that there is no need to go in search of reflections in order to know that God is there. This presence is almost continual, except when a lot of sickness weighs down on one. For it sometimes seems God wants one to suffer without interior consolation; but, never, not even in its first stirrings, does the will turn from its desire that God's will be done. This surrender to the will of God is so powerful that the soul wants neither death nor life. . . . But soon the presence of the three Persons is represented to it so forcefully that this presence provides a remedy for the pain caused by His absence. (*Spiritual Testimonies* 65.9)

Teresa explains that "never, not even in its first stirrings, does the will turn from its desire that God's will be done." As Teresa had earlier explained in *The Way of Perfection* when reflecting on the Our Father prayer, "He begins to commune with the soul in so intimate a friendship that he not only gives it back its own will but gives it His" (*The Way* 32.12). In *The Interior Castle*, she observes that the soul is now "much more occupied than before with everything pertaining to the service of God" (*Interior Castle* VII.1.8). As Edward Howells recognizes, here "the soul does not know the persons as an object like other objects in the world but knows within itself, as part of its own self-understanding."[29] It is not that the soul's will is overruled or undermined, but that the soul becomes so conformed to God that its own will, which retains its integrity and remains *its* own will, becomes conformed to the divine will. Herein the soul's participation in the life of the Trinity reaches its apogee. Its own desire, its own will, is for God's will. The soul in this final dwelling place is now Christlike, transformed and conformed to the mind of Christ, and, through him, to the will of the undivided and inseparable Trinity. As she had recounted in an earlier testimony, "Once while I was recollected in this company I always

29. Howells, *John of the Cross and Teresa of Avila*, 95.

bear within me in my soul, God seemed so present to me that I thought of St. Peter's words: *You are Christ, Son of the Living God* [Matt 16:16]. For God was thus living in my soul" (*Spiritual Testimonies* 49). The soul has now moved beyond the experience of seeing and understanding; its focus now is Christ's work in the world, that God's will be done.

Conclusion

Teresa's insights into the mystery of the Trinity emerge from her experience of the distinctly trinitarian character of the soul's mystical transformation and union with God. For her, this experience is no passing vision or ecstasy, but a habitual awareness of the distinctness and the mutuality of the indwelling divine persons in her soul. The metaphor for union is essentially—and distinctly anti-Platonist—one of descent into union with the Trinity.

Her trinitarian insights are, however, inextricably intertwined with her christological insights. She understands that, in that state of union with God, the soul's relationship to the Father is that of the Son, in the enkindling bond of the Holy Spirit. She also understands that the soul's state of union with God corresponds to Christ's hypostatic union, albeit that the hypostatic union is natural for Christ, while it is a supernatural state for the soul, attained by grace. Indeed, it is Christ's hypostatic union that grounds the possibility for the soul's union with God.

She would thus have us understand that one enters into the mystery of the Trinity through participation in the mystery of Christ. Just as the silkworm dies in the cocoon, so the soul dies with and in Christ and is conformed to Christ. Christ is the cocoon within which the silkworm-soul dies. It is in Christ that the blessed soul enters into the innertrinitarian relations and dynamism of the Trinity of the three divine persons. In the state of mystical union, each of the divine persons communicates itself to the soul and speaks to it. Knowledge of the three divine persons—knowing, loving, communicating with, and delighting in each other—is then part of the soul's self-knowledge and understanding. The soul not only sees God but sees itself—and all things—within the greatness of God. Now all of the soul's understanding is from *within* the mystery.

The soul not only differentiates the presence of each of the three persons of the Trinity abiding within it, but it knows God's will and, moreover, its own desire, its own will, is now God's will. The soul's conformity with God's will manifests itself in service of God and service to the world.

Teresa sees clearly that the three persons are distinct, relating to each other and to the soul, each in its own distinct way. At the same time, she sees with utter clarity that the Three are inseparably united, one God. She finds it impossible to think of *any* one of the Three without thinking of *all* Three. For Teresa, the mystery of the Trinity is preeminently a mystery of unity in distinction. She is sure of their unity, and just as sure of their distinction. In this intimate friendship with God, she is also in no doubt of the distinction between soul and God.

The Holy Spirit is especially vivid in her accounts, enkindling the will and drawing the soul into the bond of union between Father and Son. She recognizes that the will is crucial to spiritual growth, and urges all those who would learn from her: "The important thing is not to think much but to love much" (*Interior Castle* IV.1.7). The end of prayer, she insists, is creative and active: it is "good works, good works." She leaves us with the invitation that she herself received from that divine company that is the Trinity: "Don't try to hold Me within yourself, but try to hold yourself within Me" (*Spiritual Testimonies* 14).

References and Further Reading

Primary Sources

Teresa of Avila. *The Collected Works of St. Teresa of Avila.* Translated by Kieran Kavanaugh and Otilio Rodriguez. 3 vols. Washington, DC: Institute of Carmelite Studies, 1976–1985.

Secondary Sources

Clissold, Stephen. *St. Teresa of Avila.* London: Sheldon, 1979.

Dermot O'Donoghue, Noel. *Mystics for Our Time: Carmelite Meditations for a New Age.* Edinburgh: T&T Clark, 1989.

Dicken, E. W. Trueman. *The Crucible of Love: A Study of the Mysticism of St. Teresa of Jesus and St. John of the Cross.* London: Darton, Longman and Todd, 1963.

Green, Deirdre. *Gold in the Crucible: Teresa of Avila and the Western Mystical Tradition.* Shaftesbury: Element Books, 1989.

Howells, Edward. *John of the Cross and Teresa of Avila: Mystical Knowing and Selfhood.* New York: Crossroad, 2002.

Williams, Rowan. *Teresa of Avila.* Outstanding Christian Thinkers Series. London: Cassell Publishers, 1991.

7

JOHN OF THE CROSS
(1542–1591)

In an apostolic letter on the four hundredth anniversary of John's death, Pope John Paul II described John of the Cross as "Master in the faith and witness to the living God."[1] Few others have exercised as great and authoritative an influence on the Christian mystical tradition as John. Teresa of Avila, with whom he collaborated in the reform of the Carmelite Order, was greatly impressed by him. While she worried about his tendency to excessive austerity,[2] she lavishly extolled his virtues and gifts, saying of him, "small in stature though he is, I believe he is great in the sight of God."[3] Indeed, Teresa described him as "the father of my soul."[4] She explained: "He was so good that I, at least, could have learned much more from him than he from me."[5] She nicknamed him her "little Seneca" (*Senequita*), after the ancient Spanish philosopher.

A mystic and ascetic, he was also a man of kindness and compassion, humility and gentleness, who radiated a transparent goodness and purity of heart. He is particularly renowned for the beauty of his poetry, with its rich and suggestive nuptial imagery, and for the profundity of his insights and discernment. His poems continue to enjoy esteem, not only in the treasure trove of Spanish literature, but as preeminent expressions of Span-

---

1. See *Maestro della Fede*, at http://www.vatican.va/holy_father/john_paul_ii/apost_letters/documents/hf_jp-ii_apl_19901214_juan-de-la-cruz_it.html (accessed October 25, 2009).

2. See Teresa of Avila, *Foundations* 14.12, in *The Collected Works of St. Teresa of Avila*, trans. Kieran Kavanaugh and Otilio Rodriguez, vol. 3 (Washington, DC: Institute of Carmelite Studies, 1985).

3. *The Letters of Saint Teresa of Jesus*, trans. E. Allison Peers, vol. 1 (London: Burns, Oates & Washbourne, 1951), 52, in a letter to Francisco de Salcedo, September 1568. Also *The Collected Letters of St. Teresa of Avila*, trans. Kieran Kavanaugh, vol. 1 (Washington, DC: ICS Publications, 2001), 60.

4. *The Letters of Saint Teresa of Jesus*, trans. E. Allison Peers, vol. 2 (London: Burns, Oates & Washbourne, 1951), 625 in a letter to Ana de Jesús, December 1578.

5. *Foundations* 13.5, in *The Collected Works of St. Teresa of Avila*, vol. 3.

ish mysticism at its zenith. Together with his writings, there is his remarkable drawing, based on a vision, of Christ on the cross, which John gave to Ana María de Jesús, one of the nuns in the monastery of the Incarnation.[6] John is undoubtedly one of the greatest masters of the spiritual life, and his insights are deeply permeated by the mystery of the Trinity.

John's Life and Times

Juan de Yepes y Alvárez was born in 1542, in Fontiveros, not far from Avila in Spain. The New World had recently been discovered and colonized, sparking a new wave of missionary zeal. Spain was rising to prominence and prestige as an imperial power. It was a golden age for literature and the arts.

John's childhood, unlike that of Teresa of Avila, was marked by sadness, suffering, and poverty. John's father had been disowned by his wealthy Toledan merchant family when he married beneath his social class. John's father then died when John was two years old. Like the vast numbers of landless poor ravaged by famine in Spain at this time, the widowed mother battled to support her family of three sons. She placed John, her youngest son, in an institution for children of the poor, in the town of Medina del Campo. The institution was effectively an orphanage-cum-workhouse. The children were taught basic reading, writing, arithmetic, catechism, and elementary skills in preparation for apprenticeship to a particular craft or trade. John stayed there until he was seventeen years old. In adolescence, John also worked as an attendant in the hospital attached to the orphanage. While John showed little inclination or aptitude for a trade, he showed considerable compassion for the sick and debilitated in his work as a hospital attendant.

John proceeded to a school and there his education comprised a humanistic curriculum including Latin and Greek, grammar and rhetoric, and classical literature. When about twenty-one years old, apparently seeking a contemplative rather than an active apostolic life, John entered the Carmelite Order and was given the name Fray Juan de Santo Matía (Fray John of St. Matthias). After his novitiate year, and while continuing

---

6. An image of the drawing is on the front cover of *The Collected Works of Saint John of the Cross*, trans. Kieran Kavanaugh and Otilio Rodriguez, rev. ed. (Washington, DC: ICS Publications, 1991); an image is also available online at http://www.icspublications.org/bookstore/cross/b_cross01.html (accessed October 25, 2009). For a discussion of the image, see Graham M. Schweig, "Imagery of Divine Love: The Crucifix Drawing of John of the Cross," at http://www.icspublications.org/archives/others/cs6_13.html (accessed October 25, 2009).

his Carmelite formation, he proceeded to studies in philosophy and theology at the University of Salamanca, a greatly esteemed and flourishing center of learning, where John proved to be an outstanding student. He was ordained as a priest in 1567.

At this stage, for reasons that are not entirely clear, but perhaps because he was somewhat dissatisfied with the observance of the Carmelite Rule as he found it, John suffered a crisis with his Carmelite vocation and considered leaving the Order for a more rigorous, more solitary, and more contemplative form of religious life, such as that lived by the Carthusians. Soon after ordination, however, when returning to Medina del Campo to celebrate his first Mass, he met Madre Teresa de Jesús (Teresa of Avila), who was about twenty-seven years his senior and who had come to Medina to establish the second of her reformed Carmelite convents. A few years earlier, in 1562, she had founded a Carmelite House, which followed a new contemplative style based on the Primitive Rule (rather than the less rigorous Mitigated Rule). Teresa persuaded John to join her in the work of reform of the Carmelite Order.[7] He responded positively to her invitation to found a friars' branch of her reformed order. He was one of the first of the Carmelite friars to join Teresa's reform movement and was a vital cornerstone for it. Fray Juan de Santo Matía became Fray Juan de la Cruz (John of the Cross). The first Discalced Carmelite house for friars was founded in Duruelo in 1568.

From 1572 to 1574, Fray John was Teresa's spiritual director, counselor, and confessor. He witnessed her "spiritual marriage" to Christ on November 18, 1572, her entry into what she described as the innermost mansion of the interior castle.[8] Teresa would prove to be as significant an influence on him and his writing as he was on her. While there are clear differences between them, there is considerable affinity between Teresa and John.

John served as novice master, spiritual director, superior, and administrator for the Carmelite friars and as a spiritual counselor and confessor for

7. See Teresa of Avila, *Foundations* 3.17, in *The Collected Works of Teresa of Avila*, trans. Kieran Kavanaugh and Otilio Rodriguez, vol. 3 (Washington, DC: Institute of Carmelite Studies, 1985).

8. See Teresa of Avila, *Spiritual Testimonies* 31 in *The Collected Works of Teresa of Avila*, vol. 1 (Washington, DC: Institute of Carmelite Studies, 1976). All translations of John's work are taken from *The Collected Works of Saint John of the Cross*. We shall use the following abbreviations: *The Dark Night* (hereafter, *Dark Night*), *The Spiritual Canticle* (hereafter, *Spiritual Canticle*; 22.1, for example, means stanza 22, paragraph 1 of John's commentary), and *The Living Flame of Love* (hereafter, *Living Flame*; similarly, 1.23 means stanza 1, paragraph 23 of John's commentary on the poem).

the reformed Carmels established by Madre Teresa. John's life as a Carmelite was, however, marked by animosity, violence, intrigue, and turmoil. He suffered greatly in the tension, misunderstanding, and conflict of jurisdiction that developed between the unreformed Carmelite Order (the Calced Carmelites), which John had left when he joined the reformed order (the Discalced Carmelites, "discalced" because they did not wear shoes, but rather sandals, to symbolize the poverty to which they committed themselves). The Calced Carmelite majority remained deeply suspicious of the Teresian reform movement and considerable conflict developed over the nature and extent of reform and over questions of jurisdiction. The Calced and Discalced Carmelites were eventually formally separated by a decree of Pope Gregory XIII in 1580, which constituted the Discalced as a separate province from the rest of the Order. A papal brief by Pope Sixtus V in 1587 effected a further step toward full independence of the Discalced.

In the course of those conflicts, John suffered imprisonment and mistreatment. At one stage, in December 1577, he was captured and imprisoned by his Calced confreres and held captive for nine months in Toledo, in a state of terrible deprivation, physical mistreatment, and confinement. It was during this period of captivity that he wrote the first stanzas of *The Spiritual Canticle*. Following his escape in August 1578, he took refuge with Teresa's nuns. After his recovery from his imprisonment ordeal, he took up a series of administrative and leadership offices within the reformed order, including the ministry of spiritual direction, as well as writing his major works.

Later, as a result of tension and dissension within the Discalced Order, and after a lifetime of involvement in its government, he found himself relieved of the responsibilities of office and without assignment. Without any fuss, he retired to a life of solitude in a remote monastery. Shortly after, he succumbed to an illness, and became quite ill. When he sought assistance and refuge with a community of Discalced confreres in Ubeda, he was again treated harshly and inhospitably. He died just after midnight on the evening of December 13, 1591, not yet fifty years old. He was canonized by Pope Clement X in 1726 and declared a Doctor of the Church by Pius XI in 1926. John Paul II in 1993 proclaimed him patron of Spanish poets and Spanish composers of music.

John was a passionate character. The poverty of his childhood and his hospital work would appear to have engendered a kindness and empathy for others in need. He seems to have been especially attuned to the suffering of others. He was also a man of courage and serenity, determinedly austere in his self-discipline, and apparently utterly single-minded. In one of his most engaging images, he compares the contemplative to a turtledove (*Spiritual Canticle* 34) and in many ways this image describes John himself and his own spirituality. According to John, the turtledove does not rest at all until it finds its mate; so too the utter single-mindedness of the lover in seeking out the beloved, the contemplative in seeking God.

John was also a man of exceptional talents. He was a gifted teacher, a talented writer, a poetic genius, with a highly disciplined mind and a remarkable gift for discernment. He demonstrated exceptional psychological as well as theological insight and had a particular gift for spiritual direction. All kinds of people came to him for spiritual direction, clergy and lay, rich and poor, educated and uneducated. His role as spiritual director in the reform of the Order was of enormous importance. He himself preferred to describe himself as a spiritual teacher or guide, for, as he insisted, it is the Holy Spirit who is the soul's director. As seems to have been a common practice among Carmelite confessors and spiritual directors at the time, John would often jot down personalized notes, thoughts, or counsels for those whom he guided. It is possible that Teresa's now famous bookmark is one of these jottings:

> Let nothing disturb thee; Let nothing dismay thee; All things pass: God never changes. Patience attains All that it strives for. He who has God Lacks for nothing: God alone suffices.

John is one of the greatest masters of the spiritual life. He is renowned not only for his extraordinary mystical experiences but also for the insight and poetic genius that he brings to bear in describing the soul's journey to mystical union with God. For John, as for Teresa of Avila, the celebration of the Mass and reception of the Eucharist was often a time of special graces. The feast of the Trinity was one of his very favorite feasts. One of his contemporaries said of John in the course of the process of his beatification, "Among the mysteries for which it seems to me he had great love was that of the Most Holy Trinity and also that of the Son of God made man."[9]

John's Writings

Unlike Teresa, John received a strong formal education, culminating in his four years of study at the University of Salamanca, which equipped him with the basic tools of scholastic theology and anthropology. It is

9. *Procesos de Beatificacion y Canonizacion*, Declaration by Maria de la Cruz, in *Biblioteca Mistica Carmelitana*, XIV (Burgos, 1931), 121. Cited by John Paul II in *Master of Faith*, §9 n. 9.

hardly surprising then that John, compared to Teresa, is more systematic in his approach, conceptuality, and expression. He comes to the task of writing well grounded in his own mystical experience but also well schooled in Augustine and Thomas Aquinas and with a profound knowledge of the Scriptures.

An original and creative thinker, John seldom cites sources. In a few cases, he mentions Gregory the Great, Dionysius, Bernard of Clairvaux, and William of St. Thierry, especially in regard to the Holy Spirit. It is clear that he does not rely on any single source, but rather on a variety of sources at his disposal. Unlike Teresa, John is not subject to the kind of restrictions on freedom of expression that impacted her. We find in his writing no recourse to a rhetoric of subordination, nor need to cite numerous classical sources by way of justification of his thought. Like Teresa, he writes in the vernacular to fill the void of spiritual writing and counsel following the pronouncement of the index of prohibition of spiritual writings by Fernando Valdés in 1559.

Those of John's writings that we have were written in the latter years of his life and they demonstrate a remarkable spiritual maturity. Combining poetry as well as prose, his writings evince his scholastic training and his poetic genius. Indeed it is through poetry that he speaks of the most profound spiritual experience of union with God. His poetry is very beautiful, highly evocative, profoundly moving, mysterious and mystical, yet also systematic and theological in structure.

Unlike Teresa, John's theology is—at least at first glance—more negative, and famously so, profoundly shaped as it is by the experience of the dark night of the soul. Indeed, John is most famous for his exposition on the dark night of the soul.[10] But, in addition to *The Dark Night*, he wrote three other major prose works: *The Ascent to Mount Carmel*, *The Spiritual Canticle*, and *The Living Flame of Love*. We also have some of his poems,[11] a few letters, maxims, and spiritual counsels.

The Ascent to Mount Carmel, the longest of his manuscripts, arguably his one attempt at a systematic treatise per se, was written between 1581 and 1585 and treats the way to highest union with God and the difficulties of the way to that union. It is a prose commentary on a poem of eight stanzas (written in 1578 to 1579) and begins with the words "One dark night."

10. Note that, like Teresa, John uses the word "soul" to mean person, the self, the whole person. For both, the "soul" is inherently relational.

11. Most of John's poems are written in the Spanish ballad-meter called *romance*. A traditional Spanish verse form, the romance is often sung or chanted.

The effort was apparently abandoned by John, and the commentary-treatise comes to an abrupt end.

The Dark Night is another prose commentary, written in 1584 to 1585, on the same poem, "One dark night."[12] It takes up where *The Ascent to Mount Carmel* finishes and describes how God purifies the soul on its journey to illumination and union with God. Here John deals in more detail with the process involved in the journey to God. Like Teresa, John envisages that one's ultimate goal is union with God, such that one actually becomes divine, deiform, sharing in the divinity of God. But for Teresa, the journey to union with God is one of descent, while for John is it one of ascent.

The Spiritual Canticle, a poem of thirty-one stanzas, was written in 1578, while John was captive in Toledo (with additional stanzas added between 1580 and 1584 and a prose commentary, in second redaction, written between 1584 and 1586). Inspired by the *Song of Songs*, John, in *The Spiritual Canticle*, describes the love between the soul (the bride) and Christ (its bridegroom). With ease and elegance, without pretension or sentimentality, John describes the sublime heights of mystical union in terms of the intimacy and passion of human love. Utterly captivating in its profundity and eloquence, *The Spiritual Canticle* is arguably the finest of John's poetry.

The Living Flame of Love, a sequel to *The Spiritual Canticle*, is a poem of four stanzas with an accompanying commentary. Given that its second redaction was completed not long before John's death, in some ways it can be regarded as John's last and most vivid testament to his own mystical experience. The original poem and the commentary was written for Doña Ana de Peñalosa, whom John describes as a "very noble and devout lady" (*Prologue*). Doña Ana was a laywoman to whom John gave spiritual direction and was a generous benefactor of the reformed Carmelite Order. That John writes this for a woman, and a laywoman at that, in a time when the practice of mental prayer is regarded with suspicion, especially in regard to women, is itself remarkable.

In *The Living Flame of Love*, John writes about the union of the soul with God. The living flame serves as metaphor for the soul's loving union with God. As is his usual practice in his commentaries, John presents the entire poem first, then proceeds to a commentary on each stanza. In this text, we find a great emphasis on the Holy Spirit. Indeed in many ways, *The*

---

12. The night has different meanings at different times for John. It sometimes means suffering, sometimes purification, sometimes journey, sometimes a state beyond knowledge and/or memory.

Living Flame of Love is effectively a treatise on the Holy Spirit. In our reflections on John's insights into the mystery of God as Trinity, we shall pay particular attention to *The Living Flame of Love*, because in this work John speaks at some length on the soul's profound experience of communion with God, Father, Son, and Holy Spirit, an experience that illuminates, delights, and absorbs the soul in an embrace of love. It is somewhat surprising that *The Living Flame of Love*, both the poem and the commentary, are among the least studied of John's works, for they effectively situate the spiritual journey that John has described in his other works in its most profound context.

John's Insights into the Mystery of the Trinity

In John's commentary on his poem, *The Living Flame of Love*, we find some of John's most profound insights into the mystery of the Trinity.[13] As John himself explains in the opening sentence of his commentary on the poem, *The Living Flame of Love* treats of "a very intimate and elevated union and transformation of the soul in God." In this work, John speaks of the very heights of mystical experience, the soul's union with God, that state of enkindled love wherein the soul is so transformed that it itself becomes a living flame. John explains that he approaches the topic with considerable reluctance, for "everything I say is as far from the reality as is a painting from the living object represented" (*Living Flame* prol. 1).

"Stanzas the Soul Recites in Intimate Union With God"

1. O living flame of love
   that tenderly wounds my soul
   in its deepest center! Since
   now you are not oppressive,
   now consummate! if it be your will:
   tear through the veil of this sweet encounter!

2. O sweet cautery,
   O delightful wound!
   O gentle hand! O delicate touch
   that tastes of eternal life

13. For a most insightful and very instructive analysis of John's writings, including *The Living Flame of Love*, and the grammatical, syntactical, and linguistic logic as well as the phonic design of John's work, see Colin Thompson, *St. John of the Cross: Songs in the Night* (London: SPCK, 2002); see also Edward Howells, *John of the Cross and Teresa of Avila: Mystical Knowing and Selfhood* (New York: Crossroad, 2002).

and pays every debt!
In killing you changed death to life.

3. O lamps of fire!
in whose splendors
the deep caverns of feeling,
once obscure and blind,
now give forth, so rarely, so exquisitely,
both warmth and light to their Beloved.

4. How gently and lovingly
you wake in my heart,
where in secret you dwell alone;
and in your sweet breathing,
filled with good and glory,
how tenderly you swell my heart with love.

Fire, flame, and light are the metaphors that John uses in *The Living Flame of Love* to describe the soul's transformation and union with God. God is a living flame of love, and the soul, in the state of intimate union with God, is not only united with but absorbed into the divine flame, therein becoming enkindled and itself a living flame. As John explains, the soul in this "enkindled" state is "so inwardly transformed in the fire of love and elevated by it that it is not merely united to this fire but produces within it a living flame" (*Living Flame* prol. 4).

John returns on several occasions to the metaphor of fire and its effects. He considers, for example, the effect of fire on burning wood: "Although the fire has penetrated the wood, transformed it, and united it with itself, yet as this fire grows hotter and continues to burn, so the wood becomes much more incandescent and inflamed, even to the point of flaring up and shooting out flames from itself" (*Living Flame* 1.3). Later, in a similar vein, John draws on the distinction between glowing embers and embers that are not merely glowing but have become so hot that they shoot forth a living flame (*Living Flame* 1.16). With imagery that is reminiscent of Moses' declaration that "Our Lord God is a consuming fire" (Deut 4:24), John depicts God as a fire of love, which, "being of infinite power, can inestimably consume and transform into itself the soul it touches" (*Living Flame* 2.1).

John apparently speaks from his own mystical experience of these heights of union and its effects on the soul: "The soul feels this and speaks of it thus in these stanzas with intimate and delicate sweetness of love, burning in love's flame, and stressing in these stanzas some of the effects of this love" (*Living Flame* prol. 4). John succinctly summarizes the effects of this love in thoroughly trinitarian terms: "The Blessed Trinity inhabits the soul by divinely illumining its intellect with the wisdom of the Son, delighting its will in the Holy Spirit, and absorbing it powerfully and mightily in the unfathomed embrace of the Father's sweetness" (*Living Flame* 1.15). John later reiterates a thoroughly trinitarian understanding of the effects of this union of the soul with God, this time in terms even more closely attuned to scholastic anthropology and its understanding of the human person in terms of the faculties of memory, intellect, and will:

> "O living flame of love that tenderly wounds my soul." This is like say-
> ing: O enkindled love, with your loving movements you are pleasantly
> glorifying me according to the greater capacity and strength of my soul,
> bestowing divine knowledge according to all the ability and capacity of
> my intellect, communicating love according to the greater power of my
> will, and rejoicing the substance of my soul with the torrent of your
> delight, your divine contact and substantial union, in harmony with the
> greater purity of my substance and the capacity and breath of my mem-
> ory! And this is what happens, in an indescribable way, at the time this
> flame of love rises up within the soul. (*Living Flame* 1.17)

But, after all, as John explains in *The Spiritual Canticle*: "There would not be a true and total transformation if the soul were not transformed in the three Persons of the Most Holy Trinity in an open and manifest degree" (*Spiritual Canticle* 39.3). John understands that this transformation of the soul in the three persons of the Trinity "in an open and manifest degree" (*Spiritual Canticle* 39.3) takes place precisely in the human person's spiritual faculties of memory, intellect, and will.

John's trinitarian reflections reach to further heights in the second stanza of *The Living Flame of Love*:

> O sweet cautery,
> O delightful wound!
> O gentle hand! O delicate touch
> that tastes of eternal life
> and pays every debt!
> In killing you changed death to life.

Here, John expatiates on the mystery of the three persons of Trinity, Father, Son, and Holy Spirit, who together effect this divine work of union with the soul. John explains that the cautery (i.e., burning instrument) is the Holy Spirit, the hand the Father, and the touch of the Son. The hand (Father), the cautery (Holy Spirit), and the touch (Son) are in substance the same, he affirms, but they refer to the different *effect* that each of the persons produces in the soul in attaining this union of the soul with God.

Here John is clearly in complete accord with classical trinitarian doctrine, which understands that the three divine persons are of one substance or being, *homoousios*,[14] while distinct in their persons, relations, and roles.

John elaborates on the distinctive effect of each of the three divine persons in the work of union: "The first [effect] is the delightful wound. This it [the soul] attributes to the Holy Spirit, and hence calls him a sweet cautery. The second [effect] is the taste of eternal life. This it attributes to the Son, and thus calls him a delicate touch. The third [effect] is transformation, a gift by which all debts are fully paid. This it attributes to the Father and hence calls him a gentle hand" (*Living Flame* 2.1).

John treats the three divine persons and their effects in some detail. He expounds at length on the Holy Spirit, the cautery, and the wound of love that is the Spirit's effect. John explains that the soul, entirely transformed by the divine flame, not only feels a cautery, but itself becomes a cautery of blazing fire (*Living Flame* 2.2). Since the cautery is sweet, the wound that it causes is a wound of love and is similarly sweet, indeed delightful. As John explains: "Since the cautery is a cautery of love, the wound is a wound of sweet love and is both delightful and sweet" (*Living Flame* 2.7).

John stresses that the wound of love, caused by the cautery, cures and heals. As often as the cautery of love touches the wound of love, it deepens the wound of love, expanding the soul at its deepest level. This kind of depth imagery is also very powerful in John's writing, and he describes the journey to mystical union as a process of depthing or hollowing out of the infinite depths of the soul. Indeed, John understands spiritual knowing in terms of increasing depth of the soul, whereby the soul is deepened, so to speak, into the divine innertrinitarian dynamism. So it is that "deep calls to deep," that one abyss calls to another abyss (Ps 42:7).

Paradoxically, and contrary to our ordinary experience of being wounded, the more deeply the cautery wounds, the more it heals and cures. The wound of love becomes the cure. In the process, other wounds from other causes also become wounds of love, until eventually the entire soul is cauterized, dissolved, and transformed into a wound of love (*Living Flame* 2.7). In this way, the soul is made healthy in love, transformed by love. John stresses that the Holy Spirit never wounds except to heal and cure. The wound is for the sake of the soul's delight.

14. *Homoousios*, the Greek term meaning consubstantial (of the same being) was included in the Creed of Nicaea in 325, in response to the Arian controversy concerning the divine status of the Son in regard to the Father. The Creed elaborated: "[the Son is] God from God, light from light, true God from true God, of one being [*homoousios*] with the Father."

The hand is the merciful and omnipotent Father, and John, in his commentary, deals with this in a single short section (*Living Flame* 2.16). It is a gentle hand, loving and gracious, generous and bountiful, powerful and rich. It is the hand that embraces and caresses the soul. It is also the hand that is at work in the soul in its experience of the dark night. In comparison with his relatively fulsome description of the Holy Spirit and its effect on the soul, John is somewhat reticent in his description of the person of the Father and rather quickly proceeds to the person of the Son.

The only begotten Son is the delicate touch, the touch of the merciful hand of the Father, by which we are wounded with the force of the cautery, that is the Holy Spirit. It is a delicate and subtle touch, eminently loving, by which the Word, the Son of God, subtly penetrates the soul. It is also a delectable touch that tastes of eternal life, the things of God. John explains: "As a result the soul tastes here all the things of God, since God communicates to it fortitude, wisdom, love, beauty, grace, goodness, and so on. Because God is all these things, a person enjoys them in only one touch of God, and the soul rejoices within its faculties and within its substance" (*Living Flame* 2.21).

A deep and profound conversion of the soul occurs in attaining this state of union, and, in this conversion, the faculties of the soul—intellect, will, and memory—are transformed. Through its union with God, the soul's intellect becomes one with God's intellect. "The intellect, which before this union understood naturally by the vigor of its natural light by means of the natural senses, is now moved and informed by another higher principle of supernatural divine light, and the senses are bypassed. Accordingly, the intellect becomes divine, because through its union with God's intellect both become one" (*Living Flame* 2.34).

The soul's affection and will are similarly transformed, now moved by the Holy Spirit, and conformed to God's will. John explains: "And the will, which previously loved in a base and deadly way with only its natural affection, is now changed into the life of divine love, for it loves in a lofty way with divine affection, moved by the strength of the Holy Spirit in which it now lives the life of love. By means of this union God's will and the soul's will are now one" (*Living Flame* 2.34).

The soul's memory is also transformed, conformed to the mind of God. As John explains: "And the memory, which by itself perceived only the figures and phantasms of creatures, is changed through this union so as to have in its mind the eternal years mentioned by David [Ps 77:5]" (*Living Flame* 2.34).

John explains that the soul's natural appetite is also changed. It too is transformed, thereby conformed to the appetite of God: "its taste and savor are divine, and it is moved and satisfied by another principle: the delight of God, in which it is more alive. And because it is united with him, it is no longer anything else than the appetite of God" (*Living Flame* 2.34).

In this state of union with God, absorbed into the divine life, the soul, its faculties, and appetites are now alive and deeply and profoundly attuned to God. "Accordingly, the intellect of this soul is God's intellect; its will is God's will; its memory is the memory of God; and its delight is God's delight; and although the substance of this soul is not the substance of God, since it cannot undergo a substantial conversion into him, it has become God through participation in God, being united to and absorbed in him, as it is in this state" (*Living Flame* 2.34).

In the third stanza, John underscores the significance of the soul's transformation: "All that can be said of this stanza is less than the reality, for the transformation of the soul in God is indescribable. Everything can be expressed in this statement: The soul becomes God from God through participation in him and in his attributes, which it terms the 'lamps of fire'" (*Living Flame* 3.8).

Having received by infusion the divine attributes into its faculties of memory, intellect, and will, the soul becomes one with God. The soul's faculties, thus pervaded by God, "give forth to God in God" (*Living Flame* 3.77). John explains: "In the very manner they receive it, they return it to the one who gave it, and with the same exquisite beauty" (*Living Flame* 3.77). John elaborates, "Having been made one with God, the soul is somehow God through participation. Although it is not God as perfectly as it will be in the next life, it is like the shadow of God" (*Living Flame* 3.78). John does not mean a union of substance or being, for the soul is a creature and God the Creator, but rather a union by participation, due to the infusion of the soul's faculties by the divine attributes.

John probes even more deeply and explains that, in this state of union with God and conformity to God's intellect, memory, and will, the soul now loves God "not through itself but through him" (*Living Flame* 3.82). The soul loves God with God's own love; it loves God with the very love with which God loves it. Now participating in God, the soul is enabled to give God himself to God. John stresses the great significance of this, again in profoundly trinitarian terms: "This is a remarkable quality, for the soul loves through the Holy Spirit, as the Father and the Son love each other, according to what the Son himself declares through St. John: That the love with which you have loved me be in them and I in them [John 17:26]"

(*Living Flame* 3.82). As John explains in *The Spiritual Canticle*, the soul, now "superabounds with grace," and "loves in some way through the Holy Spirit who is given to her [Rom 5:5]" (*Spiritual Canticle* 38.3). The soul now breathes in God, the Father's breathing in the Son, the Son's breathing in the Father, and their breathing out of the Holy Spirit.

John understands, moreover, that the soul, attuned to and participating in God, loves God "not through itself but through him" (*Living Flame* 3.82), but also that it now knows and loves creatures and all creation *through God*. Everything in creation, the beauty, wonder, and freedom of each created thing, is seen and known and loved in and through God, and thus as God loves it and delights in it. There is a new delight in creation, because the soul now knows creatures *in* God. John elaborates further in stanza 4: "And here lies the remarkable delight of this awakening: The soul knows creatures through God and not God through creatures. This amounts to knowing the effects through their cause and not the cause through its effects. The latter is knowledge a posteriori, and the former is essential knowledge" (*Living Flame* 4.5). In other words, the soul now knows and loves all things, including itself, through and from God's perspective, through the wound of the Holy Spirit, the touch of the Son, and the hand of the Father. It knows and loves not God through creatures but creatures and all creation through God.

John brings his commentary on *The Living Flame of Love* to a conclusion with a reflection on the divine spiration, whereby the Holy Spirit proceeds from the Father and the Son, and the experience of the soul's "strange delight in the breathing of the Holy Spirit in God" (*Living Flame* 4.16). John again speaks of the "delightful awakening" to the presence of the Trinity that is granted to the soul in this blessed union. John explains: "And in that awakening, which is as though one were to waken and breathe, the soul feels a strange delight in the breathing of the Holy Spirit in God, in which it is sovereignly glorified and taken with love" (*Living Flame* 4.16). John hardly dares—or indeed feels able—to continue, and he explains: "I do not desire to speak of this spiration, filled for the soul with good and glory and delicate love of God, for I am aware of being incapable of doing so; and were I to try, it might seem less than it is" (*Living Flame* 4.16). His commentary culminates with a brief explanation of this experience of being absorbed, no less, into the spiration of the Holy Spirit, and he then concludes with a doxology in praise of God:

> It is a spiration that God produces in the soul, in which, by that awakening of lofty knowledge of the Godhead, he breathes the Holy

Spirit in it in the same proportion as its knowledge and understanding of him, absorbing it most profoundly in the Holy Spirit, rousing its love with a divine exquisite quality and delicacy according to what it beholds in him. Since the breathing is filled with good and glory, the Holy Spirit, through this breathing, filled the soul with good and glory in which he enkindled it in love of himself, indescribably and incomprehensibly, in the depths of God, to whom be honor and glory forever and ever. Amen. (*Living Flame* 4.16)

It is as if now, in this blessed state of union, the clouds of unknowing are drawn aside and the soul beholds, in utter and sublime transparency, the wonder and the beauty, the goodness and the glory, of God's triune being, revealed in all its grace and splendor.

In his earlier work, *The Spiritual Canticle*, stanza 39, John also refers to this spiration or breathing of the Holy Spirit in the soul, so deep and sublime as to be indescribable:

By his divine breath-like spiration, the Holy Spirit elevates the soul sublimely and informs her and makes her capable of breathing in God the same spiration of love that the Father breathes in the Son and the Son in the Father. This spiration of love is the Holy Spirit himself, who in the Father and the Son breathes out to her in this transformation in order to unite her to himself. . . . And [in] this kind of spiration of the Holy Spirit in the soul, . . . the soul united and transformed in God breathes out in God to God the very divine spiration that God—she being transformed in him—breathes out in himself to her. (*Spiritual Canticle* 39.3)

In this state of union, the soul is so profoundly united with God, so absorbed into the trinitarian communion, so conformed to the Trinity, that it participates in the innertrinitarian spiration from the Father and Son of the Holy Spirit, that living, breathing bond of love that unites Father and Son. It experiences this, not by observation from the outside, as it were, but by participation on the inside, from *within* in the relationship of the Son to the Father in the Holy Spirit. It thus enjoys a very real and conscious participation in the dynamism and mutuality of the Trinity. Indescribable though this experience of the mystery of the Trinity may be, John explains:

One should not think it impossible that the soul be capable of so sublime an activity as this breathing in God through participation as God breathes in her. For, granted that God favors her by union with the Most Blessed Trinity, in which she becomes deiform and God through participation, how could it be incredible that she also understand, know, and love—or better that this be done in her—in the Trinity, together with it, as does the Trinity itself! Yet God accomplishes this in the soul through communication and participation. This is transformation in the three Persons in power and wisdom and love, and thus the soul is like God through this transformation. He created her in his image and likeness that she might attain such resemblance. (*Spiritual Canticle* 39.4)

Transformed in power, wisdom, and love, conformed to the memory, intellect, and love of the Trinity, the soul is deiform, like God, by participation in God. Again, we see the classical psychological analogy at work in John's thinking: the three faculties of memory, intellect, and will and the three emanations of delight, understanding, and love; the three divine persons and the three divine perfections of power, wisdom, and love; the triad of the soul's faculties serving as the analogy for the triune Godhead of Father, Son, and Spirit. The image of the Trinity is imprinted in the soul in the faculties of memory, intellect, and will. In attaining union with God, the faculties of memory, intellect, and will are transformed, deiformed, so to speak, conformed to the memory, intellect, and will of God. Through this infusion into its faculties, the structure and dynamism of the Trinity is instilled in the soul. The soul thus enkindled is absorbed into God's threefold differentiated selfhood and relationality. The divine persons then are known, not as objects of its knowing, but from within the Trinity. This is the soul in the ultimate state of enkindled love. This is what it is for the soul to be so transformed in the living flame of divine love that it is "not merely united with this fire but produces within it a living flame" (*Living Flame* prol. 4). This graced union with God is the soul's fulfillment and perfection. It was indeed for this that she was created.

What emerges particularly strongly in John's reflections on *The Living Flame of Love* is the person of the Holy Spirit. The living flame is the Holy Spirit, the Spirit of the soul's bridegroom (*Living Flame* 1.3). It is the Holy Spirit who sets in motion the glorious flickerings of his flame (*Living Flame* 1.18). The Holy Spirit is the flame of the divine fire (1.19). It is the Holy Spirit who, like a cautery, wounds the soul in order to dispose it for divine union and transformation—"just as the fire that penetrates a log of wood is the same that first makes an assault on the wood, wounding it with the flame, drying it out, and stripping it of its unsightly qualities until it is so disposed that it can be penetrated and transformed into the fire" (*Living Flame* 1.19; see also 2.7). The anointings and unctions of the Holy Spirit (*Living Flame* 3.26) prepare the soul for union with God, deepening its desire for God, until the soul is so purified and prepared that it merits union with God and transformation in all its faculties. John explains: "The blessings this silent communication and contemplation impress on the soul . . . are most hidden unctions of the Holy Spirit and hence most delicate; they secretly fill the soul with spiritual riches, gifts, and graces" (*Living Flame* 3.40).

While the person of the Holy Spirit enjoys undoubted prominence in *The Living Flame of Love*, the Trinity of divine persons is ever present in John's view, as is the mystery of Christ, the Word incarnate, savior, and revealer of the trinitarian mystery of God and the soul's bridegroom. A few of John's other poems also reflect this profoundly christological and trinitarian character of John's thought. The "Song of the Soul that Rejoices in Knowing God through Faith" is a particularly rich and evocative poem, and in it we find a captivating image that is very suggestive of the freshness and vitality of the triune God, an image of God as like an eternal spring or fountain of living water, flowing in the dark of night.

> For I know well the spring that flows and runs,
> although it is night.
>
> 1. That eternal spring is hidden,
>   for I know well where it has its rise,
>   although it is night.
>
> 2. I do not know its origin, nor has it one,
>   but I know that every origin has come from it,
>   although it is night.
>
> 3. I know that nothing else is so beautiful,
>   and that the heavens and the earth drink there,
>   although it is night.
>
> 4. I know well that it is bottomless
>   and no one is able to cross it,
>   although it is night.
>
> 5. Its clarity is never darkened,
>   and I know that every light has come from it,
>   although it is night.
>
> 6. I know that its streams are so brimming
>   they water the lands of hell, the heavens, and earth,
>   although it is night.
>
> 7. I know well the stream that flows from this spring
>   is mighty in compass and power,
>   although it is night.

8. I know the stream proceeding from these two,
   that neither of them in fact precedes it,
   although it is night.

9. This eternal spring is hidden
   in this living bread for our life's sake,
   although it is night.

10. It is here calling out to creatures;
    and they satisfy their thirst, although in darkness,
    because it is night.

11. This living spring that I long for,
    I see in this bread of life,
    although it is night.

With its images of water, light, clarity, darkness, hiddenness, bread of life, and living bread, the poem is strongly redolent of the Gospel of John and especially its play on the themes of light and darkness. The nocturnal refrain—"although it is night"—reinforces these Johannine resonances and also brings to mind the dialogues in John's gospel between Jesus and Nicodemus and between Jesus and the woman of Samaria (John 3 and 4).

In "Song of the Soul that Rejoices in Knowing God through Faith," the Father is the unoriginate and bottomless font, the fountain of all being: "I do not know its origin, / nor has it one, / but I know that every origin has come from it." The Father is the one from which all else comes: "The heavens and the earth drink there," and "every light has come from it." The Father is the font from which two streams flow, the source from which the other two divine persons proceed for all eternity—the Son, through whom all things were made, and the Spirit, Lord and Giver of life. "I know well the stream that flows from this spring / is mighty in compass and power." It is the Son (verse 7). Then, the Holy Spirit, "proceeding from these two," from the Father and the Son, though without either of them preceding it: "I know the stream proceeding from these two, / that neither of them in fact precedes it" (verse 8). Finally, and somewhat surprisingly, the poem soars to a eucharistic climax (verses 9-11): The spring is concealed in the bread: "This eternal spring is hidden / in this living bread for our life's sake." In "this bread of life," wherein Christ is made present and visible, is hidden this living spring, this fountain of all life and holiness, which satisfies our thirst. And this is "for our life's sake." The fountain, "this eternal spring," that is the Trinity is truly present in the eucharistic "living bread"— and so really as to be able to be heard, tasted, and seen. In this "bread of life" is a foretaste of the trinitarian life for which the soul longs.

The mystery of the Trinity also figures prominently in a series of romances, inspired by John's reflections on the prologue of John's gospel. In this series, John situates the whole history of salvation in terms of the mystery of the Trinity and the Father's eternal begetting of the Word/Son. John engages highly suggestive nuptial imagery to describe both inner-trinitarian love and God's love for humankind. These romances, as several commentators have recognized, effectively undergird John's account of the soul's journey to union with God.

In Romance 1, "Romance on the Gospel Text, 'In principio erat Verbum,' Regarding the Blessed Trinity," trinitarian life is described in terms of the mutuality and intimacy of interpersonal love:

> As the lover in the beloved
> each lived in the other,
> and the Love that unites them
> is one with them,
> their equal, excellent as
> the One and the Other:
> Three Persons, and one Beloved
> among all three.
> One love in them all
> Makes of them one Lover,
> And the Lover is the Beloved
> in whom each one lives.
> For the being that the three possess
> each of them possesses,
> and each of them loves
> him who bears this being.
> Each one is this being,
> which alone unites them,
> binding them deeply,
> one beyond words [*un ineffable nudo*].
> Thus it is a boundless
> Love that unites them,
> for the three have one love
> which is their essence;
> and the more love is one
> the more it is love.

The divine Three are, from all eternity, united in one love, in "*un ineffable nudo*," an ineffable knot, "one beyond words." The Trinity is this mystery of love, a mutual indwelling of the Three in each other, as the lover in the beloved. John draws an analogy between the encounter of two lovers and the intimacy of their lovemaking to express the mystery of Trinity, each living in the other in boundless love.

In Romance 2, "On the Communication among the Three Persons," John describes a dialogue between the Father and the Son, "in that immense love proceeding from the two." The Father, with "great affection," addresses the Son, "you whom I love so," with imagery taken from the Nicene Creed to express the consubstantiality (*homoousios*) of the divine persons: "You are the light of my light," "you are my wisdom, the image of my substance."

> My Son, only your
> company contents me,
> and when something pleases me
> I love that thing in you;
> whoever resembles you most
> satisfies me most,
> and whoever is like you in nothing
> will find nothing in me.
> I am pleased with you alone,
> O life of my life!
> You are the light of my light,
> you are my wisdom,
> the image of my substance
> in whom I am well pleased.
> My Son, I will give myself
> to him who loves you
> and I will love him
> with the same love I have for you,
> because he has loved
> you whom I love so.

In this way, John describes the Father's love for the soul as being the very same love with which he loves the Son. Here John engages not nuptial imagery but the tender familial love of parent for child to describe the Father's love for his Son, "life of my life," "light of my light," "my image," "whom I love so."

In the third romance of the series, when the Father announces that he wishes to give the Son "a bride who will love you," John makes use of nuptial imagery to describe the love of the Son and the soul, his bride, and the intimacy with the Son, and, moreover, with God, that the soul then enjoys:

> He would take her
> tenderly in his arms
> and there give her his love;
> and when they were thus one,
> he would lift her to the Father
> where God's very joy
> would be her joy.
> For as the Father and the Son
> and he who proceeds from them
> live in one another,
> so it would be with the bride;
> for, taken wholly into God,
> she will live the life of God.

By way of this nuptial imagery, John describes the Trinity's loving embrace of the Beloved, of all humanity, whereby the Beloved is "taken wholly into God" where "she will live the life of God," and thus enter into the mystery of mutual indwelling whereby "they live in one another."

In the seventh romance, "The Incarnation," the dialogue between Father and Son resumes, and the Father reiterates, three times in just seven lines, that the perfection of love requires likeness (*semejante*) of the lover and beloved, "for the greater their likeness / the greater their delight."

> In perfect love
> this law holds:
> that the lover become
> like the one he loves;
> for the greater their likeness
> the greater their delight.
> Surely your bride's delight
> would greatly increase
> were she to see you like her,
> in her own flesh.

The reference to "likeness" has both trinitarian and christological resonances. It is primarily redolent of the perfection of love that is the Trinity of three divine persons who not only share a likeness but are consubstantial, of one and the same substance (*homoousios*). Its christological resonances are, however, no less strong. Here indeed is the rationale for the incarnation. It is not for the reparation of sin or the redemption of a debt; rather, he becomes human for the sake of the bride's increased delight, in other words, for the sake of love. Love is the reason for the incarnation.

The series of romances concludes with the nativity scene, with Mary the Mother of God gazing with sheer wonder at her babe, "God there in the manger," and marveling at the wedding in him of human and divine:

> Men sang songs
> and angels melodies
> celebrating the marriage
> of Two such as these.
> But God there in the manger
> cried and moaned;
> and these tears were jewels
> the bride brought to the wedding.
> The Mother gazed in sheer wonder
> on such an exchange:
> in God, man's weeping,
> and in man, gladness,
> to the one and the other
> things usually so strange.

Again, John uses nuptial imagery to describe the tenderness and intimacy of the exchange in him of human and divine, "to the one and the other / things usually so strange." In this way, with an exquisite simplicity, John expresses the sheer wonder of the incarnation and the love that is its source, a triune love.

Conclusion

Of all our mystics, it is John who turns to poetry to express the exquisite delights of union with God and the inexpressible mystery of God. He brings not only scholastic expertise but a highly developed aesthetic consciousness and poetic genius to his description of the soul's mystical union with God and that love beyond all telling. His poetry rightly stands as a jewel in the treasury of Spanish literature and, even more important, in the treasury of Christian mysticism. His poetry also throws into sharp relief the painful inadequacy of doctrinal formulations and theological explorations in attempting to convey the inexpressible mystery of God who is their source.

The mysteries of the Trinity, the incarnation, and, perhaps most subtly of all, the paschal mystery permeate John's thought. It is those mysteries that constitute the matrix within which he describes the experience of the soul's journey to union with God. He would have us understand that, in the embrace of love of the mystical union of the soul with God, the soul is deiformed, trinified, not just united to, but absorbed into the trinitarian dynamism wherein the Holy Spirit proceeds from the mutual love of the Father and the Son. In the trinitarian process of illumining, delighting and absorbing the soul in that loving embrace, the soul's intellect is conformed to God's intellect, its will to God's will, and its memory to God's memory. Absorbed into the trinitarian relations, yet without loss of or injury to the integrity of its creaturely humanity, the soul attains a way of knowing and indeed of being that is both human and divine. In attempting to speak of that point of sublime union, John invokes the image of breathing to render the soul's dynamic participation in the breath-like spiration of love that animates and unites Father, Son, and Spirit. Then God breathes in her, and she breathes in God. As John explains, straining to express the inexpressible, "for the soul united and transformed in God breathes out in God to God the very divine spiration that God—she being transformed in him—breathes out in himself to her" (*Spiritual Canticle* 39.3).

Where Teresa of Avila offers a kind of cartography of the soul in its descent to union, John describes the transformation of the soul that occurs in the process of ascent to mystical union. He uses a rich and evocative cluster of trinitarian images and associations, many drawn from a love of nature that imbues his thought—including light, fountain, fire, and nuptial love—to describe the process of ascent and the indescribably blissful end point of the journey. Resonances with the Nicene-Constantinopolitan Creed and with the Gospel of John are particularly strong and serve to reinforce the theological coherence of John's insights, as does his use of the faculty psychology of scholastic theology and anthropology to describe the effects of union on the soul and its absorption into the Trinity.

There is much that the Carmelite reformers, John and Teresa, have in common. For both, the Holy Spirit emerges with particular vibrancy. As John expresses it, the Holy Spirit is the spiritual director, wounding the soul in order to dispose it for divine union and transformation. With hidden and delicate unctions, the Holy Spirit fills the soul with spiritual riches, gifts, and graces. The Holy Spirit personifies the self-giving love of the Father and the Son. In the state of union, the blessed soul is absorbed into the flame that is the Holy Spirit and becomes one with the Holy Spirit. As such, it loves God with the same love with which it is loved. John's mysticism and theology is, however, more negative—indeed famously so—than that of Teresa. John understands that the ascent to mystical union with God involves "a programmatic process of sensory and spiritual negation and suffering in the dark nights."[15] Where for Teresa that final state of union is

15. Howells, *John of the Cross and Teresa of Avila*, 129.

an intimate friendship with the divine company, for John, it is a more aptly described as a continuous gazing between the soul and God, as between two lovers. Hence John's charming image of the contemplative as a turtle-dove: just as the turtledove that does not rest at all until it finds its mate, so too the soul, no matter the cost, in its yearning for its beloved, God.

References and Further Reading

Primary Sources

John of the Cross. *The Collected Works of Saint John of the Cross.* Translated by Kieran Kavanaugh and Otilio Rodriguez. Washington, DC: ICS Publications, 1991.

Secondary Sources

Collings, Ross. *John of the Cross.* Way of Christian Mystics 10. Collegeville, MN: Liturgical Press, Michael Glazier, 1990.

Hardy, Richard. *John of the Cross, Man and Mystic.* Boston: Pauline, 2004.

Howells, Edward. *John of the Cross and Teresa of Avila: Mystical Knowing and Selfhood.* New York: Crossroad, 2002.

Kavanaugh, Kieran. *John of the Cross: Doctor of Light and Love.* The Crossroad Spiritual Legacy Series. New York: Crossroad, 1999.

Matthew, Iain. *The Impact of God: Soundings from St. John of the Cross.* London: Hodder & Stoughton, 1995.

Ruiz, Federico. *God Speaks in the Night: The Life, Times and Teaching of St. John of the Cross.* Translated by Kieran Kavanaugh. Washington, DC: ICS Publications, 1991.

Tavard, George. *Poetry and Contemplation in St. John of the Cross.* Athens: Ohio University Press, 1988.

Thompson, Colin. *St. John of the Cross: Songs in the Night.* London: SPCK, 2002.

8

ELIZABETH OF THE TRINITY
(1880–1906)

Elizabeth of the Trinity was just twenty-six years old when she died in November 1906. She was just a few years younger than that other renowned daughter of Carmel, the Little Flower, Thérèse of Lisieux (1873–1897), who captured the imagination of the Christian world so quickly after her death. The two never met, although Elizabeth knew of Thérèse and, even before her own entry into Carmel in 1901, had read Thérèse's *Story of a Soul.*[1] Like Thérèse, Elizabeth achieved a sanctity characterized not by great deeds, but by a great love, lived out in the ordinariness and simplicity of her life.[2]

In her short life Elizabeth reached remarkable heights of the spiritual life. She, like Thérèse, was soon recognized as one of the twentieth century's greatest mystics. She was beatified by Pope John Paul II in 1984. She is rightly applauded as an apostle of the indwelling Trinity, having given living expression to the mystery of the trinitarian indwelling and its distinctly paschal, eucharistic, Marian, and apostolic unfolding.

1. A photograph, taken three days after Elizabeth's entrance into Carmel, shows Elizabeth kneeling beside Mother Germaine of Jesus (soon to be elected prioress, which included responsibility as mistress of novices), who holds a copy of *Story of a Soul: The Autobiography of St. Thérèse of Lixieux.* See *Letters from Carmel,* trans. Anne Englund Nash, vol. 2 of *Elizabeth of the Trinity: The Complete Works* (Washington, DC: ICS Publications, 1995), 1. (Hereafter *Complete Works* 2, with individual letters referred to by number, e.g., L132.)

2. For a comprehensive study of Elizabeth's life, see Conrad de Meester, *Élisabeth de la Trinité: Biographie* (Paris: Presses de la Renaissance, 2006). See also *Carmel: Revue Trimestrielle de Spiritualité Chrétienne* 122 (December 2006): *Élisabeth de la Trinité–L'Intériorité au Service du Monde,* the whole issue devoted to Elizabeth of the Trinity. Translations from Elizabeth's writings will be taken from *Elizabeth of the Trinity: The Complete Works,* 2 vols. (Washington, DC: ICS Publications, 1984–1995). The English translation of vol. 3 of *The Complete Works,* which includes personal notes, is yet to be published.

Elizabeth's Life and Times

Elizabeth Catez, known in the family as Sabeth, was born on July 18, 1880, in France, the first of two daughters. She was baptized on the feast of Mary Magdalene (July 22), an association that she later recognized as having great symbolic significance, discerning in it that she, like Magdalene, was very greatly loved.[3] She was apparently a lively child, with a passionate and choleric temperament, given, it was reported, to fits of rage. Her governess said that she had an iron will! Her father died when the children were young.

Elizabeth had little by way of formal education at any stage of her life. She was educated at home in her childhood, while pursuing music studies at the Conservatory of Dijon. There was no formal theological training in religious life, though there was much reading of the Scriptures, among which the writings of Paul and John were her favorites, together with the writings of various mystics, particularly Teresa of Avila and John of the Cross but also including Jan van Ruusbroec, Angela of Foligno, Catherine of Siena, and, of course, Thérèse of Lisieux.

Elizabeth enjoyed a fairly normal childhood. She showed an intense devotion to Jesus and a remarkable religious sensibility from a young age, however. As she explained: "I was very fond of prayer, and I loved God so much that, even before my first Communion, I could not understand how it was possible to give one's heart to anyone else. From that time, I was determined to love Him alone and to live only for Him."[4] Her First Communion, when she was ten, was evidently the occasion of extraordinary grace for Elizabeth, and a moment of utmost significance in her spiritual journey. She was moved to tears and, despite the long fast in preparation for reception of the sacrament, after receiving Communion she explained to her friend: "I am no longer hungry; Our Lord has fed me."[5] It was a growing intimacy with Jesus that was to lead her into the mystery of what she described as the Three guests in her soul. A meeting later that same day at the nearby Carmel of Dijon was also highly significant in the discernment of her vocation. The prioress, Mother Marie of Jesus, explained to the young girl that her name, Elizabeth, meant "House of God."

3. See, for example, Letter 121, in *Complete Works* 2. Teresa of Avila too had a special devotion to Mary Magdalene, seeing herself as Magdalene's successor in the Lord's affections. See Teresa of Avila, *Spiritual Testimonies* 28 in *The Collected Works of St. Teresa of Avila*, trans. Kieran Kavanaugh and Otilio Rodriguez, vol. 1 (Washington, DC: ICS Publications, 1976), 400.

4. *Reminiscences of Sister Elizabeth of the Trinity, Servant of God, Discalced Carmelite of Dijon*, trans. A Benedictine of Stanbrook Abbey (Westminster, MD: Newman Press, 1952), 11.

5. Ibid., 4.

From an early age, Elizabeth spent several hours in piano practice each day and demonstrated exceptional musical talent. At thirteen, she won first prize in a piano competition at the Conservatory of Dijon. A report in the local press described her as "already a distinguished pianist, with an excellent touch, beautiful tone, and a real musical feeling."[6] Her spiritual and musical development unfolded in tandem. Music became both an occasion and a form of prayer for her, an entry into a state of profound recollection that came to characterize her. While there was no piano when she eventually entered Carmel, music remained important for her, but it would then be interiorized. Elizabeth herself would become not the musician but the instrument on which the Holy Spirit as master artist plays divine harmonies.

A deep attraction to Carmel emerged as early as age fourteen and she privately consecrated herself to Christ with a vow of virginity. At fifteen, she expressed her desire to enter Carmel to her mother, who refused to give her approval. Elizabeth, her iron will now in control of her once-fiery temper, accepted her mother's ruling as an expression of God's will for her. She resolved to live out her love for God precisely there, in the world. Indeed, in many ways, Elizabeth is a model of holiness for laypeople, living out her vocation in the world for several years and making of her life, with all of its engagements and activities, a continual act of love and conformity to God's will.

During a general mission in the parish, preached by the Redemptorists in Lent 1899, her mother experienced a kind of conversion and consented to Elizabeth's entry to Carmel at twenty-one, still two years hence. Another significant milestone in Elizabeth's spiritual development occurred in the spring of 1900, as she waited to enter Carmel in August 1901. She met Père Gonzalve Vallée, OP, the prior of the Dominicans at Dijon and an esteemed preacher. In this meeting, Père Vallée explained the mystery of the trinitarian indwelling to her, in fact confirming Elizabeth's already profound experience of the Three guests in her soul. Elizabeth came to recognize the import of the religious name to be given to her in Carmel, Elizabeth of the Trinity. (She herself had initially dreamed of taking the name Elizabeth of Jesus.[7]) She wrote: "I love it [her name] so much, it expresses my entire vocation" (L185). After just a few years in Carmel,

---

6. *General Introduction, Major Spiritual Writings*, trans. Elethia Kane, vol. 1 of *Elizabeth of the Trinity: The Complete Works* (Washington, DC: ICS Publications, 1984), 13 (hereafter *Complete Works* 1).

7. Ibid., 16.

her understanding of her vocation culminated in the discernment of her mission and destiny: to be a Praise of Glory, *Laudem Gloriae*.[8] In her spiritual treatise, *Heaven in Faith*, written for her sister in August 1906, a few months before her death, Elizabeth offers a description of what it is to be "a praise of glory," and in doing so intimates the spiritual insights that she had already gleaned:

> A praise of glory is a soul that lives in God, that loves Him with a pure and disinterested love, without seeking itself in the sweetness of this love; that loves Him beyond all His gifts and even though it would not have received anything from Him, it desires the good of the Object thus loved. Now how do we *effectively* desire and will good to God if not in accomplishing His will since this will orders everything for His greater glory? Thus the soul must surrender itself to this will completely, passionately, so as to will nothing else but what God wills.
>
> A praise of glory is a soul of silence that remains like a lyre under the mysterious touch of the Holy Spirit[9] so that He may draw from it divine harmonies; it knows that suffering is a string that produces still more beautiful sounds; so it loves to see this string on its instrument that it may more delightfully move the Heart of its God.
>
> A praise of glory is a soul that gazes on God in faith and simplicity; it is a reflector of all that He is; it is like a bottomless abyss[10] into which He can flow and expand; it is also like a crystal through which He can radiate and contemplate all His perfections and His own splendor. A soul which thus permits the divine Being to satisfy in itself His need to communicate "all that He is and all that He has," is in reality the praise of glory of all His gifts.

8. Elizabeth makes a grammatical error here. It is the nominative, not the accusative, that should be used, i.e., *Laus Gloriae*. My thanks to Sr. Jocelyn Kramer, OCD, of Carmel at Varroville, NSW, for her advice, for the benefit of those who might see a connection with the OCD vows made at profession that currently conclude with the words, "and to give eternal glory to the most holy Trinity," that this is a post–Vatican II development.

9. The image of the soul as a lyre on which the Holy Spirit plays is very dear to Elizabeth. It is not entirely clear from where she draws inspiration here, although Anne Englund Nash, translator of *Letters from Carmel*, points to Thérèse of Lisieux as the source. Thérèse uses the image several times, and Elizabeth had in her breviary a picture of Thérèse with a small harp in her hand. (See *Complete Works* 2, 266 n. 12.) St. Ephrem the Syrian, Doctor of the Church, poet, and musician, who lived in the fourth century, is renowned in the Christian tradition as "the lyre of the Holy Spirit."

10. Abyss is a favorite image for Elizabeth, as it also is for Jan van Ruusbroec, Catherine of Siena, John of the Cross, Angela of Foligno, and Thérèse of Lisieux. See *Complete Works* 2, 296 n. 2. It is, of course, redolent of Ps 42:7.

Finally, a praise of glory is one who is always giving thanks. Each of her acts, her movements, her thoughts, her aspirations, at the same time that they are rooting her more deeply in love, are like an echo of the eternal Sanctus.[11]

A questionnaire completed soon after her entry to Carmel is also illuminating: Elizabeth wrote that her ideal of sanctity was "To live by love," that her motto was "God in me and I in Him," and that her chief characteristic was "Sensitiveness."[12]

Elizabeth lived only five years in Carmel before succumbing to the then incurable Addison's disease, a disorder of the adrenal glands inhibiting the normal processes of metabolism. By October 1906, Elizabeth's illness was acute. Her stomach was intolerant of food and even water. She died in November 1906.

Elizabeth's Writings

We have only a few short spiritual treatises by Elizabeth, *Heaven in Faith*, *The Greatness of Our Vocation*, *Last Retreat*, and *Let Yourself Be Loved*, all of them written in French in the last months before her death.[13] She was, however, a prolific letter writer and more than three hundred of her letters survive, many of them written to laypeople experiencing the typical struggles and sorrows of life, to whom she writes with no other concern than to offer counsel, consolation, and encouragement.[14] Written with warmth and tenderness, spontaneity and simplicity, her letters are particularly revealing of her spiritual journey and insight.

Elizabeth's Insights into the Mystery of the Indwelling Trinity

Long before she entered Carmel, and especially after her meeting with Père Vallée, Elizabeth was deeply attuned to the mystery of the indwelling Trinity. In a letter in 1901, a few months before her entry, she wrote: "I so love the Trinity; it is an abyss in which I lose myself" (L62).

Not long after her profession in January 1903, she exhorted a friend: "Let us make a solitary place for Him in the innermost part of our soul and remain there with Him; let us never leave Him, for it is His command-

---

11. *Heaven in Faith*, §43, in *Complete Works* 1, 112.
12. *Reminiscences*, 53.
13. For the set, see *Complete Works* 1.
14. See *Complete Works* 2.

ment: 'Remain in me, and I in you' [John 15:4]. Nothing will be able to rob us of this interior cell, no matter what trials we undergo: I carry my One Treasure 'inside me,' and all the rest is nothing!" (L160). To another friend, she explained: "What happiness it is to live in intimacy with God, to make our life a heart-to-heart, an exchange of love, when we know how to find the Master in the depths of our soul. Then we are never alone anymore, and need solitude to enjoy the presence of this adored Guest. . . . Oh! If you knew how good he is, how he is all Love!" (L161).[15] This indeed, she realized, was the foretaste of Heaven, Heaven within us, Heaven on earth. "It seems to me that I have found my Heaven on earth, since Heaven is God and God is [in] my soul. The day I understood that, everything became clear to me. I would like to whisper this secret to those I love so they too might always cling to God through everything, and so this prayer of Christ might be fulfilled: 'Father, may they be made perfectly one!'" (L122).

Elizabeth loved the image, also dear to Teresa of Avila, of the soul as "like a crystal in which the Trinity is reflected" (L136). As she explained to Canon Angles: "The Trinity so loves to contemplate its beauty in a soul; this draws it to give itself even more, to come with greater fullness so as to bring about the great mystery of love and unity!" (L131). A few months later, in another letter to Canon Angles, she explained: "I feel so much love over my soul, it is like an Ocean I immerse and lose myself in: it is my vision on earth while waiting for the face-to-face vision in light. He [God] is in me, I am in Him. I only have to love Him, to let myself be loved, all the time, through all things: to wake in Love, to move in Love, to sleep in Love, my soul in His Soul, my heart in His Heart, my eyes in His eyes, so that through His contact He may purify me, free me from my misery" (L177).[16]

Her letters attest to an ever keener and deeper awareness of the trinitarian indwelling, an indwelling presence that, she insisted, is offered to every believer. In 1905, to Madame Angles she explained: "*He* is always there [in the depths of your heart]. . . . He is waiting for you and wants to establish a 'wonderful communion' with you" (L249). Just a few months before her death she wrote:

---

15. Elizabeth often uses the expression "heart-to-heart" to indicate the intimacy of one's relationship to God. For example, she speaks of "that intimate heart-to-heart in which the soul flows into God and God flows into it to transform it into Himself" (L278).

16. The image of God as an ocean is redolent of Thérèse who spoke of it at the time of her First Communion. See L110 n. 3.

> I leave you my devotion for the Three, to "Love." Live within with Them in the heaven of your soul; the Father will overshadow you, placing something like a cloud between you and the things of this earth to keep you all His, He will communicate His power to you so you can love Him with a love as strong as death; the Word will imprint in your soul, as in a crystal, the image of His own beauty, so you may be pure with His purity, luminous with His light; the Holy Spirit will transform you into a mysterious lyre, which, in silence, beneath His divine touch, will produce a magnificent canticle to Love. (L269)

Toward the end of her life, she reflected: "It is this intimacy with Him [the divine Three] 'within' that has been the beautiful sun illuminating my life, making it already an anticipated Heaven" (L333).

Heaven, for Elizabeth, is total immersion, in silence and stillness, in the ocean of life and love of the Trinity. It is to contemplate unveiled this Trinity that here on earth has already been her dwelling place, and she its dwelling place. It is fellowship, an endless heart-to-heart dialogue, an eternal face-to-face with the Trinity, the Blessed Three. It is the radiant vision of divine beauty and glory. It is to be enveloped and consumed in that dazzling light, that furnace of love, that infinite abyss of love, "that infinity for which our souls so thirst" (L158). It is Light, Love, and Life.[17]

Elizabeth's profound sense of the divine indwelling was nurtured and sustained by prayer, silence, and recollection. "Always love prayer," she urged a friend, "and when I say prayer, I don't mean so much imposing on yourself a lot of vocal prayers to be recited every day as that elevation of the soul toward God through all things that establishes us in a kind of continual communion with the Holy Trinity by quite simply doing everything in Their presence" (L252). Prayer, she explained, "is a rest, a relaxation. We come quite simply to Him we love; we keep close to Him like a little child in its mother's arms, and let our hearts go out to Him."[18] "My only exercise," she described with utter simplicity, "is to enter within once again, to lose myself in Those who are there" (L179).

The prayer for which Elizabeth is renowned was found among her papers after her death and bears rich testimony to her insights into the trinitarian indwelling:

---

17. Elizabeth's last intelligible words: "I am going to Light, to Love, to Life." See Conrad de Meester, ed., *Light, Love, Life: A Look at a Face and a Heart (Elizabeth of the Trinity)* (Washington, DC: ICS Publications, 1987), 139; see also L313 and *Complete Works* 2, 260.

18. *Reminiscences*, 54.

O my God, Trinity whom I adore; help me to forget myself entirely that I may be established in You as still and as peaceful as if my soul were already in eternity. May nothing trouble my peace or make me leave You, O my Unchanging One, but may each minute carry me further into the depths of Your Mystery. Give peace to my soul; make it Your heaven, Your beloved dwelling and Your resting place. May I never leave You there alone but be wholly present, my faith wholly vigilant, wholly adoring, and wholly surrendered to Your creative Action.

O my beloved Christ, crucified by love, I wish to be a bride for Your Heart; I wish to cover You with glory; I wish to love You . . . even unto death! But I feel my weakness, and I ask You to "clothe me with Yourself," to identify my soul with all the movements of Your Soul, to overwhelm me, to possess me, to substitute Yourself for me that my life may be but a radiance of Your Life. Come into me as Adorer, as Restorer, as Savior.

O Eternal Word, Word of my God, I want to spend my life in listening to You, to become wholly teachable that I may learn all from You. Then, through all nights, all voids, all helplessness, I want to gaze on You always and remain in Your great light. O my beloved Star, so fascinate me that I may not withdraw from Your radiance.

O consuming Fire, Spirit of Love, "come upon me," and create in my soul a kind of incarnation of the Word: that I may be another humanity for Him in which He can renew His whole Mystery. And You, O Father, bend lovingly over Your poor little creature; "cover her with Your shadow," seeing in her only the "Beloved in whom You are well pleased."

O my Three, my All, my Beatitude, infinite Solitude, Immensity in which I lose myself, I surrender myself to You as Your prey. Bury Yourself in me that I may bury myself in You until I depart to contemplate in Your light the abyss of Your greatness.[19]

While an intense devotion to Jesus had developed in Elizabeth's early childhood, her sister Guite's marriage in 1902 seems to have prompted Elizabeth to reflect on what it is to be a bride of Christ. Of her bridegroom, she writes: "I have such hunger for Him. He hollows out abysses in my soul, abysses He alone can fill, and to do that, He leads me into deep silence that I never want to leave again" (L190). A growing intimacy with her beloved Spouse also coincided with a conscious conformation to the image of Christ. As she explained: "we will be glorified in the measure that we

19. See *Complete Works* 1, 185 n. 2.

are conformed to the image of His divine Son."[20] Frequently, she returns to St. Paul's words: "For those whom he foreknew he also predestined to be conformed to the image of his Son" (Rom 8:29) and "It is no longer I who live, but it is Christ who lives in me" (Gal 2:20).

The mystery of the incarnation especially fascinated her. She reflected on the action of the Trinity in the annunciation, and on the attitude and role of Mary in her *fiat* and throughout the pregnancy as she carried the Christ Child within her. Elizabeth went on to contemplate a kind of incarnation that takes place in *each and every* believer. A poem written at Christmas 1902, while she was still a novice awaiting her profession, captures her sense of this mystery:

> I saw the star that showed me by its light
> The cradle where my baby King would be:
> Then, in that calm—that mystery—of night,
> It was as though the star turned round at me:
> I heard an Angel's voice, then (how
> It charmed me!) saying "Comprehend
> This—it is in your soul that now
> The mystery achieves its end;
> God's Son, His Splendour fair,
> Incarnate now, this morn
> In you. With Mary there
> Embrace God, newly-born—
> For . . . yours he is!"[21]

The birth of Guite's first child prompted Elizabeth again to ponder the mystery of the incarnation. In a letter to her aunts at Christmastime, she wrote: "I spent my whole vigil with the Blessed Virgin awaiting the divine Little One, who this time was going to be born no longer in the crib, but in my soul, in our souls, for He is truly Emmanuel, 'God with us'" (L187). To another of her spiritual confidants, Abbé Chevignard, she spoke of the same mystery: "Let us be for Him [Christ], in a way, another humanity in which He may renew His whole Mystery." (L214).[22]

---

20. *Heaven in Faith*, §27, *Complete Works* 1, 105.

21. Poem 86, see *Barb of Fire: Twenty Poems of Blessed Elizabeth of the Trinity*, trans. Alan Bancroft (Leominster Herefordshire: Gracewing, 1991), 58. See also Poem 91 in *Barb of Fire*, 116–17.

22. Here, in the words, "another humanity in which He may renew His whole Mystery," Elizabeth echoes the words of her famous prayer, "O my God, Trinity whom I adore, my Three," written just a few days earlier, in November 1904.

She realized ever more clearly that being conformed to the image of Christ meant conformity to Christ in his *paschal mystery*. Just a few weeks before her death, she wrote to a Carmelite sister: "Before I die, I dream of being transformed into Jesus Crucified, and that gives me so much strength in suffering. . . . [W]e should have no other ideal but to be conformed to that divine Model" (L324). Love of her adored Spouse, the One crucified by love, led necessarily to conformity to him in suffering. But this was by no means suffering for suffering's sake: "I cannot say I love suffering in itself, but I love it because it conforms me to Him who is my Bridegroom and my Love" (L317). As she explained in another letter: "Never have I understood so well that suffering is the greatest pledge of love that God can give His creatures, and I did not suspect that just such sweetness was hidden at the bottom of the chalice for the one who drank it to the dregs" (L313).[23]

As death approached, she wrote to one of her Carmelite sisters: "Death entails a great deal of suffering" (L335). But, despite the fear and anguish, her suffering was also a source of joy and sweetness. As her suffering increased, her joy increased, for she was then conformed ever more closely to her Beloved, Jesus crucified. As she explained to a friend: "I do not forget you, I assure you, on my cross where I taste unknown joys. I understand that suffering is the revelation of Love, and I rush to it: it is my beloved dwelling place where I find peace and rest, where I am sure to meet my Master and dwell with Him" (L323). Such was reflected in the manner of her passing from this life to the next, as her beloved prioress, Mother Germaine of Jesus, described her dying: "Sister Elizabeth of the Trinity seemed in ecstasy rather than in her death agony. The expression on her face was wonderfully beautiful, so that we could not take our eyes off her as she seemed already gazing at the eternal hills."[24]

Elizabeth's entry into the mystery of the indwelling Trinity led her to a vivid sense of her apostolic mission, a mission by no means at odds with her contemplative calling. Her letters witness to her ongoing concern for the world, albeit in the silence, stillness, and seclusion of Carmel. Her

23. Scholars have long noted the extraordinary place of a theology of vicarious suffering, particularly its feminized form, in modern French Catholicism. For a recent discussion, see Brenna Moore, "Feminized Suffering in Modern French Catholicism: Raïssa Maritain (1883–1960) and Léon Bloy (1846–1917)," *Spiritus* 9, no. 1 (2009): 46–68. See also Richard Burton, *Holy Tears, Holy Blood: Women, Catholicism, and the Culture of Suffering in France, 1840–1970* (Ithaca, NY: Cornell University Press, 2004). For Elizabeth, though, suffering was primarily for the sake of being conformed to Christ.

24. *Reminiscences*, 165.

entry into the depths of the interior abyss, she writes, echoing the Flemish mystic Jan van Ruusbroec, "is not 'an external separation from external things,' but a 'solitude of spirit,' a detachment from all that is not God."[25] Just days before her approaching death, she explained: "I think that in Heaven my mission will be to draw souls by helping them go out of themselves to cling to God by a wholly simple and loving movement, and to keep them in this great silence within that will allow God to communicate Himself to them and transform them into Himself" (L335).

Elizabeth's abiding sense of the trinitarian indwelling also led her to a profound sense of the communion of saints, for she recognized that the mystery of the communion of saints was grounded in the trinitarian indwelling. To a young missionary priest, she explained: "Do you not find that, for souls, there is no distance or separation? This is really the fulfillment of Christ's prayer: 'Father, may they be made perfectly one' [John 17:23]. It seems to me that the souls on earth and those glorified in the light of vision are so close to each other, since they are all in communion with the same God, the same Father, who gives Himself to the former in faith and mystery and satisfies the others in His divine light" (L124). To Mother Germaine, in a letter of farewell, *Let Yourself Be Loved*, Elizabeth writes: "If you will allow her, your little host will spend her Heaven in the depths of your soul: she will keep you in communion with Love, believing in Love; it will be the sign of her dwelling in you. Oh, in what intimacy we are going to live. . . . I will come to live in you."[26] Elizabeth would have us understand that the trinitarian indwelling is the source and indeed the promise of our union in separation, even in the separation of death.

Elizabeth had no doubt that the graces that she had received were available to all: "This better part, which seems to be my privilege in my beloved solitude of Carmel, is offered by God to every baptized soul" (L129). She also recognized that, in heaven, *all* will live as "praises of glory" of the Holy Trinity, as all are predestined to be configured to Christ who is the perfect praise of glory. "'In Heaven' each soul is a praise of glory of the Father, the Word, and the Holy Spirit . . . 'its intellect is the intellect of God, its will the will of God, its love the very love of God.'"[27]

Elizabeth's mysticism, so deeply trinitarian and paschal, was also profoundly eucharistic. As she explained of a praise of glory: "a praise of glory is one who is always giving thanks. Each of her acts, her movements,

25. *Heaven in Faith*, §7, *Complete Works* 1, 96.
26. *Let Yourself Be Loved*, §4, *Complete Works* 1, 180.
27. *Heaven in Faith*, §42, *Complete Works* 1, 111.

her thoughts, her aspirations, at the same time that they are rooting her more deeply in love, are like an echo of the eternal Sanctus."[28]

Admittedly, the ecclesial dimension of Elizabeth's thought is less clearly articulated than the trinitarian, christological, paschal, and eucharistic dimensions. Hans Urs von Balthasar notes, for example, that in her famous prayer, "O my God, Trinity whom I adore," Elizabeth speaks in terms of "I" or "mine" forty-three times and makes no mention at all of the church.[29] Here Elizabeth reflects the impoverished ecclesiology and pneumatology of the post-Reformation theology of her time that relegated the indwelling of the Holy Spirit to the realm of private—as distinct from the ecclesial—domain and left ecclesiology bereft of its pneumatological and trinitarian moorings.[30] But there is really no doubting the reality—albeit not the explicit articulation—of Elizabeth's ecclesial mission, either as she understood it or as it is now appreciated in the wider domain of the church. She writes, for example to her missionary priest friend: "My soul loves to unite with yours in one single prayer for the church, for the diocese. . . . [I]nasmuch as we have an abundance of divine life, we can communicate it in the great body of the Church" (L191). The understatedness of these admittedly modest ecclesial references is understandable from the perspective of the fundamentally Marian character of her sense of vocation. Elizabeth recognized Mary as "the great praise of glory of the Holy Trinity."[31] Elizabeth explained: "I would like [to live] on earth as the Blessed Virgin did, 'keeping all these things in my heart,' burying myself, so to speak, in the depths of my soul to lose myself in the Trinity who dwells in it in order to transform me into itself" (L185).

Conclusion

Hans Urs von Balthasar, undoubtedly one of the giants of twentieth-century theology, whom Henri de Lubac described as "perhaps the most cultivated of his time,"[32] played a very significant role in drawing recognition

28. Ibid., 112.

29. Hans Urs von Balthasar, *Elizabeth of Dijon and Her Spiritual Mission: An Exposition of the Teaching of the French Carmelite Mystic*, trans. A. V. Littledale (New York: Pantheon, 1956), 19. Von Balthasar also suggests that the prayer is not so much a prayer of adoration as a petition for the power to adore.

30. See Yves Congar, *I Believe in the Holy Spirit*, trans. David Smith, vol. 1 (New York: Seabury, 1983; London: Geoffrey Chapman, 1983), 151–64.

31. *Last Retreat*, §40, *Complete Works* 1, 160.

32. Henri de Lubac, "A Witness of Christ in the Church: Hans Urs von Balthasar," in *The Church: Paradox and Mystery*, trans. James R. Dunne (Shannon: Ecclesia Press, 1969), 105.

to Elizabeth's insights. In a strong defense of the originality of her insights and their doctrinal caliber, he writes:

> It might be urged that she had nothing really original to say, so closely were her views related to those of previous writers. Such an objection is not conclusive. However dependent on others, her own thought has its unique characteristic resonance. Its originality lies in the combination of a loftiness of conception with a sparseness, an asceticism of treatment, and this latter is due not to any narrowness of mind, but to her intense concentration on the end in view. This results in a work of very high rank, both spiritually and theologically, an organic and vital growth from a single germinating idea. It pulsates with a vigour and confidence which are not to be found in any of her predecessors, in spite of their eminence as theologians. Admittedly, it is narrow in range, but this makes for a magnificent simplicity and concentration of force. The "one thing necessary"[33] is held steadily in view, until we are convinced that this is all that matters, the treasure for the sake of which all else is to be left. Her subject-matter she may have drawn from Père Vallée . . . but her treatment is unique. It points to the reality of her true, underived doctrinal mission.[34]

Von Balthasar's assessment stands to challenge those who might suggest that Elizabeth has nothing fresh or innovative to offer to the Christian tradition and its understanding of the divine indwelling. In regard to his comment on her subject matter, however, one must take issue. Elizabeth's primary subject matter—the mystery of the indwelling of the Three—is in fact demonstrably Elizabeth's own, a remarkable grace evidently granted to her in her childhood, long before her encounter with Père Vallée, indeed possibly long before her encounter with John of the Cross, Teresa of Avila, Thérèse of Lisieux, and the other saints and mystics whose writings she so loved. Her source was her own intense experience of being drawn ever deeper into the immense abyss of God, in solitude and silent recollection. By no means the source of her subject matter, Père Vallée merely confirmed and encouraged what was already a profound consciousness and a lived reality for Elizabeth. One can agree with von Balthasar, however, to the degree that Père Vallée provided Elizabeth with a *style of expression* of the mystery, as Conrad de Meester suggests.[35]

---

33. See Elizabeth's Poem 83, where she writes of the Carmelite: "She has found the One Thing Necessary" (Conrad de Meester, *Light, Love, Life*, 87).

34. Hans Urs von Balthasar, *Elizabeth of Dijon*, 14–15.

35. See Conrad de Meester, *Élisabeth de la Trinité*, 499ff., also 597ff.

At the core of Elizabeth's witness is the experience of the transcendent mystery of love and awe, drawing her to desire to be, for all eternity, a *Laudem Gloriae* to the Blessed Trinity. Her insight into the mystery of the trinitarian indwelling is truly extraordinary. Utterly focused on this mystery of the trinitarian indwelling that so captivates her, she writes with an assured and impeccable theological orthodoxy. The doctrinal caliber of her insights is all the more remarkable for one so young and theologically untutored. Admittedly, the immediacy of Elizabeth's experience of God is clearly communicated in her letters to her many correspondents and in her spiritual writings was not to—and indeed could not—find theoretical or systematic expression in her hands. But, for Elizabeth, experience, expression, and reflection came together in the singular integrity of her vocation to witness to the mystical center of all Christian life, the mystery offered to each and every Christian. She is rightly applauded as an apostle of the Trinity lovingly dwelling in every heart.

References and Further Reading

Primary Sources

Elizabeth of the Trinity: The Complete Works. Vol. 1. *General Introduction, Major Spiritual Writings.* Translated by Elethia Kane. Washington, DC: ICS Publications, 1984.
Elizabeth of the Trinity: The Complete Works. Vol. 2. *Letters from Carmel.* Translated by Anne Englund Nash. Washington, DC: ICS Publications, 1995.
Reminiscences of Sister Elizabeth of the Trinity, Servant of God, Discalced Carmelite of Dijon. Translated by A Benedictine of Stanbrook Abbey. Westminster, MD: Newman Press, 1952.
Barb of Fire: Twenty Poems of Blessed Elizabeth of the Trinity. Translated by Alan Bancroft. Leominster Herefordshire: Gracewing, 1991.

Secondary Sources

Balthasar, Hans Urs von. *Elizabeth of Dijon and Her Spiritual Mission: An Exposition of the Teaching of the French Carmelite Mystic.* Translated by A.V. Littledale. New York: Pantheon, 1956.
Meester, Conrad de, ed. *Light, Love, Life: A Look at a Face and a Heart (Elizabeth of the Trinity).* Washington, DC: ICS Publications, 1987.
———. *Élisabeth de la Trinité: Biographie.* Paris: Presses de la Renaissance, 2006.

CONCLUSION

Looking back over our studies, what first strikes us is that our mystics show considerable variation in their respective insights into the mystery of the Trinity. Indeed, they offer a rich tapestry of perspectives on the mystery. While the architecture of their thought is thoroughly and profoundly trinitarian, they first demonstrate that there is no one form of trinitarian mysticism. They speak of different experiences giving rise to their insights and images: in some cases there are visions while for others it is a matter of mystical encounters of other kinds. We, of course, have no direct access to their actual experiences, only to their writings and, for Hildegard, to her illuminations. Their educational background and their previous spiritual reading are clearly influential in their articulation of their experiences and insights. Their mystical writings include a plentiful array of metaphors and linguistic devices to express God's unutterable mystery. For example, the immense love of God to which all attest is variously expressed in nuptial imagery, the relationship of friendship, and the familiar familial communications of hearth and home. Other images abound: the silkworm, entry into a castle, light, flame, and fountain. It is not surprising that this rich kaleidoscope of images promises no easy synthesis, although their insights are complementary and, with very few exceptions, thoroughly orthodox. Any generalization must, therefore, be somewhat tentative.

The mystics do not offer abstract theological insights, but accounts of intensely personal mystical experiences, more poetic than systematic in expression. We find no great investment of effort in trinitarian analogies or in theological expositions of the mystery. There is no wrestling with an explanation of the mystery of the three-in-oneness of God. Certainly, at times, there is a concern to refute errors, such as occurs in William of St. Thierry's refutation of the errors of Peter of Abelard or in Bonaventure's *Disputed Questions*. But their aim is not primarily teaching *about* the Trinity per se, but rather an urging to enter more deeply into the mystery and thus to be ever more closely conformed to it and transformed by it. As for the gospels, these mystical meanings are revealed to you, the reader of the mystical texts, that you might believe and, in believing, enter into this mystery of salvation.

These mystical writings are thus quite unlike the classical trinitarian expositions of Augustine and Thomas Aquinas in their orderly treatment of the mystery of the Tri-unity of God, while dealing with such questions as how to distinguish the procession of the Holy Spirit from that of the Son. Similarly, except in their scholarly treatises written for the academy, the mystics show no great concern for the technical language of trinitarian theology. We find no concerns in regard to the word "person," for example. In other words, the mystics' focus is not on a systematic exploration of the mystery per se.

For the mystics, the mystery of the Trinity stands as the *datum* of faith, so to speak, intimated in the Scriptures, worshiped and adored in prayer and liturgy, defined in creeds and statements of church doctrine, and explicated in such classic explorations as that of Augustine. Indeed, what shines forth from the mystical consciousness that unfolds in and through those profound mystical encounters is an abiding sense of the *donum* of the mystery, the sheer gift that is this intensely personal encounter with the three-personed God. While they write according to different styles of theology, and cast somewhat different lights on the mystery, all of them are captivated by the encounter—be the metaphor one of *ascent* or *descent*—of the soul with God and entry into union with God. For none of them is this discourse a merely speculative investigation or explication of the mystery; it is rather a discourse about their deeply personal, intimate, and ongoing engagement with these Three. Perhaps Hans Urs von Balthasar best described it when he spoke in terms of a *kneeling* theology, as distinct from a *sitting* theology.[1]

The trinitarian image and likeness in the human person is a very strong motif in their thinking, another *datum* of faith. For most, there is a strong sense of the trinitarian image, imprinted, indelibly, from the moment of creation in the human person. The psychological image of the human person in terms of the operations or faculties of memory, intellect, and will pervades their thought, a testament to its usefulness and to Augustine's genius in applying the psychological analogy to the mystery of the Trinity. But that psychological analogy would count for little were it not for the consciousness that is ignited through direct encounter with God, an encounter that throws

---

1. Peter Henrici, "Hans Urs von Balthasar: A Sketch of his Life," *Communio* 16 (1989): 329.

into sharp relief the trinitarian nature of both human and divine being. It is as if, in that most intense and radiant state of union of the blessed soul with God to which the mystics so powerfully attest, the trinitarian constitution of both God and the human person, both divine and human being, is intensified, heightened, thrown into unmistakable relief.

For many, Meister Eckhart being a notable exception here, there is a keen consciousness of the trinitarian indwelling. What comes to the fore in all of their descriptions of the soul's state of union with God is a lively sense of the Three and the soul's relationship to each of the Three, conversing with them, communicating with them (for example, William of St. Thierry and Teresa of Avila). Entry into union with God, according to the mystics, is an entry into the very midst of the Three, an entry into the trinitarian relations, and an entry into the divine knowing and loving. Indeed, for John of the Cross it is an entry into the breath-like triune spiration of love that is the Trinity. In that state of sublime union, the blessed soul knows the Trinity not from the outside, so to speak, but from within it. In that state of mystical union with God, the mystic speaks not *about* the Trinity as some object of knowledge, but from *within* the mystery. This union of the soul with God effects a profound transformation of the human person, a new consciousness of God, of self, and of everything else, and a new way of knowing and loving. Now, as John of the Cross in particular captures so clearly, the blessed soul knows and loves all that is in creation from within the mystery.

The mystics show notable variation in their understanding as to how that entry into union with the Trinity takes place. For some, there is a keen sense of the role of the Holy Spirit in effecting the union, as in William of St. Thierry, Hildegard, Teresa of Avila, and John of the Cross. But for Eckhart, for example, entry is via the Son, indeed it is grounded in the birth of the Son in the soul. For Bonaventure, the second person as Word, center of the Trinity, also stands at the center, though in a very different way. For some, then, there is a greater focus on the Holy Spirit in this process of entry into union; for others, it is on Christ as point or avenue of entry into the mystery. For all of them, the Father remains as the source, the font.

All are thoroughly orthodox, with the possible exception of Meister Eckhart at that point when he strains to express the ultimate mystery of union, of oneness, expressed in that groundless ground, that is the *grunt*, and with it the daring notion of God beyond God and a union of indistinction. Fairer, I suggest, to give the Meister the benefit of the doubt, for he, more than most, was keenly aware of the radical inadequacy of all of our language about God. It is interesting to note that, while the mystics are not particularly averse to considerations of God *ad intra*, the immanent Trinity, the very distinction between God *ad extra* and God *ad intra* would seem to be of little relevance for the soul in mystical union with God. None seems concerned by the blurring of the distinction between the immanent and economic Trinity, the action of the Trinity *ad intra* and *ad extra*. Indeed, the mystics would seem to suggest that the distinction breaks down, dissolves, or is simply redundant in that state of union wherein the soul perceives things from within the Trinity, so to speak, not from without. Similarly, in contrast to the classical understanding of the strategy of appropriation, the mystics strain to express much more than mere appropriation of roles and traits, which is not so surprising given their vivid consciousness of the Three in their distinction. Through it all, there is, however, an unwavering sense of the unity of the Godhead.

Perhaps somewhat paradoxically, given the mystical heights to which they soar, the mystics generally share a strong soteriological focus. They want us to know, to understand, to follow them, to take up the invitation to entry into the mystery of the Trinity. It is not a matter, however, of understanding for understanding's sake, but for love's sake: it is to know, to recognize, to love, to converse, to accompany, to worship, and to invoke the Three. The reason for the incarnation, as it emerges, for example, in Hildegard, is for the sake of revelation of this immense love. The passion and death of Jesus, as Julian of Norwich saw so clearly in her first and programmatic showing, is not primarily for reparation of sin but revelation of love. For Meister Eckhart, it is for the sake of the birth of the Son in the soul, that we be this same Son and, as son, enter into relationship with the Father. What they would all have us understand, above all else, is the Trinity as mystery of love, the innertrinitarian love of the Three for each other, and their distinctly threefold love for us and for all creation. It is a three-personed love that seeks out the human person and invites each and every one into conversation and communion.

Some Methodological Reflections

We began our exploration with challenges posed by Karl Rahner, SJ, who spoke in terms of "how religious experiences of a spiritual or mystical kind can overflow and be transposed into the idiom of theological reflection,"[2] and issues raised by Michael J. Buckley, SJ, who highlighted

---

2. Karl Rahner, *Experience of the Spirit, Source of Theology*, trans. David Morland, *Theological Investigations*, vol. 16 (New York: Crossroad/Seabury Press, 1979), 72 n.12.

the lacuna "that theology neither has nor has striven to forge the intellectual devices to probe in these concrete experiences the warrant they present for the reality of God and make them available for so universal a discipline?"[3] Here is the challenge for those of us disposed to learn from them: to find in the consciousness and insights of the mystics a *locus theologicus*, a source and a resource for theological reflection on the mysteries of Christian faith.

Bernard Lonergan's methodological insights offer some assistance, first, in highlighting the range of realms of meaning, each with its own language and categories and distinct mode of apprehension, from which the mystics speak about the mystery of the Trinity—the realm of common sense, the realm of theory, the realm of interiority, and the realm of transcendence; second, in terms of the different functions of meaning that are variously served, be it the cognitive, the constitutive, the communicative and the effective; and third, in terms of the different differentiations of consciousness the mystics bring to their writings, most particularly the affective-symbolic and the cognitive.[4]

Lonergan's reflections on the transcendental imperatives, which culminate in the state of "being in love with God,"[5] accord closely with the mystics' own accounts of their experience. For example, Elizabeth of the Trinity herself described it: "I live in love, I am immersed in it, I am lost in it" (L107). For her and for our other mystics, this state of being in love with God is a state of being in love in an unrestricted fashion, without limits or qualifications, without conditions or reservations. The mystics epitomize what Lonergan describes when he writes of that state of "being in love with God": "Though not the product of our knowing and choosing, it is a conscious dynamic stage of love, joy, peace, that manifests itself in acts of kindness, goodness, fidelity, gentleness, and self-control (Gal 5:22)."[6] These indeed are the virtues to which their contemporaries attested. Recall, for example, the accounts of those close to them of the virtues of John of the Cross, Teresa of Avila, and Elizabeth of the Trinity. In this, the mystics provide a warrant for Lonergan!

Lonergan elaborates further on this state of being in love with God: "Because the dynamic state is conscious without being known, it is an

---

3. Michael J. Buckley, Presidential Address, *The Catholic Theological Society of America Proceedings* 47 (1992): 77.

4. Bernard Lonergan, *Method in Theology* (New York: Seabury, 1972), 271–76, 302–5.

5. Ibid., esp. 101–24.

6. Ibid., 106.

experience of mystery. Because it is being in love, the mystery is not merely attractive but fascinating; to it one belongs; by it one is possessed. Because it is an unmeasured love, the mystery evokes awe. Of itself, then, inasmuch as it is conscious without being known, the gift of God's love is an experience of the holy, of Rudolf Otto's *mysterium fascinans et tremendum*."[7] Classical theology would describe the experience in terms of "the state of sanctifying grace." It is that state that, as Lonergan explains, is characterized by "the easy freedom of those that do all good because they are in love."[8] In other words, it is that graced state in which one is motivated to do good, not from a desire for goodness or virtue, but purely and simply out of love, because of one's being-in-love. Such too is manifest in the lives of the mystics.

One of the challenges that the mystics pose to theology is the rich and diverse array of metaphors and linguistic devices that they employ to express the inexpressible mystery of God that has so captivated them. They offer essentially poetic metaphorical discourse rather than literal accounts of experience or theoretical systematic discourse about the mystery. As such, they demand a different kind of reading and probing, a kind of *lectio divina*, rather than a linear analysis. For many of them, the notion of the spiritual senses provides an apt means by which to express what we could describe as the "saturated phenomenon" that is their encounter with the divine mystery and which, by its very nature, simply defies description. Their writings strain to express the experience of a supersaturation of the senses, a quickening and delight to overfilling of the senses, which is also promised to the reader who yields to the invitation. Once again, Meister Eckhart stands as an exception, showing little if any interest in the language of the spiritual senses, or indeed in the language of the trinitarian indwelling.

These then are the rich seams of data for systematic theology that the mystics offer to us. It remains a challenge for theologians disposed to learn from them, and most especially, perhaps, given today's burgeoning interest in spirituality and indeed its interfaith dimensions.

7. Ibid.
8. Ibid., 107.

Index of Names

Abelard, Peter, 4, 5, 7, 8, 9, 13, 15, 16, 19, 182
Ahlgren, Gillian T. W., 123n4, 128n14
Alan of Lille, 48n2
Albert the Great, 76
Alexander of Hales, 51
Anderson, John, 2n4
Angela of Foligno, 169, 171n10
Anselm of Canterbury, viiin2, 5, 50, 56, 115
Anthony of Padua, 8, 129
Augustine of Hippo, vii, xii, 3, 6, 6n10, 7, 9, 15, 18, 19, 21, 31, 56, 57, 61, 62, 63, 65, 69, 70, 71, 79, 80, 84, 94, 111, 113, 114, 115, 125, 126n10, 129, 140, 149, 183

Balthasar, Hans Urs von, 88, 179, 180, 181, 183
Bell, David N., 4n7, 6n10, 6n22
Bernard of Clairvaux, x, 1, 2, 3, 4, 5, 6, 7, 8, 28, 36, 37, 49, 129, 149
Boethius, 21n20
Bonaventure, x, 8, 48ff., 80, 84, 97, 182, 184
Brooke, Odo, 2, 6, 14, 15n12, 22
Buckley, Michael J., ix, 185, 186
Burke, Greg, 124n6
Burton, Richard 177n23
Bynum, Caroline Walker, 115n17, 117n19

Camille, Michael, xiiin8

Catherine of Siena, 128, 129, 169, 172n10
Chaucer, Geoffrey, 99
Clissold, Stephen, 143
Collings, Ross, 167
Congar, Yves, 179n30
Council, Fourth Lateran (1215), xii, 61n19, 100
Council, of Constantinople (381), 43
Council, of Ferrara-Florence (1138–45), xii
Council, of Trent (1545–63), 122, 123, 128n16
Council, of Vienne (1311–12), 76n10
Council, Second Lateran (1139), 31
Council, Second of Lyons (1274), xii, 49, 53, 55
Cullen, Christopher

Day, Dorothy, 98
Déchanet, J. M., 6n10
Delesalle, Jacques, 17n14
Delio, Ilia, 71
Dermot O'Donoghue, Noel, 143
Derolez, Albert, 34n23
Dicken, E. W. Trueman, 143

Eliot, T.S., 98
Elizabeth of the Trinity, x, 168ff, 186
Emperor Frederick I (Barbarossa), 25
Ephrem the Syrian, 171n9

Flanagan, Sabina, 26n9, 29n13, 47
Francis de Sales, 8

Francis of Assisi, 49n6, 50, 51, 52, 54, 55, 57, 62, 67, 68, 70, 129
Francisco de Osuna, 125, 128
Führkötter, Adelgundis, 37n28, 46, 47

Gerken, Alexander 53n11
Gilson, Étienne, 2
Glasscoe, Marion, 105n10
Gnadenstuhl, xiii, 46
Green, Deirdre, 143
Guibert of Gembloux, 24, 26, 27, 30, 33n21

Hardy, Richard, 167
Hayes, Zachary, 48n1, 48n2, 49, 50n9, 57, 66n23, 70n31, 71, 72
Hellmann, J. A. Wayne, 49n3, 49n4, 72
Henrici, Peter, 183n1
Henry of Ghent, ixn5
Henry Suso, 78, 89n33
Herrera, R. A., 122n1
Hide, Kerrie, 115n17, 121
Hildegard of Bingen, x, xi, 23ff, 182, 184, 185
Hollywood, Amy, 97
Howells, Edward, 131n20, 141, 143, 151n13, 166n15, 167
Hunt, Anne, viin1
Hurtado, Larry, viin1
Huxley, Aldous, 98

Izbicki, Thomas M., 35n24, 46

Jan van Ruusbroec, 8, 169, 171n10, 178
Jantzen, Grace, 121
Joachim of Fiore, 56, 61
John of the Cross, viii, x, 21, 144ff, 169, 171n10, 180, 184, 186
Jones, E. A., 101n4
Julian of Norwich, viii, x, xi, xii, 98ff, 185
Jutta von Sponheim, 25, 26, 27, 32

Kempe, Margery, 99, 102
Kramer, Jocelyn, 171n8

Langland, William, 99
Lerner, Robert E., 77n13
Lubac, Henri de, 179

Mary Magdalene, 131, 169
Matthew, Iain, 167
McGinn, Bernard, ixn5, xiv, xv, 2, 6, 21n20, 22, 28n11, 31n16, 33, 34n22, 49n5, 72, 73n1, 75, 78n18, 79, 80, 82, 84, 85, 89n33, 96, 97
Meester, Conrad de, 168n2, 174n17, 180, 181
Meister Eckhart, x, xii, 73ff, 184, 185, 187
Merton, Thomas, 20, 74, 98, 99n3
Migne, Jacques Paul, 31
Monti, Dominic, 72
Moore, Brenna, 177n23
Moore, Sebastian, viin1
Murdoch, Iris, 98

Newman, Barbara, 25n5, 32, 35n25, 36, 46, 47
Newman, Cardinal John Henry, 98n2
Nuth, Joan M., viin2, 109n12, 121

Odo of Soissons, 23
Olson, Mary, 109n12
Os, Henk van, xiiin8

Pelphrey, Brant, 109n13
Pennington, Basil, 3n6
Perez-Romero, Antonio, 123n4
Pope Clement X, 147
Pope Eugenius III, 24, 28, 31, 33
Pope Gregory the Great, Gregory I, 18n15, 149
Pope Gregory VII, 31
Pope Gregory IX, 30
Pope Gregory XIII, 147
Pope John XXII, 73, 77

Pope John Paul II, 24, 49, 50, 73, 91,
    144, 147, 148n9, 168
Pope Leo XIII, 49
Pope Pius XI, 147
Pope Sixtus IV, 28n28
Pope Sixtus V, 147
Pope Urban VIII, 139n28
Porete, Marguerite, 76, 80
Principe, Walter, 68, 68n29
Pseudo-Dionysius, 56, 57, 58n16, 70,
    80, 83, 149

Rahner, Karl, viii, ix, 185
Ratzinger, Joseph, 48n2, 56n14,
    61n18
Richard of St Victor, vii, 56, 57, 63, 70
Ruiz, Federico, 167
Ryan, Patrick, 18n16

Sacks, Oliver, 26n9
Schipperges, Heinrich, 37n28, 47
Schroeder, Joy A., 47
Schürmann, Reiner, 97
Schüssler Fiorenza, Elisabeth, 31n16
Schweig, Graham M., 145n6
Staley, Lynn, 103
Synod of Reims (1148), 31
Synod of Trier (1147–48), 28

Tauler, John, 78, 89n33
Tavard, George, 167
Tengswich, Mistress, 29n12
Teresa of Avila, x, xi, xii, 98, 122ff,
    144, 145, 146, 147, 148, 149, 150,
    166, 169, 169n3, 173, 180, 184,
    186
Thérèse of Lisieux, 168, 169, 171n9,
    171n10, 180
Thomas Aquinas, viii, 20n19, 21n20,
    49, 50, 53, 54, 57, 62, 63, 70, 73,
    75, 76, 76 n.9, 80, 81, 84, 94, 149,
    183
Thompson, Colin, 151n30, 167
Tobin, Frank, 81n22, 97

Valdés, Fernando, 123, 128, 149
Vallée, Gonzalve, 170, 172, 180
Volmar of St. Disibod, 27, 28, 32, 33

Weber, Alison, 123n4, 132n21
William of St. Thierry, x, 1ff, 89, 103,
    149, 182, 184
Williams, Rowan, 136n26, 143
Windeatt, Barry, 104n8
Wyclif, John, 99, 100

Yeats, William Butler, 98